Francis Grose

Supplement to the Antiquities of England and Wales

Francis Grose

Supplement to the Antiquities of England and Wales

ISBN/EAN: 9783337329129

Printed in Europe, USA, Canada, Australia, Japan

Cover: Foto ©ninafisch / pixelio.de

More available books at **www.hansebooks.com**

SUPPLEMENT

TO THE

Antiquities

OF

ENGLAND

AND

Wales.

By Francis Grose Esq. F. A. S.

LONDON. Printed for S. HOOPER, N.º 25, Ludgate hill. M DCCLXXVII.

ADVERTISEMENT.

ON the completion of my fourth volume of the Anti-quities of England and Wales, I proposed to have taken leave of the publick, and to have laid down my pen and pencil, for the reason mentioned in the preface to that volume, namely, left a further continuation might have betrayed the original encouragers of the work into a greater expence than they at firft expected or intended.

This reafon, cogent as it feemed to me, has not by the majority of the purchafers been deemed fufficient, and ever fince the laft publication I have been flattered with repeated folicitations from a great number of refpectable perfons, all requiring an extenfion of the work. In anfwer to my fcruples they have given it as their opinions, that as the book has been regularly clofed, a Supplement will not fubject the original encouragers to the inconvenience I apprehended.

This, with my own fondnefs for the fubject, has induced me to refume my labours, and I will promife the purchafers that all the plates fhall be executed in a manner at leaft equal to the beft in the former volumes.

Whether this fupplement will confift of one or two volumes depends on the opinion of the publick, which will be interpreted from the degree of encouragement it meets with. The fubjects, fome very capital ones excepted, will chiefly be felected from thofe counties hitherto omitted, or flightly touched on.

F R O N T I S P I E C E.

Placed at Page

THIS very curious drawing reprefents Caftle Cornet, in the ifland of Guernfey, in the ftate it was before the year 1672, when the powder magazine being fet on fire by lightening, the great tower or keep here feen, with many houfes and other handfome buildings, were blown up and demolifhed. This accident happened at midnight on the 29th of December ; the particulars are mentioned in the account of this caftle in the body of the work. *Page*

THE exact refemblance obfervable in this drawing to the parts of the fortrefs which efcaped that misfortune, and are now remaining, affords fufficient teftimony of the accuracy of the draftfman to befpeak our credit for the likenefs of the whole.

P U B L I C.

I T is with the profoundeſt gratitude, for the many indulgencies I have experienced from the encouragers of this work, that I inform them it is at length finiſhed ; and hope I have, on my part, fulfilled my promiſe, that the Supplement ſhould be better executed than the preceding volumes. It now only remains for me to mention the aſſiſtance I have received in deſcriptions and drawings, for which I here beg leave to return my moſt hearty thanks.

BURNHAM ABBEY, in Bucks, plates I. and II.; Leiceſter Abbey, plate II.; the Gate in Old Ford, Middleſex, called King John's Houſe ; the ruins near Crowhurſt; thoſe at Robert's Bridge, both in Suſſex ; Egleſton Abbey, and Harwood Caſtle, plates I. and II. in Yorkſhire, were all drawn by James More, Eſquire.

LUTON TOWER, Bedfordſhire, and Cardigan Caſtle, were drawn by Paul Sandby, Eſq. and, by Mr. Grimm, Pontifract Church, Roach Abbey, Clifford's Tower, and the Chapel on Rotherham bridge, Yorkſhire ; Bolſover Caſtle, Derbyſhire ; the two plates of Beaurepaire, or Bear Park ; Gretham Hoſpital ; St. Cuthbert's Oratory, on Coquet Iſland, and Monks Weremouth, all in Durham ; Tinemouth Priory, Northumberland ; the Biſhop's Palace, Lincoln ; Lanthony Priory, Monmouthſhire, and the Epiſcopal Palace at Southwell. Arundel Caſtle ; the inſide of Bodiam Caſtle ; Brede Place ; the Crypt at Boſham Church ; the Town Hall of Chicheſter, the Vicar's College, at the ſame place ; Eaſtburne Priory ; the four plates of Hurſtmonceaux ; the Great Hall at

A   Mayfield

Mayfield Place ; Stanstead Place ; Verdley Castle and Plan ; Winchelsea Gate ; Ipres Tower at Rye, all in Suffex ; from the collection of William Burrell, Esq. for that county The castle of Longharne, Llanstephen, Caernarvon, and the Gate of Pembroke Castle, with the Monasteries of Haverford-West ; Strata Florida, Margham, and the Palace of St. David, were likewise drawn by that ingenious artist.

To my ingenious friend, Samuel Lysons, Esq. F. A. S. I am obliged for the following drawings : the Cross at Iron-Acton ; the Kitchen of Stanley ; St. Leonard's Priory ; St. Swithen's Church, Gloucestershire ; Uske Castle, Monmouthshire ; Stoke Castle, Shropshire ; Charlecombe Church, Somersetshire ; plate III. of Malmsbury Abbey, and Malmsbury Cross, in Wiltshire ; Great Malvern Priory, Worcestershire ; Brecknock, Montgomery ; Penline and St. Quintin's Castles ; the Cathedral of St. Asaph, and Powis Castle, plate II. .

By Samuel Ireland, Esq. I was favoured with his drawing of Medenham Abbey, Buckinghamshire ; and by the Rev. Mr. Street, with the drawing and account of Warblington Castle, Hants ; to Mr. Day, junior, of York-street, Covent-Garden, I am indebted for the two views of the Chapel in the Savoy ; and to Mr. Richards for that of Combe Sydenham, Somersetshire.

The views of St. Germain, plate I. ; Port Eliot and Trematon Castle, all in Cornwall, were drawn by Mr. Payne of the drawing-room in the Tower, who bids fair, as an artist, to arrive at great eminence in his profession.

The view of Haghmond Abbey in Shropshire, was drawn by Mr. Russel, and that of Tickencote Chapel (by permission) from a view, taken on the spot, by Mr. Carter of College-street, Westminster.

To Thomas Pennant, Esq. I am obliged for the following drawings taken by his draughtsman Mr. Moses Griffiths. The Castle of Newark, Nottinghamshire ; Beaumaris Castle, plate III. ; the Great Gate of Caernarvon Castle ; Clynog Church ; Dolwydellan Castle ; Llandegai Church ; Denbeigh Castle ;

Bangor

Bangor Monachorum, Flint Caftle; Dolforwyn Caftle; Montgomery Caftle, plate II. and the Tinewald Hill, in the Ifle of Man, plate II.

St. Germain's Church, plate II. I owe to the favour of the Reverend Mr. Chancellor Carrington, of St. Helion's, near Exeter. It was drawn by the Hon. Mifs Eliot. To him likewife I am obliged for a defcription of that venerable edifice.

Maxtoke Castle, Warwickfhire, was engraved from a drawing made by that well-known artift, Mr. Miller; Ravenfworth Caftle, Yorkfhire, from a view taken by my worthy friend the late Lieutenant-Colonel Hicks of the 70th regiment.

Snape Hall, Helmefley Caftle, Caterick Bridge, the Keep of Richmond Caftle, Ravenfworth Caftle, plate II. Tanfield Caftle, and the Vignette to the fixth volume were all taken from the drawings of Mr. Rowe of Perfhore in Worcefterfhire.

The Abbey of Sallay in Yorkfhire, and King John's Houfe at Clypefton, in Nottinghamfhire, were drawn by my much refpected friend Major Hayman Rooke; Knarefborough Caftle, Yorkfhire, by ——— Tarrent, Efq. of the corps of engineers, and communicated by Thomas Maude, Efq. and the Church of Walton-on-the-Naize by Mr. Beck, of the drawing-room in the Tower; Clare Caftle, Suffolk, by the Rev. Mr. Jones; and the defcription was given me by Tho. Ruggles of Clare, in Suffolk, Efq.

Mayfield Place, Plates I. and II. were drawn by that excellent draughtf-man Mr. Kenyon, author of the Antiquities of Herefordfhire. The plan of Richmond Caftle was made by Mr. Bailey, whom I have before mentioned; he alfo drew Branfpeth Caftle, Durham.

Eastbury House, Waltham Abbey, Rye Houfe, plates I. and II. and Latton Priory, with the defcriptions, were all given me by ——— Forfter, Efq.

to

to whom I have had occasion in a former volume to make my acknowledge-ments for similar favours. The drawing of Our Lady's Mount, near Lynn, in Norfolk, was sent me by the late Rev. Mr. Tyson; for the account I am be-holden to Governor Pownal.

For Plate I. of Leicester, I am obliged to Mr. John Throsby of that place, and for St. Sampson's Church, in the Isle of Guernsey, to J. Gosselin, Esq. of that Island. Queenborough Castle was taken from an original drawing by Holler, and the view of Castle Cornet, before its demolition by the blowing up of the magazine, from an ancient drawing; and Plate I. of Restormel Castle, from an original picture belonging to the owner, ——— Masterman, Esq.— All the rest of the views were drawn by myself.

13th Sept. 1787.

Dunstable Priory. Bedfordshire. Pl. 1.

DUNSTAPLE OR DUNSTABLE PRIORY, BEDFORDSHIRE.
(PLATE I.)

THE fite of this monaftery, was, it is faid, at the time of the conqueft, a wild wafte, over-run with wood, ferving as a fhelter to divers bands of outlaws and robbers. King Henry I. in order to prevent their depredations and to deftroy their fhelter, refolved to caufe the woods to be grubbed up, and the place to be fettled with inhabitants; he therefore iffued procla-mations, inviting people to fettle here, and informing them that they fhould have land at the annual rent of twelve-pence the acre, with the fame privileges for themfelves and heirs as were enjoyed by the citizens of London, or any other town in England. He alfo built here a royal palace call.d Kingfbury, which ftood near the church; where in 1123 he held his Chriftmas in great ftate, with his whole court, and received an embaffy from the earl of Anjou. He made the town a borough, beftowed on it a fair and a market, whence fome derive its name, as compounded of Dun, a hill, and ftaple, a place of merchandize or com-merce. Others, indeed, deduce it from Dunning, a famous robber, who lurked about thefe woods; thence, as they fay, called Dunning's ftable. The town being built, was in the king's hands, as a free borough, feventeen years and a half. The burgeffes were by the king made free throughout England, and were not liable to anfwer before the king's juftices itinerant, or any other of his fervants out of the town or liberty; but the juftices went thither, and deter-mined all fuits without any foreign affeffor, by the oath of twelve of the townfmen. Thefe privileges, when the town was in the hands of the monks, were feveral times called in queftion by th. juftices and king's fervants, particularly in 1286.

THE laft ftep towards completing the fettlement of this place, was the foundation and endowment of this monaftery; which Tanner fays was done towards the latter end of the reign of this king, or according to other writers, fometime after the year 1131; it confifted of black canons, and was dedicated to the honour of St. Peter. To them, Henry granted the whole manor of Dunftaple, with the lands pertaining to the town, viz. four culturæ of land round the town, the market and fchools of the faid town, with all its liberties and free cuftoms; *fac, foc, tol, theam, infangenethef, guthbrith, hamfocne, clodxith, forftal,* and *flemenes*

ford, right of Cadendone, Kenſworth, and Totenhoe; and the four ways (quadraria) of the
ſaid town, with ſafe paſſage to the market, under pain of forfeiting 10 l. He further granted
them leave to hold what they could purchaſe, and exemption for themſelves and ſervants for all
taxes due to the ſhire and hundred, county fines for murder, tollage, pleas, geld and dane-
gelds, hydage, toll, paſſage, pontage, ſtallage, and all cuſtoms and ſecular exactions, and
worldly ſervices through the realm. The king reſerved to himſelf only his houſes in the
town, and the garden where he uſed to lodge. This charter is witneſſed by Robert biſhop
of Hereford, Simon biſhop of Worceſter, G. Chancellor, Robert de Sigillo, N. the biſhop's
nephew, Milo of Glouceſter, Humphry de Bohun, G. Fitz Paine, Robert Fitz John, Drago
de Moncei, and Maurice de Windſor, at Cumba [Comb Abbey].

These grants were confirmed by Henry II. Henry III. and John. The latter prince gave
them his royal palace here, and a fair for three days on St. Frehemund's feaſt, as did Henry III.
the pleas and fines of the town, and appointed that the prior ſhould ſit with the king's
juſtices, and have his clerk and enrollment of writs. All theſe ſeveral privileges were enjoyed
by the convent and town, and many of the inhabitants were tenants in capite and other tenants
in fee to the prior. The church was all along taxed at 100 s. the town at the ſame ſum, and
the profits of the market at the ſame. Three parts of the town ſtand on the fee of Houghton,
(now a mean village below Dunſtable to the ſouth, in a deep chalky ſoil) for which Hen. I.
gave the tenants of that place part of his wood at Buckwood; the fourth part to the ſouth,
is reputed of the fee of Kenſworth.

In this priory were altars dedicated to St. Mary, St. Frehemund king and martyr, St.
Nicholas, and St. James; and about Eaſter 1212, ſay the annals of this houſe, many miracles
were wrought here by God and St. Frehemund. It ſeems that the reliques of this ſaint were
on their way to Canterbury, but by ſome miracle they could get no farther than Dunſtaple.

In June 1221 the roof of the preſbytery, which had been repaired the autumn before, fell
in; and in December fell down two towers in the front of the church, one on the prior's
hall, and deſtroyed moſt of it; the other on the church, which it ſhattered.

The priors of this houſe, recorded by Browne Willis in his Hiſtory of Mitred Abbies,
are

Thomas, who occurs 1196, died 1205.

Richard de Morins, elected September 1203, died 1242.

William, prior of Dunſtaple, 1233. Galſridus de Barton, canon of Dunſtaple, reſigned 1263. Simon
de Eton, died 10 cal. Novembris 1274. William de Breton or Brothon, confirmed prior 8 id. Novembris
1274, lived ſeven years after he reſigned, 1280, and dying 1288, was buried in the Chapter-houſe. William
de Wederhous, Wederhoſe, Wederour or Waderhyr, nominated 8 cal. Februarii 1280, on the reſignation of
Breton. He reſigned 1302 or (as Chron. Dun. p. 658) 1303. John de Chedington, confirmed 8 id. De-
cembris 1304, died 1341. John de London, elected 1341, reſigned 1348. Roger de Gravenhurſt, confirmed
2 id. Aprilis 1348, died 1351. Thomas Marſhall, elected and admitted 7 id. Octobris 1351, died Oct. 12,
1413. John Aſton ſucceeded, and died in ſix weeks. John Saxton or Royſton, confirmed Dec. 28, 1413.
Thomas Giles reſigned 1482. He had been preſented by John Broughton, eſq. to the church of Leighton
Boſard, on the reſignation of John Gyrton, July 28, 1473. Richard Cuarnock, October 31, 1482,
occurs 1494, and quitted it for the priory of Chriſt-Church, London, April 28, 1473. William Weſthall,
confirmed 1497, occurs 1501, died 1525. Gervas Markham the laſt prior. He was an active man in Henry
VIII.'s divorce, which was tranſacted in his monaſtery, as divers of our hiſtorians can teſtify; and in Rymer's
Fœdera may be ſeen ſome commiſſions directed to him, October 17, 1534. 26 Henry VIII. he with Thomas
Claybrooke and eleven others, ſubſcribed to the king's ſupremacy; and continuing till the diſſolution 1539,
had, on the ſurrender of his monaſtery, a penſion of 60 l. aſſigned him for life. He appears to have been poſ-
ſeſſed of it in 1553, and was buried in the church here, September 23, 1581.

At the diſſolution, the revenues of this priory were rated in a valuation taken a little before
that event, at 344 l. 13 s. 3 d. per ann. according to Dugdale; Speed eſtimates it, 402 l. 14 s. 7 d.
ob. The ſite was granted, 1ſt of Mary, to ſir Leonard Chamberlayne; it has ſince belonged
to Mr. Crawley, —— Cook, eſq. and Mr. Vaux.

By letters patent, 6 Ed. VI. the rectory and advowſon of the vicarage of Dunſtaple were
granted to Windſor College. It is now in the crown, and worth about 100 l. per ann. and
was not charged in the king's books; the certified value 50 l.

Annual Penſions paid to the following Monks of this Houſe:

Thomas Cleybroke 9 l. Richard Kerke 8 l. Auguſtine Curtis 8 l. George Edwards 7 l.
John Stalbworth 7 l. Richard Bowdood 7 l. Edward Green 6 l. Robert Somer 6 l. John Nyxe
5 l. 6 s. 8 d. Nicholas Cleybroke 2 l. John Percivall 2 l.

This view, which ſhews the north-weſt aſpect, was drawn A. D. 1760.

Dunstable Priory, Bedfordshire. Pl 2

DUNSTAPLE OR DUNSTABLE PRIORY.

(PLATE II.)

Of this priory little remains but part of the conventual church, and a small distance south-west of two arches of a porter's lodge or gateway.

The front of the church is fingular and picturefque. The great door is under a femi-oval arch, richly ornamented with various grotefque fculptures, reprefenting human figures, animals and foliage; the capitals of many of the columns are decorated in the fame tafte: the leffer door, which ftands north of it, is likewife much ornamented. Between them is a row of interfecting circular arches, whofe columns, Mr. Pennant obferves, confift of fingular greater and leffer joints, placed alternately, not unlike one fpecies of the foffils called Entrochi. Over the leffer door is a range of pointed arches, fupported by cluftered columns, forming niches, which from the remains of divers pedeftals, feem to have had ftatues in them. Above thefe, are fix larger and higher pointed arches; which, with three of greater dimenfions over the grand door, form the front of a gallery called the Rood loft; from whence, on holidays, probably fome miraculous crofs or crucifix might be exhibited to the multitude. Four of the lower of thefe arches are furmounted by five fmaller ones, and over them this face terminates with a battlement.

THE tower is annexed to the north-weſt angle of the building. Its turret, incloſing a ſtair-caſe, projects a little beyond the weſt-end face. Mr. Pennant thinks that this, and a correſponding tower on the ſouth-eaſt angle, were thoſe mentioned to have fallen down in the year 1221, when they deſtroyed the prior's hall and part of the church. The Annals ſay, "the body of the church was repaired in 1273 by the pariſhioners, but one Henry Chadde was the principal contributor;" but do not mention the re-building of any tower.

THE inſide of the church is ſupported by ſix round arches, all plain except one. The roof is of oak, beautifully carved with knots, flowers, &c.—the beams ſupported by angels, horizontal and perpendicular. The upper ſtory of windows are alſo ſemi-circular. Mr. Pennant obſerves, "that either the date of the re-building is wrong, or the Saxon or round arched mode muſt have continued longer than is generally allowed."—Might not the architect, who ſuperintended the repairs, either be directed or chuſe to reſtore the building to its priſtine form, without attending to the ſtile then in faſhion.

THE church is ſaid to have been originally in the form of a croſs, with a tower in the center. Two of the vaſt pillars which ſupported it, are ſhewn in this drawing at what now forms the eaſt end.

DIVERS ſtone coffins, one with a chalice and patten, have been found by different perſons digging for ſtone in the ſite of the ancient eaſtern part of the church, particularly in 1745, about two feet under ground and about three from the ſide wall, and the feet cloſe to a croſs wall, was found a ſtone coffin ; the lid compoſed of four ſtones ; the piece at the foot, a ſeperate one ; the head, ſides and bottom, of one ſtone ; under the head, an eminence inſtead of a pillow, in a hollow or niche correſponding to the head. The ſkeleton was entire except the ribs, which had fallen in ; the head inclined to the left : between the upper bone of the left arm and the back bone, was a glaſs urn, fallen down and the lid off, ſtained with deep brown, on the inner ſide of that part which lay over the ſtone : about the feet were pieces of leather very rotten, which by the holes appeared to have been ſewed together. An ancient ſpur was found here.

IT is ſaid that after the diſſolution, Henry VIII. pitched on this church to found one of his cathedrals, and had nominated Dr. Day to be the firſt biſhop thereof ; but for ſome reaſon, now unknown, that deſign was laid aſide, and all the conventual part of the church was demoliſhed ; for the part now left ſtanding is only the nave and two ſide ailes of the church, from the weſt end to the tranſept, the length meaſuring no more than an hundred feet.

HERE are many ancient tombs and braſſes ; many of them are deſcribed in No. VIII. of the Bibliotheca Topographica Britannica, wherein are ſome very curious extracts from the Annals of Dunſtable, publiſhed by Hearne, from which ſeveral particulars here mentioned are tranſcribed.

THIS view, which ſhews the north-eaſt aſpect of the church, was drawn A. D. 1787.

Gate of Dunstable Priory, Bedfordshire.

THE GATE OF DUNSTABLE PRIORY, BEDFORDSHIRE.

THE two remaining arches of the priory gate before mentioned in Plate II. are here delineated ; by their ſtile they do not ſeem much older than the time of Henry VII. Theſe led to the lodgings and offices of the priory, which ſtood on the ſouth ſide of the church.

AT this priory and the town of Dunſtable, many important affairs were tranſacted. A. D. 1247, the former was viſited by king Henry III. and his family, when the monks preſented the king with a gilt cup, the queen with another, and their ſon and daughter, prince Edward and the princeſs Margaret, each with a gold claſp. In return their majeſties beſtowed on the church eight pieces of ſilk, and the king gave an hundred ſhillings for the making of a thurible and a pix. A number of tournaments were held at this town in different reigns, and the buſineſs of the divorce of king Henry VIII. was here agitated.

THIS view, which ſhews the north or outſide of the gate, was drawn A. D. 1787.

The Tower, at Luton, Bedfordshire.

LUTON TOWER, BEDFORDSHIRE.

This tower is reputed to be of great antiquity: it was the summer residence of the Abbots of St. Albans. After the diffolution of religious houfes it was purchafed by the family of Napier, and is now the property of the Earl of Bute, who has erected near it a moft magnificent manfion, and laid out the grounds with a tafte and propriety that always mark his Lordfhip's improvements.

This tower was very high, and of great ftrength, and had within it a fpiral flope, which ferved for afcending to the top inftead of ftairs. It is faid to have been entire when purchafed by Sir John Napier, who near fifty years ago began to pull it down, and that there was then found a whifpering place, communicating from the bottom to the top. By the remains of this tower and its appendages, it feems to have been a very extenfive building.

Remains of the Tower at Luton, Bedfordshire.

Published according to Act of Parliament by G. Kearsley in Fleet Street, March 1784.

View of the Remains of the TOWER, at LUTON, in BEDFORDSHIRE.

Drawn by PAUL SANDBY, Efq; R. A. and Engraved by Mr. ROOKER.

THIS Tower is faid to be of great antiquity, and from the femblance of the red and yellow pavings, to thofe in the font of Luton Church, it is conjectured to be built about the fame time, which is above 500 years ago, and that it was the fummer refidence of the abbot of St. Alban's, before Henry the VIII. alienated the revenues of that abbey. It was many years afterwards purchafed by the family of Napier, who was defcended from a noble family of that name in Scotland, and came into England about the time that James the I. afcended the throne. It is now the property of the earl of Bute.

The tower has been very high, and of great ftrength, and before the invention of gunpowder, impregnable. There was a cavity in the wall, called a whifpering pipe, from the bottom to the top, which was intire before Sir John Napier began to pull down the tower, which is about forty years ago, part of which now remains, and alfo the walls of the chapel, and other ruins, which have been very extenfive.

Burnham Abbey, Bucks.

BURNHAM ABBEY, BUCKINGHAMSHIRE. (PLATE I.)

BURNHAM, is a village, which gives name to the hundred in which it ſtands, and is ſituated about five miles to the north eaſt of Eton, and about two miles eaſt of Maidenhead, in Berkſhire. Here A. D. 1165, Richard, King of the Romans, began a nunnery of the order of St. Auguſtine, which was dedicated to the Bleſſed Virgin Mary, and conſiſted of an Abbeſs and ſeven or eight nuns. Their yearly revenues, in tax Linc. amounted to 56l. 16s. 11d. in 26 Hen. VIII. to 51l. 2s. 4d. q Dugdale 91l. 5s. 11 ob. Speed. At the diſſolution Browne Willis ſays, here was an Abbeſs, nine nuns, and thirty-ſeven ſervants. The following is a liſt of Abbeſſes, as given by that gentleman. Joan de Bedware died 1314; Idonea d'Audeley, elected 1314, died 1324; Joan de Somerville, elected 1324; Joan de Dorney, elected 1339; Agnes Frankeleyn, elected 1367, reſigned 1393; Eliz. Ward, elected 1393; Alice Golafree, elected about 1406; Agnes Gower, occurs 1457, as does Agnes Sturdys, about 1459; Joan Radcliff, reſigned 1506; Margaret Gibſon, ſucceeded 1507, and reſigned 1536.

THIS view was drawn anno 1786.

Burnham Abbey, Bucks: Pl.2.

BURNHAM ABBEY, BUCKINGHAMSHIRE. PLATE II.

This view shews the aspect of the monastery. To the account given in the former plate may be added the following particulars, which occur in the additions to Browne Willis's History of Abbeys.

BURNHAM. Margary de Louch was abbess temp. Edward III. in which reign she was succeeded by Joan Turner.

THE first abbess of this place was Margery de Eston, elected anno 1265. She was succeeded anno 1273 by Maud de Dorkcester. The two last were Margaret Gibson and Alice Baldwin. The instrument of surrender is dated September 1539, and signed by the abbess and nine nuns; the four last of which were surviving anno 1553, and enjoyed their pensions, which were appropriated as follows, viz. Alice Baldwin, abbess, 13 l. 6 s. 8 d. Anne Benfield 4 l. Alice Cells 2 l. 6 s. 8 d. Margaret Browne 3 l. Elizabeth Woodforth 2 l. Elizabeth Loo 2 l. Anne Norys, Margaret Mosse, Bridget Woodward, Luce Packett, 2 l. each. In the Augmentation-Office is the original surrender, too long to be inserted here, and a letter from the visitors, in the same nature as that of Bitlesdon, recommending the religious to the king's favour, on account of their readiness to yield to the king's measures; and the following survey of this house, taken amongſt the returns of the leſſer houſes. " The monaſtery of the order of St. Auſtin, value 51l. 12 s. 4 d. nuns 9, incontinent none, all deſire to go into religious houſes; ſervants 37, whereof prieſts 2, hinds 21, women 14. Bells and lead, worth 40 l. 16 s. 8 d. the houſe in good eſtate. The value of the moveable goods, 45 l. 17 s. 9 d. Stocks and debts none. Woods 160 acres, whereof in woods under 20 years of age 80 acres, old woods 80 acres."

THE manſion-houſe of the convent ſeems to be entirely ſtanding; 'tis built in ſhape of an L, and made uſe of to hold huſbandry implements and produce, viz. corn, hay, &c. the tenant dwelling in a little houſe near it, where probably the chief hind anciently lived. I could learn no account of the church, viz. when it was pulled down, the arms of this convent were as I find, Or on a chief Argent, Three Lozenges Gules.

Malenham Abbey near Henley on Thames.

MEDENHAM, OR MADENHAM ABBEY, BUCKINGHAMSHIRE.

MEDENHAM abbey is pleasantly situated on the banks of Thames, about four miles south west of Great Marlow.

THIS Manor being given before the second of King John, by Hugh de Bolbec, to the Cistertian Monks of Woobourne, in Bedfordshire, they placed some of their society here about the year 1204, and it became a small abbey of that order, being rather a daughter (as the writers of that order express themselves) than a cell to Woburn. It was dedicated to the Virgin Mary, and valued 26 HENRY VIII. (when here were only two monks) at 20l. 6s. 2d. per ann. Dugdale 23l. 17s. 2d. Speed. In 29 Hen. VIII. it was made part of the endowment of the new abbey at Bustlesham, or Bisham, in Berkshire; and after the suppression of that house, it was granted to Robert Mone and others, 38 Hen. VIII. These are the particulars of this house given by Tanner, to which the following are added by Browne Willis: The account of the Abbots, says he, is very imperfect, being a cell to Woobourne, and so subordinate to their government; all I meet are, Roger, anno 1256, and Peter, anno 1295, in which year he was elected to this office September 11. The next that occurs, as yet to me, is Henry, ann. 1416, after whom I find no other, save that Richard, whose surname I find not, presided ann. 1521, and was, as I conceive, on many accounts, the last prior. Here was then only one monk, whose name was Guy Strenshill. Temp. Hen. VIII. the commissioners returned that " This monastery was of the order of St. Bernard, the clere value 20l. 6s. 2d. Monks then two, and both desyren to go to houses of religion ; servants none, bells, &c. worth 2l. 1s. 8d. the house wholly in ruine ; the value of the moveable goods, 1l. 3s. 8d. woods none, debts none."

Here remains still standing the walls of the north isle of the abbey church, it is in length sixteen yards, and in breadth four. It seems by this to have been a neat stately building, well wrought with ashler work ; the windows high and spacious. It probably consisted of a body, and two side isles and chancel, and had a tower at the west end. The house that is now called the Abbey house seems to have been patched up after the dissolution. Since Browne Willis wrote, most of the remains he mentions have fallen, or been taken down, the adjacent grounds elegantly laid out and planted, and the abbey house repaired, and made again conventual, by a society of gentlemen who lived together in a kind of monastic state; their abbot was a noble Peer. The rules observed by these monks have not been published, but from some of them which have transpired, we may venture to suppose they were not quite so rigid as those of their brethren of La Trape. This was in some measure indicated by the motto over their door, which carved in large letters still stand thus: FAY CE QVE VOVDRAS.

This view was drawn July 1786.

PYTHAGORAS, HIS SCHOOL, CAMBRIDGE.

For the following very ingenious differtation and defcription of this ancient building, I am obliged to a clergyman in the neighbourhood of Cambridge, well verfed in Englifh antiquities, and particularly in thofe of the county wherein he refides.

Before I attempt to dive into the very obfcure origin of this ancient ftructure, it may be ufeful to trace its transfer from its remoteft owners, down to its prefent proprietors: and this from authentic documents in the archieves of Merton College, to whom it now belongs.

The Priory of St. Giles, in Cambridge, was founded about 1092, by Picot, Baron of Brunne, with Hugolina his wife, near the place where the church of St. Giles now ftands: but the fituation being found to be too ftrait and confined, it was removed, fome twenty years after, to a place called Bernewelle, on the other fide of the river. Whether this building was any part of that foundation, I believe is more than can be afcertained: certain it is, however, that it was part of their poffeffions. For Laurence de Stanfield, prior, with the convent of Bernewelle, demifed the premifes, formerly granted to Algar Nobilis of Cambridge, to Hervey Fitz Euftace, of the fame place; this was about the year 1233, as it is witneffed by Jeremiah de Caxton, then fheriff of the county. Much about the fame time, Baldwin, the fon of Baldwin Blangernun, of Cambridge, conveys this meffuage to Hervey Fitz Euftace, for one of the witneffes to the conveyance, was Geoffrey de Hatferd, high fheriff of the county: now he was in that office from 1224, to 1232. The fame perfon alfo grants the faid meffuage, with an holme, to the faid Hervey: this was towards the end of the reign of Hen. III, as Jer. de Caxton is a witnefs, together with Henry de Colvyle, then fheriff; but as he was in that office, both in 1236, 1240 and 1250, it may be difficult to afcertain the precife year. In the copy I have feen of this conveyance, the fheriff is called Hen. de Colȳ; but as no fuch perfon ever was fheriff, and a Hen. de Colvyle, an old family, ftill in being, was evidently fo, about this time, I have no difficulty to fuppofe him to be the perfon meant, and that the tranfcriber made a miftake. Together with the meffuage, was conveyed an holme: this I make no doubt, are the fwampy low grounds and pondyards, lying on the bank of the river, and extending towards the library of St. John's College, on this fide of the river.

About the year 1256, John Shotley, prior of Bernewelle, with his convent, demife the faid premifes to Euftace Fitz-Hervey, probably fon of the former, which formerly had been in the occupation of Henry, the fon of Edward Froft, whom I take to have been the original founder of St. John's Hofpital, in Cambridge, about 1210, by giving the fcite on which the hofpital was built. So that the college of St. John the Evangelift, now grafted on that hofpital, and ftill enjoying its poffeffions, may juftly be accounted the firft of our prefent colleges.

By an indenture, dated at Cambridge 41 Hen. III, anno 1256, Euftace, the fon of Hervey Dunning, of Cambridge, leafes to Mag. Guy de Caftro Bernardi, the meffuage that belonged to his father Hervey, and in which he lived, with other lands, &c. except the capital meffuage which he had purchafed of Baldwin Blangernun: And in the fame year, the faid Euftace mortgaged his eftate, together with this capital meffuage, to the abovefaid M. Guy de Caftro Bernardi, an ancient family in Cambridge; on whofe deceafe, Richard, fon and heir of Euftace Fitz-Hervey Dunning, feifed, as lord of the manor, the faid premifes into his hands: whereupon William de Manefend, nephew and heir of the faid M. Guy, brought it into the King's Bench, where it was tried before Sir Rob. Fulco, Chief Juftice of that Bench, where the caufe was traverfed, and given againft the faid Richard Dunning. This happened about 1270, and probably brought on, on purpofe to create a clear and legal title to the eftate: for in the fame year, this William de Manefend, conveyed the fame to the prefent proprietors.

About the year 1256, it appears that the houfe was in the occupation of St. John's Hofpital, in Cambridge; for about that time, the mafters and brethren of that Hofpital, grant to Henry Fitz-Euftace, and his heirs for ever, two beds with their neceffary coverlids, for the ufe of infirm perfons, in their ftone houfe, obliging themfelves to find a chaplain, and to celebrate mafs, efpecially for the foul of Euftace Fitz-Hervey, in acknowledgment for the lands granted by him to their hofpital, lying in Cambridge, Chefterton and Madingley. No doubt he was a confiderable benefactor to that religious houfe, though omitted as fuch by the worthy Mr. Baker, in his excellent hiftory of that foundation: for fo late as the year 1284, when Richard Cheverel was mafter, they oblige themfelves to find and maintain a chaplain, one of their brethren, for the above purpose, within their own houfe. This was after Merton College was in poffeffion of the meffuage, but yet for the lands which he had conveyed to them, they were obliged to celebrate for him as a benefactor. The manor was fettled on the college by Bifhop Walter de Merton in 1270, as appears by this defcription of it by the founder in his fecond charter, and the title he added to it. Terr. & Redd. quondam Rici Dunning & Wilkelmi de Manefeld, quos ipfi in Cantebrigia & Portibus adjacentibus mihi dimiferunt. And they were the chief perfons the college was concerned with in the purchafe.

THE great difficulty is ftill behind, I mean the original ufe and deftination of the building and by whom erected. That it was not defigned for any religious purpofe is plain, for its having no one part of it proper for an altar to be placed in, and its having only one entrance would be equally inconvenient. My firft thoughts were, and I have not altered them, that it was a part of Picot's foundation for a prior and fix canons: where the fcite being found too confined, Pagan Peverel removed them to Bernewelle, whofoever looks at St. Giles's Church, which has all the marks of one of our moft ancient buildings, muft be convinced, that could not be the fcite of Picot's foundation, both as the choir and church would be too fmall; but more efpecially, as it is bounded and hemmed in on two fides, the fouth and weft by the king's highway, and to the north by the precincts of and afcent to the caftle. The way alfo from them to the river, muft confequently have been acrofs the road to Chefterton, which would have been inconvenient.

POSSIBLY the priory might receive its denomination of St. Giles's from its vicinity to this parifh church, even from the founders: in the fame manner as Corpus Chrifti College acquires its ufual one from the adjoining church of St. Benedict.

BUT even allowing the fituation of this priory to have been where I would rather fuppofe it to have been placed, ftill they muft have been much cramped and confined, which probably occafioned their removal, for on one fide was the common road, and to the eaft, a range of buildings conftituting the ftreet oppofite Magdalene College; and to the fouth a morafs with a branch or cut of the river by it, now filled up. At prefent I conceive, nothing pofitive can be faid on a fubject too much in the dark, till farther difcoveries are made to throw more light upon it.

HOWEVER that may be, this building bids faireft to authenticate the antiquity of the univerfity of Cambridge of any in the place, as it feems moft likely to have been the ftructure where the Croyland monks gave their lectures to their fcholars: and from them has retained the name of fchoic, from that period to this very time.

THE undercroft is exactly in the fame ftyle of building with that given by T. Hearne for St. Grymbalds church, except in a plainer and more fober way, confequently more likely to be the antienter of the two; and that this has only a single row of pillars which run in a line from one end to the other, which by the plan and section taken by Mr. Richard Well in 1739, and published by Mr. Masters some years after, seem to have their plinths or bases hidden and sunk into the ground. Of these pillars there are only five round and short with pilasters on each side and end, opposite to every one of them. The arches are semicircular and spring from the pillars to the walls, which are of a great thickness, and contain on one side only four narrow windows. The capitals are of no positive order, but of the plain style of the unornamented sort in Grymbalds crypt and that under the choir of Canterbury Cathedral. It seems to me that the use of it might be in the last instance whatever its original one was, to have been to read lectures of philosophy and the sciences in, and to have been made use of as scholes of learning, with rooms over it for the same purpose, in various branches. If this is allowed it will carry up the date to 1109, when the Benedictine monks from Croyland Abbey came to Cambridge for that intent: some few years after which, about 1112, the canons of St. Giles's left Cambridge for Bernewelle. On their retreat, it is no strained inference to suppose, that they might accommodate these professors with a building that would be so convenient to them and was of no use to themselves, at their first coming hither they were contented with worse accommodations.

Mr. Gostling in his account of the crypt under the choir of the cathedral of Canterbury as Mr. Hearne in his of that under St. Grymbalds, seem to aim at very high antiquity in their respective relations of them. I can hardly suppose either of them so ancient as the 10th century: Hearne has a system to complete, which was never out of his head: but Mr. Gostling was of a soberer and more rational understanding. However their conjectures may turn out, or whatever may be the age of either of their crypts, it must be in favour of Pythagoras his schole: for the same sort of building with pillars and arches of the same style, will equally prove that this at Cambridge is of as high antiquity as either of the other.

This View was drawn, Anno 1777.

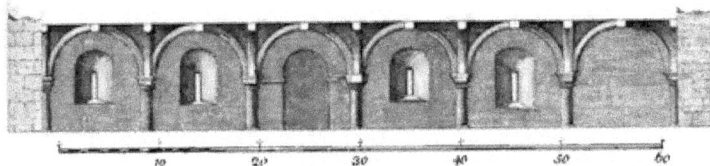

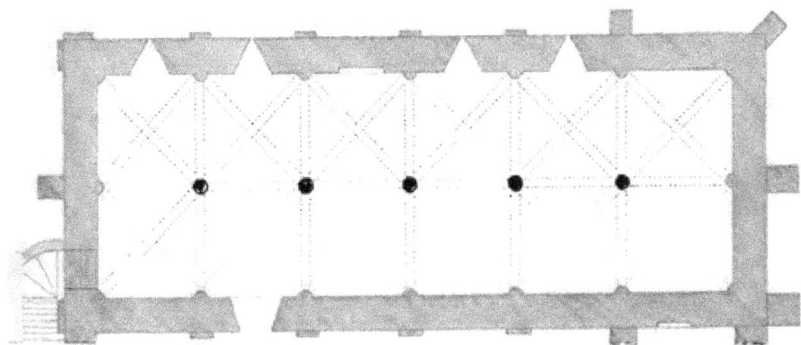

Viris Rev. HENRICO BARTON S.T.P. Custodi et Scholaribus
Collegij de MERTON in OXON.
hanc Ichnographiam et Sectionem AULÆ de MERTON in CANT.
(vulgo vocat. 'PYTHAGORAS SCHOOL)
humillime dicat R. Masters.

■

ARWENACKE HOUSE, AT FALMOUTH, CORNWALL.

ALTHOUGH both Leland and Carew mention this mansion, neither of them give any information respecting its builder, or time of erection. The former describes it in the following words: " And a quarter of a mile farther I came to Arwennak, Mr. Keligrew's place, standing on the brimme or shore, within Falmouth haven.

" THIS place hathe beene of continuance the ancient howse of the Killegrewes.

" THE R was another howse of the Keligrewis descending out of this, and it was in the town of Penrine : now both these houses are joined in one."

MR. Crew says of it, " After the declining hill hath delivered you downe from this castle (i. e. the castle of Pendennis) Arwenacke entertaineth you with a pleasing view : for the same standeth so farre within the havens mouth, that it is protected from the sea stormes,

and yet fo neere thereunto, as it yeeldeth a ready paffàge out ; befides, the cliffe on which the houfe abbateth is fteep enough to
fhoulder off the waves, and the ground about it, plaine and large
enough for ufe and recreation.

It is owned by mafter John Killigrew, who married the daughter
of Monck, and heire to her mother, and was fonne to Sir John
Killigrew, who matched with Woulverftone ; the ftocke is ancient,
and diverfe of the branches (as I have elfewhere remembred) growne
to great advauncement in calling and livelyhood by their greater
defert : their armes are argent, an eagle with two heads, difplayed
within a bordure bezanty fable.

The prefent ftate of this building will be beft underftood by the
annexed view ; fome parts of it, or at leaft of an ancient building
adjoining to it on the north, are ftill inhabited.

Tradition fays, When the parliamentary forces befieged the
adjacent caftle of Pendennis in 1646, the General took up his
quarters at this manfion.

Adjoining to the north fide of this building is a fine grove, and
in it a handfome ftone pyramid, faid to have been erected in memory
of fome perfon of the family of the Killigrews, but it has no infcription.

This view was drawn July 1786.

Town, Haven, & Castles of Fowey Pl. 1

THE TOWN, HAVEN, AND CASTLES OF FOWEY, OR FAWEY, CORNWALL. (PLATE I.)

THIS haven, town, and their environs, afford a variety of picturesque views. Their history and situation are thus related, and described by Leland in his Itinerary.

" THE town of Fowey ys a market town, walled defensably to the se cost, and hath gates alfo. Yn the town is but one chyrche, but the howfes of the towne be well buylded of ftone and yl enhabited. Alfo at the entery of the haven on the W. fide is a blockke howfe, and a chapel of S. Catherine by the fame. Alfo ther is on the fame fyd a towre with ordinans for the defens of the haven.

" AT the eaft fyde of the haven's mouth of Fowey ftondeth a tower for the defens thereof, and a chapel of S. Savyor a lytle above the fame. Ny by the faid towr ftondith a fifhar village cawled Polruan. Vol. 7, p. 122.

" THER is at the weft point of the haven of Fawey mouth, a blok houfe, devifed by Thomas Treury, and made partely by his coft, partely by the town of Fawey. A little higher on this point of the hille is a chapel of St. Catarine. And hard under the roote of this hille a litle withyn the haven mouth is a litle bay or creke bearing the name of Catarine.

" ABOUT a quarter of a mile uppe on the weft fide of Fawey haven is a fquare toure of ftone for defence of the haven, made about King Edward the 4. tym, and a litle above this towr on the fame fide is Fawey town, lying along the fhore, and builded on the fide of a great flatty rokkid hill.

" IN the middle of the town upon the fhore itfelf is a houfe builded quadrantly in the haven, which fhadowith the fhippes in the haven above it, from 3 partes of the Haven mouth, and defendith them from ftormes.

" THE name of the town of Fawey is in Cornifh Conwhath. It is fet on the north fide of the haven, and is fet hangging on a maine rokky hille, and is in length about a quarter of a mile.

" The towne longid to one Cardinham, a man of great fame, and he gave it to Tywartraith Priorie, of the which fum fay that Cardinham was founder, fum fay Campernulph of Bere.

" But at this gift, Fawey was but a finaul fifchar toun.

" The paroch church of Fawey is of S. Finibarrus, and was inpropriate to the priorie of Tywartraith.

The glorie of Fawey rofe by the warres in King Edward the firft and thirde, and Henry the V. day, partely by feates of warre, partely by pyracie, and fo waxing riche felle al to Merchaundice, fo that the town was haunted with fhippes of divers nations, and their fhippes went to al nations.

" The fhips of Fawey fayling by Rhie and Winchelfey about Edward the 3 tyme, woud vale no bonet beyng required, whereupon Rhy and Winchelfey men, and they faught, wher Fawey men had victorie, and thereupon bare their armes, mixed with the armes of Rhy and Winchelfey, and then rofe the name of the gallants of Fawey.

" The French men diverfe tymes affailid this toun, and laft moft notably about Henry the VI. tyme, when the wife of Thomas Treury the 2d, with her men, repelled the French out of her houfe in her houfebandes abfence, whereupon Thomas Treury buildid a right fair, and ftrong embatelid towr in his houfe ; and embateling al the waulles of the houfe, in a maner made it a caftelle, and unto this day it is the glorie of the town building in Fawey.

" In Edward the IV. day, two ftronge towers were made a litle beneth the town, one on eche fide of the haven, and a chayne to be drawen over.

When warre in Edward the IV. days feafed betwene the French men and Englifch, the men of Fawey ufed to pray, kept their fhippes, and affalid the French men in the fea agayne, King Edwardes commandement, whereupon the captaines of the fhippes of Fowey were taken and fent to London, and Dartemouth men commanded to fetche their fhippes away, at whiche tyme Dartmouth men toke their in Fawey, and toke away, as it is fayde, the great chaine that was made to be drawen over the haven from tour to towr. Thomas Treury, now livinge, and the towne, made a blocke-houfe on St. Catherine's hille botom. Vol. 3. p. 15.

Carew fays, that " The townfmen vaunt, that for the refkuing certaine fhips of Rye from the Normans in Henrie the thirds time, they beare the armes, and enjoy part of the priviledges appertaining to the Cinque Ports, whereof there is fome memorie in their chauncell window, with the name of Fifart Bagga, their principall commaunder in that fervice. Moreover, the prowefse of one Nicholas, fonne to a widdow neere Foy, is defkanted upon, in an old three mans fongs, namely, how he fought bravely at fea, with John Dory (a Genowey, as I conjecture) fet forth by John the French king, and after much bloudfhed on both fides, tooke and flew him, in revenge of the great ravine and crueltie, which he had fore-committed, upon the Englifh mens goods and bodies."

This view, which was drawn September 1786, from the hill on the north fide of the outer, or St. Catherines caftle, fhews the two towers built by King Edward the Fourth, two fmall batteries lately erected for the defence of the haven having fheds to cover the guns ; and laftly, parts of the church and town.

Town, Haven & Castles of Fowey, Cornwall, Pl. 2.

THE TOWN, HAVEN, AND CASTLES OF FOWEY, CORNWALL. (PLATE II.)

HAVING in the defcription, plate I, tranfcribed the account of this place given by Leland, I fhall here add fuch additional particulars as occurred to me in vifiting the fpot.

FIRST, then, with refpect to the two towers built by king Edward the IVth, they are both extant, though in ruins, all the floors being fallen in. Two links of the boom or chain, which ran crofs the harbour, were taken up by a trawl boat about the year 1776; they were ftrongly incrufted with ftones, fhells and other bodies, and are now preferved in the grotto of Philip Rafhley, Efq; at Menabilly, near this town.

TREFFERY Houfe, called the Place, the caftellated manfion mentioned by Leland, is ftill ftanding, though much out of repair. The tower on the north-eaft angle has fallen down, and many other parts feem likely to follow. It was a handfome building, the outfide highly decorated with ornaments cut in the ftone. It has a very fine old hall, with a flat oaken ceiling, richly carved, and under a coat of arms in ftucco is the date 1575. In another room are diverfe coats of arms in old painted glafs; among them one with the plume of feathers, having on each fide of it the letters E. P. probably fignifying Edward Prince of Wales. Under it is the motto, thus mif-fpelt, *Hic Dien.* Several parts of this houfe have been repaired in the modern ftile. The chief entrance to it is from the church-yard, up three flights of fteps, and through a ruined gate, with a ftrong wicket, flanked by a lodge pierced with loop holes; the gardens run along upon an eminence, overlooking the town and harbour.

THE church, which ſtands a ſmall diſtance ſouth from it, is a handſome edifice; the tower adorned all over with carving. In it are ſeveral monuments, chiefly for the Treffrys and Raſhleys, ſome of them having the figures of knights in armour engraved on ſtone, in the ſame manner as practiſed on braſs. There are alſo a few braſs plates; but neither thoſe nor the ſtone monuments are older than the latter end of the ſixteenth century, and ſome even of the ſeventeenth.

THERE are alſo ſeveral ſculptured monuments in marble and other ſtone; ſome of them mural, and but indifferently executed. One, a table monument, for Mr. John Raſhleighe, is in a better ſtile; his figure lies on the top, as big as life, habited in a kind of bonnet, ruff and gown. The ſides are adorned with eſcutcheons of arms, figures, and an inſcription in verſe; but ſo blocked up by pews, as to prevent its being read. On one of the eſcutcheons is a ſhip with four maſts. A whimſical epitaph is ſhewn here for one of the Treffry family, ſaid to have been written by himſelf, and put up whilſt he was living. It is inſcribed on a marble tablet :

Our nature by order of Providence divine,
Will have its period to which it doth incline;
From birth to fatall death ſummons us to the grave,
Where equally doth lye the ſimple, fooll, and brave.

Eccleſiaſtes, chap. ii. ver. 16.

Here, in this chancell do I ly,
Known by the name of John Treffry,
Being made and born for to dye,
So muſt thou, friend, as well as I;
Therefore good works be ſure to try,
But chiefly love and charity;
And ſtill on them with faith rely,
So be happy eternally.
Soli Deo Gloria.

THE roof of the church, which is coved ſemicircularly, is adorned with diverſe carvings in wood, of angels holding armorial ſhields, and other devices, as are alſo the beams, and ſome of the pews. There is likewiſe kept here, a very ancient carved chair. Although the town of Fowey has many very good houſes, and is the reſidence of many reſpectable gentlemen, no wheeled carriage can come into it, owing to the narrowneſs and ſudden turnings of the ſtreets.

THIS view, which was drawn A. D. 1786, is taken from the haven ſide, a little to the ſouth-weſt of the town, at the place where the ferry-boat lands paſſengers from Polruan. It exhibits one of king Edward the IVth's towers, and a diſtant view of the harbour's mouth, and St. Catherine's caſtle.

North side of Fowey Castle, Cornwall. Pl. 1.

THE OUTER, OR ST. CATHERINE's CASTLE, AT FOWEY, IN CORNWALL. (PLATE I.)

THIS view prefents the north fide of the Outer, or St. Catherine's Caftle or Blockhoufe, built, as Leland fays, at the joint charge of Mr. Thomas Trefry, and the townfmen of Fowey. It is ftill kept up at the expence of the corporation, there being no allowance or efta-blifhment from government for that purpofe. As Mr. Trefry was, according to Leland, living when he wrote his Itinerary, this blockhoufe muft have been erected towards the latter end of the reign of King Henry the eighth ; indeed its conftruction carries the appearance of the military architecture of that time.

THIS view was drawn September 1786.

Fowey Outer, or St Catherine's Castle Cornwall East Aspect.

THE OUTER, OR ST. CATHERINE's CASTLE, AT FOWEY, IN CORNWALL. (PLATE II.)

THE east view of this castle is here given, as it appears in the way from the town. Its picturesque and Romantic situation and appearance will, it is hoped, apologize for a second plate of a building of so little importance, either as to antiquity or architecture.

This view was drawn September 1786.

St. Germains Priory, Cornwall. Pl. 1.

ST. GERMAIN'S PRIORY, CORNWALL. (PLATE I.)

THIS Priory is supposed to have been founded by King Ethelstan, and dedicated to St. Germaine, Bishop of Auxere in France, a famous preacher, and a strenuous opposer of the Pelagian Heresy, for which purpose he came over into Britain with Lupus, Bishop of Troy, A.D. 429.

HERE were at first Secular Canons, and King Ethelstan is said to have appointed one Conan to the bishoprick of their see, A.D. 936; but Tanner and Borlace both think it more probable that the Episcopal See for Cornwall, was not fixed here till after the burning of the Bishop's house, and Cathedral Church at Bodmin, Anno 981, after which King Canute more amply endowed this Church; and about the year 1050, Levfric who was Bishop here, and of Crediton, having united both Bishopricks in the Church of St. Peter at Exeter, changed the Seculars here into regular Canons, and appointed the Bishop of Exeter, for the time being, perpetual Patron. The yearly revenues of this Priory were valued, 26 Henry VIII. at 243 *l.* 8 *s.* 0 *d.* Dugdale. Speed makes it 227 *l.* 4 *s.* 8 *d.* Clare MS valor; the Scite was granted 33 Henry VIII. to Kath. Champernoun, John Ridgway, &c.

CAREW in his History of Cornwall, among other particulars respecting this Priory, relates a pleasant story of the manner in which was acquired by Champernoun. The whole passage is here transcribed in his own words:

"THE Church towne mustreth many inhabitants, and sundry ruines, but little wealth, occasioned either through abandoning their fishing trade, as some conceive, or by their being abandoned of the religious people, as the greatest sort imagine: for in some times, the Bishop of Cornwall's See, was from St. Petrock's in Bodwyn removed hither; as from hence, when the Cornish Diocess united with Devon, it passed to Crediton; and laftly, from hence to Excefter. But this firft loffe receyved reliefe through a fucceeding Priory, which, at the general fuppreffion, changing his note with his Coate, is now named *Port Eliot*, and by the owners charity diftributeth *pro virili*, the almes accuftomably expected and expended at fuch places. Neither will it (I thinke) much difpleafe you to heare, how the Gentleman's anceftors, of whom Mafter Eliot bought it, came by the fame. John Champernoune, fon and heir apparent to Sir Philip Devon, in Henry the VIII's time, followed the Court, and through his pleafant conceits, of which much might be fpoken, won fome good grace with the King. Now when the golden fhowre of the diffolved Abbey lands rayned welnere into every gaper's mouth, fome two or three Gentlemen of the King's fervants, and Mafter Champernowne's acquaintance, waited at a doore where the King was to paffe forth, with purpofe to beg fuch a matter at his hands: Our Gentleman became inquifitive to know their fuit, they made ftronge to import it. This while out comes the King; they kneele down, fo doth Mafter Champernowne: They preferre their petition; the King grants it; they render humble thanks, and fo doth Mafter Champernowne: Afterwards he requireth his fhare; they deny it; he appeals to the King; the King avoweth his equal meaning in the largeffe, whereon the overtaken companions were fayne to allot him this priory for his partage.

THE parish church anfwereth in bigneffe, the large proportion of the parifh, and the furplufage of the Priory; a great part of whofe chauncell, anno 1562, fel fuddenly downe, upon a Friday, very fhortly after publicke fervice was ended, which heavenly favour of fo little refpite, faved many perfons lives, with whom immediately before it had bene ftuffed; and devout charges of the well difpofed parifhioners quickly repayred this ruine.

ROBERT SWIMMER, Prior. Nich Gyft fub-prior. Richard Tyn, with four others, fubfcribed to the King's fupremacy, Aug. 13, 1534. 26 Hen. VIII. The fame Prior, viz. Robert Swymmer furrendered his Convent, with feven Monks, March 2, 30 Hen. VIII. Their names were Stephen Sackogmore, Richard Trowt, Robert Vyan, Will Lowee, Robert Kappit, John Ryche, Martin Powtravyr. Penfions, An. 1550. To Robert Swimmer Prior, 66l. 13s. 4d. over his name is wrote, he hath changed his penfion for a benefice. I prefume his benefice was the Rectory of Southill, in this County, to which the borough town of Kellington is a chapelry: and my reafon for this is, becaufe he was a good benefactor to the faid chapel.) Stephen Segenore, 5l. 6s. Robert Vyen, 5l. 6s. 8d. Robert Capel, 2l.

BORLASE fays, this Monaftick church is as ancient a building, as any at this time extant in Cornwall, and was formerly inclofed by the Priory. This likewife appears from the following paffage in Leland's Itinerary, Vol. VII. p. 123. " Alfo upon another creke, weft of the faid river, (Tamor) and nerer up, is a towne cawled S. Germaynes, wherin is now a Priori of Black Canons, and a paroche Churche yn the body of the fame. Befide the hye altare of the fame Priori, in the ryght hand, ys a tumbe yn the walle, with an image of a Bifhop, and over the tumbe a XI. Bifhops, paynted with their names and verfes, as token of fo many Bifhops beried theere, or that there had beene fo many Bifhoppes of Cornwalle, that had theyr feete theer: and at this day the Bifhop of Exeter hath a place cawled Cudden Beke, joining hard upon the Sowth-Eaft fide of the fame towne.

THIS view was drawn 1786.

St Germains Priory, Cornwall. Pl. 2

ST. GERMAIN's PRIORY, CORNWALL.
(PLATE II.)

The former plate contained such information respecting this priory, as could be collected from printed books: For the following particulars I am indebted to the Rev. Chancellor Carrington, and Mr. Penwarne, minister of the parish.

The church of St. Germain consists of a nave and two aisles; the southernmost aisle is compass-roofed, as well as the nave, and is nearly of an equal heighth, breadth and length, with it; the northern aisle is low and narrow, with a slanting roof, which does not reach to the height of the wall by several feet. It is ten feet wide within, and formerly extended the length of the building. The church measures 104 feet 6 inches in length, by 67 feet 6 inches in breadth, within the walls. There is one stall remaining, which has commonly been called the bishop's chair; but seemingly without reason, as it rather appears to have been the seat of one of the monks. Several of the same kind are still preserved in Bodmin church. It is accompanied by a piece of carved timber, on which is the coat of arms of the priory, a sword and key crossed. Concerning these arms, there is the following article in Tanner's Notitia Monastica, among the notes on the armorial bearings of the different monasteries:

" St. Germain's: the priory is the manfion of Mr. Elliot; in the great hall are the arms of the priory on painted glafs of a large bow window, viz. a fword and two keys endorfed in Saltire. Mag. Britan. Antiq. et nov. p. 347, a. It feems to be the fame with Plimpton, the fecond coat of Bath Abbey, or the arms of the bifhoprick of Winchefter, and might perhaps formerly be the arms of the bifhop of this diocefe." It does not appear that this was ever any part of the chair or feat, on which is carved the figure of a hunter, with game on his fhoulder, and accompanied by dogs. It is now removed to a niche in the chancel, and placed on part of a teffalated pavement, found about 50 feet from the prefent eaft window: this pavement was about ten feet fquare. Nearly ten feet eaft of it, was the foundation of a wall, which from its thicknefs and materials feems to have been the original extent of the building.

In the wall of the fouth aifle there are three niches, two at the eaftern end high and narrow, which have been ornamented at the top; and about the middle of the fame aifle, there is one of a very different figure, which is fuppofed to have belonged to a more ancient monument; it is ornamented all round, and alfo in front to the height of two feet and a half from the floor of the church, where the recefs of the wall is covered with a ftone 7 feet 6 inches long, and 1 foot 9 inches broad. This ftone has many marks on the face of it, as if fome metal had been let into it; none is at prefent remaining, nor do the marks defcribe any intelligible figure. Refpecting this monument there is no tradition whatfoever. In the chancel are feveral monuments of the Moyle and Scawen families, of different dates.

The priory of St. Germain's, and other lands in the vicinity, were obtained by an exchange made in the year 1565, between John Eliot, efq. and Mr. Champernoune; the former giving for the priory, &c. an eftate called Coleland's in Devonfhire.

This plate exhibits the weft front of this venerable pile. It was drawn about the year 1779, before the clock given by lord Eliot, was fet up. This clock is feen in Plate I. About the fame time that this clock was given, lord Eliot, then Mr. Eliot, procured a faculty from the bifhop, for levelling the church-yard, and making a new cemetery at a little diftance towards the weft, which has been ufed for that purpofe ever fince, and the old church-yard now forms a kind of lawn between the church and the manfion-houfe.

S.t Germain's Priory, now Port Elliot, Cornwall.

ST. GERMAIN'ṣ PRIORY, NOW PORT ELLIOT, CORNWALL.

THIS plate prefents a view of the feat of lord Elliot, formerly the lodgings and offices of the priory of St. Germain's, which having been purchafed by one of his anceftors in the reign of queen Elizabeth, has continued ever fince in the poffeffion of the family, and has by them been improved to its prefent ftate. This family have been confiderable benefactors to the town of St. Germain's, having endowed a public fchool there, repaired the feffions-houfe, and beautified the old conventual, now parochial church, where one of them lies buried under a fine monument of Italian marble, erected to his memory by his widow.

THIS view was drawn A. D. 1787.

LAUNCESTON CASTLE, CORNWALL. (PLATE I.)

LAUNCESTON, according to Leland, was called Loftephan, and alfo Dunevet; the laft, perhaps, from fome allufion to the family of the Nevets, or Knivets, who might either give their name to it, or be ftiled De or Du-Nevet after it.

BORLACE, in his antiquities of Cornwall, fuppofes this caftle to be older than the year 900, and fays, It is not improbable that this fpot might have been fortified by the Romans. There was undoubtedly a caftle here before the conqueft, of which Othamarus de Knivet was hereditary conftable, and was difplaced by the Conqueror, who gave both it and the town to Roger earl of Moreton, with the earldome of Cornwall, and many other manors and eftates. William, his fon and heir, kept his court here, and probably made fo many alterations and additions, that he has by fome been confidered as the founder. From him it fell to the crown, with his other lands, and was at length made, and ftill continues aparcel of the eftates of the duchy of Cornwall.

LELAND treating of this caftle fays, the hill on which the keep ftands is large, and of a terrible height, and the arx (i. e. keep) of it, having three feveral wards is the ftrongeft, but not the biggeft that I ever faw in any ancient work in England.

BORLACE, who feems to have examined this building with great attention, thus defcribes it : " The principal entrance is on the north-eaft, the gateway 120 feet long, whence, turning to the right, you mount a terrace running parallel to the rampart, till you come to the angle, on which there is a round tower, now called the Witches Tower, from which the terrace runs away to the left, at right angles, and continues on a level parallel to the rampart, which is nearly of the thicknefs of twelve feet, till you come to a femicircular tower, and, as I fuppofe a guard room, and gate: from this the ground rifes very quick, and, through a paffage of feven feet wide, you afcend the covered way betwixt two walls, which are pierced with narrow windows for obfervation, and yet cover the communication between the bafe court and the keep or dungeon. The whole keep is 93 feet diameter. It confifted of three wards; the wall of the firft ward was not quite three feet thick, and therefore I think could only be a parapet for foldiers to fight from, and defend the brow of the hill. Six feet within it ftands the fecond wall, which is twelve feet thick, and has a ftaircafe three feet wide at the left hand of the entrance, running up to the top of the rampart. The entrance of this ftaircafe has a round arch of ftone over it; paffing on to the left you find the entrance into the innermoft ward, and on the left of that entrance a winding ftaircafe cafe conducts you to the top of the innermoft rampart, the wall of which is 10 feet thick, and 32 feet high from the floor; the inner room is 18 feet fix diameter, it was divided by a planching into two rooms. The upper room had to the eaft and weft, two large openings, which were both windows, and (as I am inclined to think) doors alfo in time of action, to pafs from this dungeon out upon the principal rampart, from which the chief defence was to be made; for it muft be obferved, that the fecond ward was covered with a flat roof at the height of that rampart, which made the area very roomy and convenient for numbers. Thefe openings, therefore, upon occafion, ferved as paffages for the foldiers to go from one rampart to the other. In the upper room of the innermoft building there was a chimney to the north, underneath there was a dungeon which had no light. The lofty taper hill on which this ftrong keep is built, is partly natural and partly artificial; it fpread farther in the town anciently than it does now, and by the radius of it, was 320 feet diameter, and very high. (*)

NORDEN gives us a wall at the bottom of this hill, and though there is no ftrefs to be laid on his drawing, yet it is not unlikely that it had a wall or parapet round the bottom of it, towards the town, for the principal rampart of the bafe-court breaks off abruptly fronting the town, and feems patched and maimed, and to have loft fome works at this place. The bafe-court (half of which, or more, as I judge, is now covered with the houfes of the town) had formerly in it the affize-hall, a very fpacious building, a chapel, and other buildings, now all gone, but the county gaol. At the weftern end there is another gateway into the town, but more modern than the reft.

THIS view, which reprefents the north afpect, was drawn anno 1786.

* I took the height of it by a quadrant, and made it from the bafe-court to the parapet of the dungeon, 164 feet perpendicular; but as it rained violently, I cannot depend on the obfervation, though I believe it is pretty near the truth.

Launceston Castle, Cornwall. Pl. 2.

LAUNCESTON CASTLE, CORNWALL.

(PLATE II.)

THIS view fhews the keep of this antique caftle as it appears from one of the upper rooms in the White Hart Inn, whence it was drawn in the year 1786.

THESE circular keeps feem almoft peculiar to this county; one however, tho' not raifed aloft on a mount, is to be found in Wales; that is in Flint Caftle; where the keep confifts of a large round tower, having an open circular area or well in its center.

St Michael's Mount. Cornwall. Pl.1.

ST. MICHAEL'S MOUNT, CORNWALL. (Plate I.)

This romantic mount is situated in the bottom of Mount's Bay, about half a mile south of the town of Marazion, from which place there is a dry passage to it over the sands, from half ebb to half flood ; at other times the only communication is by means of a boat.

This mount is by Ptolomy called Ocrinum, by the Cornish men Karah-Luz, en-leuz, that is the grey, or hoary rock in the wood, from a number of trees formerly growing between it and Penzance, many of which are said by Leland to have been found thereabouts ; and others have been discovered within a few years, i. e. A. D. 1757. It was called in the book of Landaff, Densul, a compound word, signifying a hill dedicated to the sun ; and in the sixth century, Michael Stow, in latin St. Michael de Monte, and as Scawen says, St. Michael de Magno Monte.

It is doubtful when this mount was first appropriated to religious uses ; it is however certain, it was deemed a holy place as early as the 5th century ; for St. Keyna, daughter of Braganus, King of Brecknockshire, in Wales, is said to have come hither in a pilgrimage about the year 490 ; and some years afterwards to have been joined by Cadoc her nephew, who, as may be seen in Capgrave, miraculously produced a fountain in a dry place, on which a church was erected to his honour. King Edward the Confessor found here a few Monks, and gave them by charter the property of the mount, and other lands, on condition that they should observe the rule of St. Benedict. After the accession of William the Conqueror, the duchy of Cornwall being by him bestowed on Robert Earl of Morton, he out of regard to Normandy, his mother country, made this monastry a cell to the abbey of St. Michael de Periculo Maris (situated on a mount on the coast of Normandy, extremely similar to this) a cistertian monastry of the reformed kind, called Gilbertines, from its founder Gilbert, of Semperingham, in Lincolnshire by which rule Monks and Nuns were placed in the same house, and accordingly here were both a priory and nunnery. Here was also, as Léland " a lytel chapel yn the land near by the town toward the mount," at which probably the pilgrims stopped to offer up their orisons, as a preparation to purify them for the holy mount. A stack of rocks near half way between the town and mount still bear the name of the chapel rock.

This monastery was seized by King Edward III. among the other alien priories, and was afterwards restored and made Denizon, on condition of paying to the King the sum annually remitted to its superior foreign convent ; but by an after ordonance all religious houses, not conventual, were directed to be taken into the king's hands, when notwithstanding the prior of this house appeared to the summons, and gave sufficient proof that it was actually conventual, the Bishop of St. David's, then treasurer to the king, set it to farm at 20l. per annum, which the king remitted, retaining only ten pounds a year, to be paid half yearly, so long as this nation should continue at war with France. The reason assigned in the the deed, which is printed in Rymer, was, that under that rent the Monks could not afford to repair their buildings, which were greatly decayed, a matter that might be extremely detrimental to the king's service, that mount being the fortress of the adjacent country.

About this time the priory was valued at 200 marks a year ; there were only six stalls in the choir, and consequently the priory could have no more Monks, even when complete, which was not always the case, for it was visited A. D. 1336 by Grandison, Bishop of Exeter, and the conduct of the prior censured for remaining one month without a Monk, letting the lands beneath their value, and suffering delapidations.

When king Henry VI. built King's College, in Cambridge, he gave it this priory, which was afterwards by Edward IV. granted to the nunnery of Sion, in Middlesex.

At the dissolution of religious houses it was valued at 110l. 12s. per annum. King Henry the VIIIth gave the revenues and government of it, for it had been many ages before a garrisoned fort, as well as a religious house, to Humphry Arundell, Esq. a branch of the family of Lanherne, who enjoyed it till the first of Edward VI. After his death goverment granted a lease of it to John Milton, Esq. under the description of the farm house of the mount and island, with the appurtenances, for the yearly rent of 40 marks. It afterwards came into the family of St. Aubyn, and is at present the property of Sir John St. Aubyn, Bart.

This view, which was drawn from the town of Marazion, a little to the westward of the passage to the mount, shews the north side of the mount, chapel, and mansion of Sir John St. Aubyn ; the fishermens houses below, and the pier. On the left is seen the passage, which rises like a causeway, and is formed of large loose stones.

THIS view was drawn anno 1786.

S.ʳ Michaels Mount Cornwall Pl.2.

ST. MICHAEL'ı MOUNT, CORNWALL. (PLATE II.)

Iɴ the defcription annexed to the former plate, this mount was confidered in its monaftic capacity; the objeĉt of the prefent fhall be to inveftigate it as a fortefs, and to relate the different military operations there tranfaĉted.

Tʜᴇ firft inftance of any material confequence happened in the reign of King Richard 1ft. whilft that monarch was detained prifoner by the Emperor of Germany, when Hoveden fays, Henry de la Pomeroy furprifed this place, expelled the monks, and fortified it, but learning that his fovereign had recoverd his ilberty, and fearing a juft punifhment for this aĉtion he became his own exceutioner. After his death it was furrenderd to the Archbifhop of Canterbury for the King.

Aᴄᴄᴏʀᴅɪɴɢ to Carew, in his hiftory of this county, the defcendants of this Pomeroy relate this ftory very differently ; for they affirme (fays he) that a Serjeant at Armes of the Kinges, came to their anceftor, at his caftle at Berry Pomeroy in Devon, received kind entertaynment for certaine days together, and at his departure, was gratified with a liberal reward, in counterchange whereof, he then, and no fooner, revealing his long concealed errant, flatly arrefted his hoafte, to make his immediate appearance before the King for anfwering a capital crime, which unexpeĉted and il-carryed meffage, the Gentleman tooke in fuch defpite as with his dagger he ftabbed the meffenger to the heart, and then well knowing in fo fuperlative an offence, all hope of pardon foreclofed : he abandons his home, gets to a fifter of his abiding in.

this mount, bequeatheth a large portion of his land to the religeous people there for redeeming his fowle; and laftly caufeth himfelf to be let bloud unto death, for leaving the remainder to his heir. From this time forward this place continued rather a fchoole of mars than the temple of peace.

A. D. 1471. In the 13th of Edward IV. John de Vere Earl of Oxford, an active partizan for the houfe of Lancafter after the defeat at the battle of Barnet, took fhipping for this place, attended by a few faithful followers, and under the difguife of pigrims to the holy mount, furprifed the garrifon and feized the fortrefs, which he for a long time defended, againft the Kings forces, flaying in one of the attacks John Arundel, of Trerife, who was buried in the chapel, but at length furrendered it on reafonable conditions. This laft circumftance is contradicted in one of the letters to the Pafton Family, wherein it is faid only his life was granted, the words are, " It'm men faye that the Erle of Oxenfford hathe ben conftraynyd to fewe ffor hys pardon only off hys lyffe, and hys body, goodes, londes with all ye remenaunt at ye Kinges wyll and foo fholde in all hafte nowe come in to ye King, and fome men faye yt is goon out of ye mounte, men wot not to what plaie and yeit lefte a great Garuyfon theer weel furnyfhyd in oytayll and all other thynge.

DURING the late Cornifh commotion fays Carew, diverfe gent. with their wives and families fled to the protection of this place, where the rebels befieged them, firft wynning the plaine at the hils foote by affault, when the water was out, and then the even ground on the top, by carrying up great truffes of hay before them, to bleach the defendants fight and dead their fhot, after which they could make but flender refiftance, for no fooner fhould any one within, peepe out his head over thofe unflanked wals but he became an open marke to a whole fhowre of arrowes.

THIS difadvantage, together with womens difmay and decreafe of victuals, forced a furrender to thefe Rakehels mercy, who, nothing guilty of that effeminate vertue, fpoyled their goods, imprifoned their bodies, and were rather by Gods gracious providence, than any want of will, purpofe, or attempt, reftrayned from murdering the principal perfons.

IN the 13th of Henry VII. heere alfo was Lady Catharine Gordon (an unfit yoke fellow for that counterfeit prince Perkin Warbeck) taken by the Lord Daubeney and conveyed to the King.

THE mount had its fhare in the troubles under Charles I. as we learn from Sprigges treatife, entitled England's Recovery, where it is related, that about the middle of April 1646, it was taken by Colonel Hammond, after confiderable defence; the Governor was Sir Arthur Baffet. The Marquis of Hamilton was prifoner in it. Here were found fifteen pieces of ordnance, and great ftore of ammunition and provifions; this is, fays he, a place of great ftrength, the tyde flowing about it twice a day which rendered the reduction of it a fervice of great difficulty and confequence, and redounding much to the honour of Colonel Hammond, who underwent the fame.

THIS view fhews the north fide of the buildings, as feen from the bottom of the mount, fouth of the fifhermen's houfes.

THE church and tower are placed on the summit of the rock; the nunnery and house for the monks, stand lower in point of height, and spread to the east, south and west, for the most part at equal distances, but to the south-west end, contiguous to the church; the whole making together a kind of oblong square, consisting of projecting and receding rectangles. These buildings have of late received many modern repairs. The following description is as they stood about forty years ago, before the alteration.

As you ascend the outer gate, fronting the west, you have a wall, or rather some part of one, on each hand of the steps; that on the right-hand has a stone door-case and part of a large window standing, which shews the building formerly extended farther towards the west. At the top of the steps you enter the first gate, which is very low, and the portcullis with which it appears to have been guarded, needed not to have been more than four feet high; five steps within the gate, lead you into the passage or entry, about twelve feet wide, (on the left of which is the guard-room or dungeon) till you come to a large wooden gate, whence leaving the church door on the right and a narrow embattled terrass on the left, in about seventy feet eastward you come to a grey coarse marble door-case, carved in a better gothic style than the opening of the church, and therefore more modern; over it is a window of the same stone and workmanship, exactly well plac'd; the door lets you into an apartment distinct from the other parts of the monastery, about fifty foot long and eighteen wide, consisting of one chamber or more (for the partitions were all down) to the west, over a passage somewhat more than half the length, i. e. twenty-five feet; and lets you into a chapel dedicated to St. Mary, with a little area to the east of it. This was the nunnery, and in the aforesaid passage, on the left hand, there is a narrow stair-case, by which the nuns retired to their chambers over the passage. The planching of the chambers was fallen into the passage below, through which over carved beams and rubbish, we got to the end of the building with difficulty, and in the eastern end of the chapel found a fair marble window which gave light to the altar; one stone of the same grey marble projected from the south wall, it had two escutcheons embossed; the first had three castles, two and one garretted, the arms at present of the town of Merazion, and formerly perhaps the arms of this priory. The second escutcheon had a chevron between the fleurs de lis; this stone served no doubt to support part of the image of the Holy Virgin. The chapel was peculiar to the nunnery, and from the chamber the whole of the chapel might be seen, and the ordinary duties of devotion performed, without descending or opening the gratines of the chambers. In the eastern hall behind the altar, there was a small door of three feet and a half high, which is the only entrance into a little open court or belvidere, of no more than six paces long and three wide, with a little terrass or banquet to look over the garretted wall to the east. By the carved fragments of stone, with some other marks of distinction and neatness, this apartment shews itself to have been erected with much cost.

This view was drawn A. D. 1786.

St. Michaels Mount. Cornwall. Pl. 3.

ST. MICHAEL's MOUNT. PLATE III.

THE eastern part of this romantick building is here given, seemingly overhanging the almost perpendicular rock whereon it stands, from the summit of which there is a most extensive and beautiful prospect over the bay. The height from low water mark to the top of the buildings, is said to measure two hundred and thirty-eight feet. The distance from Merazion, half a mile. The present proprietor bids fair greatly to augment the beauty of the scene by judicious plantations of firs over the face of the mount, most of which seem to thrive.

AT the bottom of the rock, on the north side, is a handsome pier and bason, capable of receiving upwards of fifty sail of fishing vessels. It was erected in the year 1425, when it is recorded in the register of the bishops of Exeter, that Edmund, then bishop, granted forty days indulgence to all those who should contribute, or otherwise assist the inhabitants of Merazion in building the stone pier, then begun. Possibly some wooden or other mole, might have before existed.

THIS pier has been since rebuilt by Sir John St. Aubyn, the third baronet of that name, in the years 1726 and 1727. The entrance is in the middle of the north front, by an opening of forty feet. The west front of the wall is 481 feet, towards the north and east it measures 445 feet. Occasionally ships of considerable burthen may be here.

THE manuscript before-mentioned, which was written by Mr. Borlace about the year 1730, gives a description of the state of the buildings of this monastery before repaired, to the following purport:

St. Michael's Mount, Cornwall. Pl. 4.

ST. MICHAEL's MOUNT, CORNWALL. Plate IV.

The weft front of this venerable pile is here delineated. The entrance, up a flight of fteps, lies behind the great tower; over it appears the tower and flag-ftaff of the church; part of its weft end is alfo feen over the middle of the building between the two towers.

The whole of this edifice is in a compleat ftate of repair, and affords a moft delight-ful fummer refidence to the prefent owner, who commonly retires hither from his feat at Clowance for a few weeks. Indeed the peculiar romantic fituation of the building, the beauty of the furrounding fcene, and the operations of the pilchard fifhery, prefent a variety of rich profpects, fcarcely to be conceived by thofe who have not had the pleafure of feeing them. The polite reception and hofpitable entertainment given by fir John to ftrangers vifiting the place, is not often equalled, and cannot be exceeded.

This ifland is ftill in fome degree a fortrefs, as on different parts of it there are feveral batteries furnifhed with cannon, fome of them capable of refifting a privateer. The fifhermen refiding near the pier, would on any emergency furnifh plenty of gunners and men able to perform the other duties of a garrifon.

PROBABLY the buildings here underwent some confiderable repairs between the years 1641 and 1660; as a large room, formerly the refectory of the monks, is fitted up with a very extraordinary frize, whereon in ftucco is reprefented different huntings of the wild boar, bear, bull, ftag, oftridge, fox, hare and rabbit. At the upper end of this room are the royal arms and fupporters over the date 1641, beneath this is the motto Dieu et Mon Droit, and under it the date 1660; at the other end of the room are the arms of St. Aubyn.

DIVERS ancient fpear heads, and a match lock to a mufket, have been found here in digging. Human bones are alfo frequently digged up all over the mount; at prefent a fpot of ground is fet apart for a cemetry, this place having been adjudged extra-parochial.

THE taking of this place by the parliamentary forces, about the 18th of April 1646, has been already mentioned. The fame Chronicle, in a part ftiled The Burning Bufh not confumed, page 412, has thefe additional particulars, "that the governor, fir Arthur Baffet, and the reft of the garrifon, had liberty to retire to the ifles of Scilly, and that here were found an hundred barrels of powder, 500 mufkets, 100 pikes, 30 pieces of ordnance, 3 murthering pieces, and eighty tons of wine, with ftore of other provifions." It is here ftiled "that impregnable and almoft inacceffable fort."

THIS view was drawn A. D. 1786.

Chapel of S.t Michaels Mount, Cornwall.

THE CHAPEL OF ST. MICHAELS MOUNT, CORNWALL.

THIS view shews the south-side of the chapel, with part of the long gallery that runs through the house. The small projection seen over the battlements of the tower, is the remains of a lantern, vulgarly called St. Michael's Chair, mentioned in the general description of this place, as supposed to have the virtue of conferring the reins of domestic government on that person, man or wife, who shall have courage to ascend to it, and seat themselves in it.

THIS view was drawn in 1786.

Inside View of the Chapel of St. Michaels Mount.

INSIDE OF THE CHAPEL OF ST. MICHAEL's MOUNT, CORNWALL.

This view shews the inside of the chapel as it appears from Sir John St. Aubyn's pew at the east end of the building. It was drawn anno 1786.

This edifice was repaired by the father of the present proprietor about sixty years ago; its state before that reparation is described in a manuscript preserved in the family, from whence we learn that it was divided by the lattice-work of the rood loft into an aile and a choir, and that the rood loft was carved and painted with the history of Christ's Passion, not inelegantly executed considering the time when it was done.

On each side of the entrance into the choir, were three stalls; and at the altar two tall eastern windows, and over them as a finishing at the top, one in the shape of a rose. It had also three windows with pointed arches on each side wall, and another handsome rose window at the west end. The chief door or entrance is up a flight of steps on the north side.

The aile or anti-chapel is forty-eight feet long, the choir measures twenty-one; both are of the same breadth. On the right of the altar there was a little door, which by twelve steps led down to a well arched stone vault, nine feet square; this, from a very small aperture or listening place, in the south wall, appears to have been intended for the purpose of hearing confessions.

THE walls are thick and well built, and which is fuppofed a mark of antiquity, have no buttreffes. The bell tower ftands in the center of the building. In this tower are five tuneable bells, four of them feemingly of fome antiquity. On the firft or fmalleft, is written in a very neat old Englifh character, Ordo Poteftatuum.

ON the fecond, ⊕ I. Sancte Nicholae Ora pro Nobis ⊕ I, O, S, Ordo Principatuum. On the third bell, Spiritus Sanctus eft Deus—Gabriel, ⊕ Sanctae Paule Ora pro Nobis. Ordo Virtutum. Maria. On the fourth bell, Filius eft Deus. Raphael ⊕ Sancta Margarita Ora pro Nobis. Ordo Archangelorum. On the fifth bell, which is not fo neat as the others, is, in indifferent Roman characters, Soli Deo Detur Gloria. 1640, with the impreffion of four pieces of coin, commonly known by the title of broad pieces; on one of them, the letters CAR. are plainly to be feen. This bell was, it is likely, in the room of one more ancient, probably chriftened St. Michael; and as the two other perfons of the Trinity are mentioned in the third and fourth bells, had the following infcription: Pater eft Deus. Michael, St. — Ora pro Nobis. — Ordo Cherubini & Seraphim.

ON the top of the tower, in one of the angles, are the remains of a moor-ftone lantern, kept in all likelihood by the monks, who had a tithe of the fifhery, to give direction to the fifhermen in dark and tempeftuous weather. This is vulgarly called St. Michael's chair, and will only admit one perfon to fit down in it. The afcent to it is dangerous; but it is, neverthelefs, fometimes afcended, out of a foolifh conceit, that whofoever fits therein, whether man or woman, will thenceforth have the maftery in domeftic affairs.

AT prefent there are no remains of the ftalls, rood loft, painting or carving, they having been removed at the time of making the repairs before-mentioned; fince which time a pulpit and organ were put up, and when the prefent baronet is refident at the Mount, he pays a clergyman for performing divine fervice every Sunday, when few parifhes can boaft a more numerous or decent congregation.

The old Fort at S.t Michaels Mount, Cornwall.

THE OLD FORT ON ST. MICHAELS MOUNT, CORNWALL.

THE Old Fort, feen in plate II. of this place, and which en-
filades the way afcending to the caftle, is here drawn on a
larger fcale; it feems to have been intended for ordnance by the
fize of its embrazures or apertures. Its ftate and ftile befpeak it of
no very modern conftruction: the adjoining building to the left,
was alfo garnifhed with loop holes, forming with it a crofs fire, the
path to the entrance of the buildings on the mount paffing between
them.

THIS view was drawn A. D. 1786.

Mounts Bay. Cornwall.

ST. MICHAEL's MOUNT, AND MOUNT's BAY, CORNWALL.

THIS plate shews the eastern side of Mount's Bay, with the head land near the Lizzard Point, the small town of Merazion, or Market Jew, and the north west side of St. Michael's Mount, as they appear from an eminence near the village of Gulwall. The tower of its parish church is here seen near the fore-ground.

THIS view was drawn anno 1786.

Pendennis Castle N. West aspect, Cornwall.

PENDENNIS CASTLE, NEAR FALMOUTH, CORNWALL.

THIS fortrefs, which is very advantageoufly fituated, was firft conftructed by king Henry the VIIIth, when he fortified the fea coafts, and afterward ftrengthened and enlarged by Queen Elizabeth. Leland, in the third volume of his Itinerary defcribes it in the following words: " The very point of the haven mouth being an hille, whereof the king hath builded a caftel, is called Pendinant, and longgith to Mr. Kiligrewe. It is a mile in compace, by the compace, and is almoft environed with the fe ; and where it is not, the ground is fo low, and the cut to be made fo little, that it were infulated."

In 1646 this caftle was bravely defended againft the parliamentary forces by John Arundel of Trerice, then near eighty years of age : he was affifted by his fon Richard, a colonel in the royal army, afterwards created Lord Arundel of Trerice, and many other loyal gentlemen of the county of Cornwall, this garrifon refufed to treat till they had not provifion for twenty-four hours, and then negotiated with fuch feeming indifference, and infifted fo firmly on the articles required by them, that the enemy, ignorant of their fituation, granted them their own conditions, which were as good as had been given to any garrifon in the kingdom. This, with Ragland caftle, were among the laft garrifons held for the king. Lord Arundel, of Trerice, was Governor here in 1672.

THIS fortrefs has lately undergone great repairs, and is at prefent garrifoned by a company of invalids. The grand entrance is on the weft fide.

	£.	s.	
Its eftablifhment is a Governor, at	300	0	per ann.
A Lieutenant Governor, at - -	91	5	per ann.

The prefent Governor is Major General Robert Robinfon.
The Lieutenant Governor Major Nevifon Pool.

THIS view was drawn Auguft 1786.

Pengersick Castle, Cornwall.

PENGERSWICK CASTLE, CORNWALL.

PENGERSWICK caftle is fituated in a bottom near five miles fouth-eaft of Marazion, and about a mile fouth of the high road leading from that place to Helftone.

THE prefent remains of this caftle confift of the walls of the keep, a fquare tower of three ftories, with a fmaller one annexed to the north-eaft fide, containing a flight of winding ftone fteps, leading to the top of the building, which is covered with lead; the whole faced with fquared ftone.

MANY of the floors are fallen in, and all are much decayed. The girders which fupported them are remarkably large. On the firft floor fome of the wainfcot is remaining, on which are diverfe verfes, and moral fentences, written in the ancient black letter, one comparing a mifer to an afs loaded with riches, who notwithftanding his precious burthen, fatisfies himfelf with a thiftle. This has, however, given rife to a foolifh tradition, that the perfon who built this caftle had made a great fortune at fea, and landed fo much treafure, which he loaded on an afs, in order to convey it hither, that it broke the back of the poor animal. It is faid the figure of an afs was painted over the fentence before-mentioned; if it was, it is now expunged.

UNDER the ground floor is a large vaulted room pierced with loop holes for difcharging arrows or mufkets.

OVER the great door, which is on the north-fide of the tower, is a machicolation, for pouring boiling water, or melted lead, on the heads of affailants attempting to force it open.

NORTH of the tower are several ruinous walls of different appartments covered with ivy; and on the north-east, the remains of a window and door. Neither Leland, Carew, Hals, nor any other of the topographical writers, who mention this place, give any information respecting the builder, or time when this castle was erected; nor could the occupier of it give any tradition respecting it, except the foolish story of the ass.

AT present the property of these remains are divided into several parts: Lord Caermarthen is the chief proprietor. The castle, together with a small farm, is rented for ten pounds per annum. Several parts of this structure, such as door cases and window frames, have been taken down and used to refit the neighbouring cottages.

NEAR the castle is a pretty rill of water, and from the leads of the tower there is a beautiful prospect, taking in the sea, which is distant about a mile. The greater parts of this building do not bear the marks of any very remote antiquity, and probably are not; the tower in particular much older than the reign of Henry VIII.

MR. Carew mentions this place by the appellation of " a fayr house in an unfruitful soyle ;" whence it is evident it was entire when he wrote his survey of Cornwall, which was published A. D. 1602. Mr. Hals, in his parochial antiquities of Cornwall says, this Barton and Manor was purchased in the latter end of the reign of king Henry VIII. by Mr. Milliton, who having slain a man, privately made that purchase in the name of his son, and immured himself in a secret chamber of the tower, seeing none but his trusty friends, so that he died, without being called in question for that offence.

THIS son John Milliton, was 1st of Ed. VI. made Governor of St. Michael's Mount, in the room of Humphrey Arundell, executed for rebellion. He married the daughter of the Godolphin family, by whom he had William Milliton, sheriff of Cornwall, 7 Eliz. 1565, who dying without issue, being lost, as Carew says, in travaile beyond the seas, the estate devolved to his six daughters, who married into the following families: 1. To Erisey and Sir Nicholas Parker. 2. To Lanine. 3. To Tresusis and Tregodeck. 4. To Trewwith, Arundel and Hearle. 5. To Bonithon. 6. To Abbot. From some of these co-heiresses Sir Nicholas Hals purchased their parts of this manor, and obtained leases from the rest, and for some time made it and Trewinard the places of his residence. His son and heir John Hals, cut down the timber, which tradition says, was here in great quantity. The land was sold to Godolfin and some others. Pen-gers-wick signifies the head ward or command, fenced, or fortified place, or pen-gweras-ike, the creek, cove, or bosom of waters-head help.

THIS view was drawn September 1786.

Restormel Castle Cornwal.

RESTORMEL CASTLE, CORNWALL.

WILLIAM of Worcester, a monk, who wrote an Itinerary the latter end of the fifteenth century, mentions this castle by the name of Reformel Castle, all he says of it is, that it is situated between the towns of Laftydielle and Lanceston.

IT is also described by Leland in his Itinerary, vol. iii. page 17. thus: " The park of Reftormel is hard by the north side of the town of Loftwithiel.—Tynne workes in this parke.—Ther is a caftel on an hill in this park, wher fumtymes the erles of Cornewal lay. The base court is fore defaced. The fair large dungeon yet ftondith. A chapel caft out of it a newer work then it, and now ontofid. A chapel of the Trinitie in the park not far from the caftelle." And in vol vii. page 122. a. " The little round caftel of Leftormel ftandith in the kinge's park ny to Lofwithiel."

BORLACE in his Hiftory of Cornwall, gives an elevation of the infide of this caftle fronting the entrance, accompanied with a plan and the following defcription : " One of the principal houfes of the earls of Cornwall, was Reftormel Caftle, about a mile north of the town of Loftwythyel. This caftle ftands not on a factitious hill, for the architect finding a rocky knoll, on the edge of a hill overlooking a deep valley, had no more to do than to plane the rock into a level, and fhape it round by a ditch, and the keep would have elevation enough, without the trouble of raifing an artificial hill, (like that at Trematon) for it to ftand on. The bafe court was fore defated, as Le-land fays, in his time fome few ruins were to be feen in the lower part, (in Mr. Carew's time) where the ditch is very wide and deep, and was formerly filled with water, brought by pipes from an adjoining hill ; on the higher fide alfo leading to the principal gate, there are traces of building to be found. The keep is a very magnificent one ; the outer wall or rampart is an exact circle, a hundred and ten feet diameter within, and ten feet wide at the top, including the thick-nefs of the parapet, which is two feet fix. From the prefent floor of the ground-rooms to the top of the rampart is twenty-seven feet six, and the top of the parapet is seven feet higher, garreted quite round. There are three stair-cases leading to the top of the rampart, one on each side of the gateway, ascending from the court within, and one betwixt the inner and outermost gate. The rooms are nineteen feet wide, the windows mostly in the innermost wall, but there are some very large openings (in the outmost wall, or rampart) now walled up, shaped like Gothick church windows, sharp arched, which were formerly very handsome and pleasant windows, and made to enjoy the prospect, their recesses reaching to the planching of the rooms: these large openings are all on the chamber floor (where the rooms of state seem to have been) and from the floor of these chambers you pass on a level to the chapel. This chapel is but twenty-five feet six, by seventeen feet six, but that it might be the more commodious, there seems to have been an anti-chapel. This chapel, as Leland well observes, is a newer work than the castle itself; and I may add, that the gateway and the large windows in the rampart wall, are also more modern than the keep, for they were not made for war and safety, but for pleasure and grandeur; and yet, as modern as these compared with the rest may appear, they must at least be as ancient as Edmund, son of Richard king of the Romans (temp. Edward I.) for since his death, I cannot find that any earl of Cornwall resided here. Richard king of the Romans kept his Court here, and in all probability made these additions temp. Henry III. The offices belonging to this castle lay below it in the base court, where signs of many ruins to the north and east are still apparent, and with the ruins on either hand as you come towards the great gate from the west, shew that this castle was of great extent; there was an oven (as Mr. Carew says) of fourteen feet largeness among the ruins in the base court, and may serve to give us some idea of the hospitality of those times. This noble keep still holds up the shell of its turreted head, but within equals the ruinous state of the base court below, over both which the following is Mr. Carew's lamentation, in his somewhat antiquated but nervous style: "Certes (says he, p. 138) it may move compassion, that a palace so healthful for air, so delightful for prospect, so necessary for commodities, so fair, in regard of those days, for building, and so strong for defence, should in time of secure peace, and under the protection of its natural princes, be wronged with those spoilings, than which it could endure no greater at the hands of any foreign and deadly enemy; for the park is disparked, the timber rooted up, the conduit pipes taken away, the roof made sale of, the planchings rotten, the walls fallen down, and the hewed stones of the windows, dournes and clavels plucked out to serve private buildings; only there remaineth an utter defacement to complain upon this unregarded distress." [*]

"The castle and honour has never been alienated, as far as I have learned, from the inheritance of the dukes and earls of Cornwall. There was a park round it, well wooded, and suitable to the quality of the ancient owners; but with several other parks in this county (there having been formerly belonging to this earldom nine parks, and one chace or forest) disparked by Henry VIII. at the instance of Sir Richard Pollard."

In the act of Resumption, 4th Edward IV. it appears, that William Sayer was on the third of March, in the preceding year, appointed to the offices of constableship of the king's castle of Rostormell and parkership of the same.

This castle and park is held of the Dutchy of Cornwall, under a lease for three lives, by William Masterman, Esq; member of parliament for Bodmyn; his immediate predecessor in this possession, Thomas Jones, Esq; was at a considerable expence in clearing the building from the rubbish and bushes with which it was encumbered and over-ron; a laudable example he has strictly followed by giving great attention to the protection and preservation of this venerable piece of antiquity, which before had, for time out of mind, been abandoned to the depredations of the under-tenants.

This view was drawn from an original picture, the property of Mr. Masterman.

[*] I THINK this castle must have been built since the Norman conquest, for in the Exeter Domesday it is not named, nor in a list of the earl of Moreton's lands and castles, communicated by Francis Gregor, Esq; from a MS. in the Ashmolean library, among the Dugdale MSS.

Restormel Castle, Cornwall 1786.

RESTORMEL CASTLE. (PLATE II.

THIS view shews the east-side of the castle, with the projecting building opposite the gate supposed by Mr. Borlace to have been the chapel; the windows, and indeed the whole building, is so overgrown with ivy, as to have very little of the stone visible.

THIS view was drawn anno 1786.

Trematon Castle, Cornwall.

TREMATON CASTLE, CORNWALL.

THIS is fuppofed to have been one of the caftles of the ancient dukes of Cornwall before the Conqueft. The builder, and time of its erection, are equally unknown. After the Conqueft, it appears by Domefday-book that it belonged to William earl of Moreton and Cornwall, who refided here and had a market. It was beftowed by the Conqueror on Robert, father of the faid William, who difpoffeffed Candorus, (or as Camden calls him, Cadocus) the laft of the ancient Britifh earls of Cornwall; according to Borlace, fometimes ftiled dukes and fometimes kings of that county.

MR. Carew mentions, that in the church of St. Stephen, which belonged to the caftle, the body of a big man was digged-up, enclofed in a leaden coffin. This, by an infcription on a plate of the fame metal, was faid to be the corps of a duke, whofe heir was married to a prince. This he conjectures to have been Orgerius, who lived A. D. 954, from the circumftance of his daughter having been married to Edgar; but this Orgerius, according to William of Malmfbury, was buried in the monaftery of Taviftock. Mr. Borlace fuppofes it to have been the body of Cadocus, whofe only daughter and heir, Agnes, was married to Reginald Fitz-Henry, natural fon of Henry I.

UNDER Robert earl of Moreton and Cornwall, according to the Exeter Domefday, Reginald de Valle-Torta held the caftle; but the inheritance came to William earl of Cornwall, from whom it paffed by attainder to the crown, with his other eftates;

then, as some think, Cadorus, son of the Candorus before-mentioned, was restored to his paternal estates and dignities, and lived and died at this castle.

From Reginald Fitz-Henry, with one of his daughters and co-heiresses, this lord-ship of Trematon came to Walter Dunstavil, baron of Castle Comb in Cornwall; with whose daughter, in default of issue male, it went to Reginald de Valle-Torta, temp. Rich. I. who from evidences in the red book of the Exchequer, appears to have had 59 knight's fees belonging to the honor of Trematon.

His son John had issue Roger, by some called Reginald, whose eldest daughter Eglina, married ⸺ Pomeroy, of Bury Pomeroy in Devonshire, on whose issue he settled this lordship. — Her son, sir Henry Pomeroy, knight, or a son of his of the same name and title, by a deed bearing date the 11th of Edward III. did, in consideration of an annuity of 40 l. payable out of the Exchequer, release to Edward the black prince, then created duke of Cornwall, all his right to this honor, castle and manor; since which time it has continued a part of the estates of the dutchy of Cornwall.

This castle stands in the parish of St. Stephen, near Saltash, and on the northern side of the river Tamar. It consists of a base court, having on one side of it a circular keep, mounted on an artificial hill. The base court contains about three quarters of an acre; in it were formerly several buildings now all gone. The gateway is in a square tower; Mr. Borlace thinks it of more modern workmanship than the rest of the building. The walls of the base court are surrounded by a ditch, and are pierced with loop-holes of different constructions; some being long chinks, some square, and others in the form of a cross.

The keep stands at one end of this court, mounted on the top of a conical hill, which by the dipping of the valley becomes of a considerable height on the outside, but next the base court is not above thirty feet high. The building is an oval, whose interior conjugate diameter measures nearly sixty feet; its transverse fifty: it has no windows, but was probably aired and illuminated by openings made into a small internal area or court in its center, called by builders a well. This would indeed afford but very little light; but in castles that conveniency was sacrificed to strength: from the want of light, Borlace supposes the keeps of castles were called dungeons. The wall of this keep is ten feet thick, and round the top runs a crenellated parapet of two feet thick; the other eight form the terre pleine of the rampart. The entrance is on the west side, through a semicircular arch. The top of the parapet is above thirty yards from the area within; which area, when Mr. Borlace saw it, was converted into a garden for pot-herbs; but the man who then shewed the castle remembered a chimney and some ruins of walls standing, of which no traces are left.

The holes for receiving the beams that supported the roof, are in two rows, but both so near the top of the parapet as to shew there was but one flight of rooms; the double holes being designed to give strength to the roof, on which the soldiers were to work the mangonels and other projectile machines.

This view was drawn A. D. 1786.

Bolsover Castle Derbyshire.

BOLSOVER CASTLE, DERBYSHIRE.

THIS castle stands on an eminence, and commands a most beautiful prospect. It anciently belonged to the Hastings', Lords of Abergavenny, and by an exchange with King Henry III. from them it came to the Cavendish's and Hollis', Dukes of New-castle, and by a female, went to the Earl of Oxford. At present it belongs to his Grace the Duke of Portland, whose father married the heiress of the Oxford family.

HISTORY does not inform us at what time, or by whom this castle was built. We, however, learn from the public records, it was in being as early as the reign of King John ; for by his patent, in the 17th year of his reign, Bryan de L'Isle, a great Ba-ron of that time, was made Governor thereof, and in the same year accounted for the fermes of the honour of Peverel and Bolsover. In the next year, the said Bryan had the command of the King's forces raised against the Barons, and was ordered to fortify the Castle of Bolsover, and to hold it against them ; but if he could not make it te-nable, then to demolish it, whereby they might not have the advantage of it.

IT seems as if the Castle was found defensible, and therefore not demolished in con-sequence of that order, but the command given to some other person ; for in the se-venth of King Henry the Third, Bryan de L'Isle was appointed Governor of it, together with that of Peke; after which, by some means or other, he appears to have again vacated, at least, one of these offices; for in the 18th of the same reign, he was once more made Governor of Bolsover Castle, in which year he died.

From that time nothing remarkable occurs respecting this Castle, till about the year 1629, when divers repairs were made, and new buildings added here by the Marquis of Newcastle, in order to receive King Charles the First. The initials H S. C D. and A F. with the date 1629, appear cut on different stones, set up on these buildings; probably they were the names of the persons employed as architects. The chief of the additions here mentioned, was a gallery of stone, seventy-two yards in length, and seven yards four inches in breadth, within the ceiling; it has battlements on the top, and is a handsome regular structure.

The following account of the taking of this Castle, by the parliamentary forces, during the troubles under King Charles I. is given in a Parliamentary Chronicle, published by Vicars, intitled the Burning Bush not consumed. "Shortly after, i. e. after August 16, 1664.) The noble Major General having left Colonel Bright a commander of my Lord Fairfaxe's, and a party of foot in the Castle (Sheffield) by order from the most noble Earl of Manchester, advanced towards Bowzan, alias Bolsover Castle, about eight miles from Sheffield. It being another strong house of Marquesse Newcastle's, in Derbyshire, which was well manned with soldiers, and strengthened with great guns, one whereof carried eighteen pound bullet, others nine pound, and it had strong works about it; yet this Castle also upon summons, was soon surrendered up to my Lord's forces, upon faire and moderate articles granted to them. It pleased God to give us in this Castle of Bolsover an hundred and twenty muskets, besides pikes, halberts, &c. Also one iron drake, some leaden bullets, two mortar pieces, some other drakes, nine barrels of powder, with a proportion of match, some victuals four our souldiers, and some plunder."

This view was drawn 1778.

Garrison at Plymouth.

THE FORT OR GARRISON OF PLYMOUTH.

PLYMOUTH is situated at the mouth of the small river called Plym, whence it takes its name. This river, at a small distance, falls into a bay of the English channel, called Plymouth Sound; on its opposite side is the river Tamar.

THE first fortress erected here, is said to have been built by one of the Valtort's, who were lords of this part of the town; others say, by Edmond Stafford bishop of Exeter, and chancellor of England under king Edward III. Godwin does not mention this erection in his life of that bishop.

LELAND, in his Itinerary, vol. vii. p. 22, describes a fort then existing, in these words: "The mouth of the gulph wherein the shippes of Plymouth lyeth, is waullid on eche side, and chainid over in tyme of necessitie; on the south-west side of this mouth is a blok house, and on a rokky hille hard by it, is a stronge castel quadrate, having at eche corner a great rounde tower. It seemith to be no very old peace of worke."

CAREW, in his survey of Cornwall, says queen Elizabeth built a fort here; whether it was a new erection, or only a repair or addition to a former fortress, is uncertain. During the civil wars, Plymouth was in the hands of the parliamentarians, and was several times unsuccessfully attacked by the royalists.

THE prefent fort was built by king Charles II. who had experienced the importance of its fituation, as it both commands the town and defends the harbour. It is fuppofed to have been built on the fite of the old caftle. It is of an irregular figure, having towards the land fide, three baftions, a ditch, ravelins and a couvert way, with divers irregular works towards the water. Within the fort are barracks for the garrifon, and a houfe for the governor. Its walls are faid to include about two acres of ground.

In the Hiftory of the firft fourteen Years of King James I. there is the following Entry refpecting this Fort:

To fir Fardinando Gorges, captain of the new fort at Plymouth,
for himfelf and foldiers there, 56s. per diem, which cometh
unto per annum — — — — — £.1022 0 0

A. D. 1659, the Eftablifhment of this Garrifon and its Dependencies, was

	£.	s.	d.	
A governor, at — — — — — —	0	8	0	
A ftore-keeper, at — — — —	0	2	0	
Two gunners, each at — — — —	0	1	8	
Three gunner's mates, each — — —	0	1	4	
Eight matroffes, each — — — —	0	0	10	
A boatman — — — — —	0	1	0	Per diem.
Fire and candle for the guards — — —	0	3	4	
Two companies of foot, confifting of two captains, each at —	0	8	0	
Two lieutenants, each at — — — —	0	4	0	
Two enfigns, each at — — — —	0	3	0	
Four ferjeants, each at — — — —	0	1	6	
Six corporals and two drummers, each at — —	0	1	0	
Two hundred foldiers, each at — — —	0	0	8	

Its prefent Eftablifhment, is a governor, whofe annual falary is — £.1289 2 6
A lieutenant-governor — — — — 182 10 0
Fort-major — — — — — 73 0 0
Chaplain — — — — — 121 13 4

With a Mafter and other Gunners.

THIS view was drawn A. D. 1787.

IVY BRIDGE near PLYMOUTH.

DRAWN BY PAUL SANDBY, Esq. R. A.
Engraved by Mr. CHESHAM.

THIS bridge stands a few miles from the entrance into Plymouth, upon a small descent, from which, though there are no extensive prospects, the whole forms a pleasing assemblage of neat buildings, and improved grounds.

PLYMOUTH is situated to the south of this bridge, at the mouth of a small river called Plym, which at a little distance falls into a bay of the English channel, called Plymouth-Sound, on one side of the town, as the river Tamar does on the other. It is a large and populous place, containing near as many inhabitants as Exeter. The streets are very compact, and well supplied with water, though it is brought from a spring seven miles distant, which was done at the expence of that great navigator Sir Francis Drake. Not many ages ago, it was a small fishing-town; but it has received its increase from the conveniency of the harbours, which are fit to receive vessels of any burden. It was, however, a well-frequented town in the reign of Edward the Third; but it was laid in ashes in the time of Henry the Fourth, when the French invaded these parts, and burnt three hundred of the houses. It is now well known to be a flourishing place, and to be one of the chief magazines for sea-stores in the kingdom. The most remarkable things in it, are its port, castle and forts, the dock and the churches.

Its port, consisting of two harbours, capable of containing a thousand sail, has rendered it one of the chief magazines in his Majesty's dominions.

The castle is supposed to be built by the Valtorts, who were lords of this part of the town; or, as some say, by Edmund Stafford, bishop of Exeter, and chancellor of England. King Charles II. modernized it, and turned it into a strong citadel, in which there is generally a garrison, consisting of two companies of soldiers, under the command of a governor and lieutenant. Its walls include at least two acres of ground. It has five regular bastions, mounted with 167 guns, and contains a large magazine of stores. But the greatest security of the town and the forts about the entrance of the harbours, wherein are about 100 guns, exclusive of those just mentioned. The inlet of the sea, which runs some miles up the country, at the mouth of the Tamar, is called the Hamouze; and that which receives the Plym, is called Catwater. About two miles up the Hamouze, are two docks, one dry and the other wet, with a basin 200 f. et square; they are hewn out of a mine of slate, and lined with Portland stone. The dry dock is formed after the model of a first rate man of war, and the wet dock will contain five first rates. The dock and basin were chiefly constructed in the reign of king William the Third, and finished in that of queen Anne. They keep clean walls about them, so that they are equal to any in England. There are here conveniences of all kinds for building; and any being ships; and the whole forms as complete an arsenal as any in the kingdom. There are only two churches, of which St. Andrew's is a very spacious building, and has a very high, handsome tower, at the west end, adorned with pinnacles, and containing six large bells. The body of the church is equally large and beautiful, as are also the side files of the chancel. Charles's church, so called from its being dedicated to the memory of Charles I. is a good building, with a handsome spire, covered with lead. Though there are several meeting-houses, each of these churches has so large a current soul, that the parish clerks, till very lately, took deacons orders, to enable them to perform the sacerdotal functions; the profits of these pews go to the poor.—The fortifications of this town are now augmenting, in consequence of the visit which the French fleet paid us off this coast last summer.

THE KING'S TOWER, CORFE CASTLE, DORSETSHIRE.

THE KING'S TOWER, CORF CASTLE, DORSETSHIRE.

THIS view shews the king's tower or keep of that ancient castle, as viewed from the east; the whole of which bears indisputable testimony that violent means have co-operated with the slower ravages of time and weather to bring it to its present ruinous state. In some of those monstrous fragments scattered all around it, which could only have been disjointed by gun-powder, there are pieces of herring-boned work, such as are found in the oldest part of Guildford castle. Indeed, by a careful investigation of these ruins, architecture of every age and stile may be traced out, from that species called Saxon, to that used in the days of Elizabeth and James the First.

This view was drawn anno 1781.

John of Gaunts Kitchen, Dorsetshire.

JOHN OF GAUNT'S KITCHEN, AT GREAT CANFORD, DORSETSHIRE.

THE buildings here chiefly reprefented were part of the offices of the ancient manfion of the lords of the manor of Great Canford; at prefent known by the appellation of John of Gaunt's Kitchen. The fmall building feen in the corner of the view, is part of the prefent manfion, occafionally inhabited by Sir John Web, to whom the manor now belongs.

HUTCHINS, in his Hiftory of Dorfetfhire, fuppofes the ancient feat to which thefe offices belonged, to have been built by William Montacute, the firft Earl of Salifbury, or his father William; both great builders. The former lived in the reign of King Edward the Second.

OF thefe ancient remains, as they ftood before the year 1765, Hutchins gives the following defcription. In that year part of them were pulled down, but not the whole, as he fuppofes; for the kitchen was ftanding in 1785, when this view was taken.

"ADJOINING to the north, was till very lately, a long range of the moft ancient in the county, the remains of the feat of the ancient lords of this manor.

" Near the eaſt end were the remains of a very large gate, with a tower over it, of
" which only the ſtair-caſe remained. In the ſtable was a very large chimney
" without any funnel, and a vaſt ſquare window, reaching from the top to the
" bottom of the houſe, projecting above three feet; over this, another room,
" aſcended to by narrow winding ſtone ſtairs, perhaps the dining-room, in which
" was a chimney like the former.

" Towards the weſt end, was a large old kitchen, called by the country people,
" John of Gaunt's Kitchen. It was made a brew-houſe, and had a remarkable
" large chimney, eighteen feet broad and ſix feet and a half high in the crown
" of the arch. The windows, though for the moſt part walled up, were ſome
" eliptical and ſome ſquare, but did not project. On the outſide of the eaſt end,
" were three very large chimneys entire, very broad at the bottom, but narrowing
" upwards by ſeveral inbenchings. The funnels were indented or embattled on the
" top; the doors were ſmall and low; ſome ſquare, and the arches of others
" eliptical or circular; the walls in general four feet thick. Theſe buildings being
" entirely taken down 1765, a ground plot of them is here inſerted, &c. &c."

The manor of Great Canford, very early after the conqueſt belonged to Peter
Lucyan. In Domeſday-Book, Cheneford was held by Edward of Sariſburie; and by
marriage afterwards came to Henry Earl of Lancaſter. 16th Edward II. the King
granted it to Hugh de Spenſer, on whoſe attainder it eſcheated to the crown, and
1ſt of Ed. III. was granted by that King to John Earl of Warren and Surry, and
Johanna his wife, for their lives. 16th of Ed. III. the King made a reverſionary
grant of it to Alice Counteſs of Lincoln for life, but ſhe ſeems never to have poſſeſſed it. 35th Ed. III. the manor was poſſeſſed by the Montagues, in the 4th of
Henry VI. was granted to the Duke of Bedford, and in the 17th of the ſame reign,
to Henry, Cardinal of Wincheſter, for life.

In the 4th of Ed. VI. Canford was granted to the Duke of Somerſet, and by his
attainder reverting to the crown, it was in 1ſt of Mary granted to the Marchioneſs of
Exeter in fee, who by her will dated Aug. 27, 1557, bequeathed it to James Lord
Montjoy. She died A. D. 1558. In the year 1611, it was purchaſed by Henry
Earl of Huntingdon, and by him ſold to Web.

Canford Magna is about two miles ſouth-eaſt from Winborn Minſter, on the
ſouth ſide of the river Stour, in the eaſt part of the hundred, and belonged formerly
to the Dutchy of Lancaſter. Here were formerly two parks.

In the manſion houſe, probably at the eaſt end, was a chapel value 10 l. one chalice
of ſix ounces, two ſilver ſpoons of two ounces; Robert Reade incumbent.

In the park adjoining to the garden, are four large cheſnut trees, one of them
meaſuring 37 feet round, ſtill bearing fruit plentifully, though much ſhivered and
decayed by age; in a field eaſt of the cheſnuts is an oak called the Mountjoy Oak,
apparently very ancient.

Pomery or Poundbury Camp Dorsetshire

POMERY, OR POUNDBURY, DORCHESTER.

THIS was a Roman camp, and is described by Dr. Stukeley, in his Itinerarium Curiosum, in the following terms: "It stands half a mile west of Dorchester, in a pasture called Pomery, upon the brink of the river, which is very steep; the form square, the rampart high, but the ditch inconsiderable, except at the angle by the river, because standing on high ground, they dug the earth clear away before it, and threw it entirely into a vallum; so that its height and steepness, wherein its strength consists, is the same as if a regular ditch was made in level ground: the chief entrance was on the south side. There was another next the river made with the greatest art, for a narrow path is drawn all along between the edge of the precipice and the vallum; and beyond the camp west for a long way, a small trench is cut up on the said edge, which seems designed to prevent the ascent of cavalry, if they should pass the river. The ground rises in the middle, as was usual among the Romans. Near the south side is a tumulous too, which is probably Celtic, extant before the camp was made. The name Poundbury is taken from its enclosure round this tumulus as a pound."

COKER, Camden, and Speed, (fays Hutchins in his History of Dorfetfhire) with more probability make it a Danifh work, raifed by Sweno, King of Denmark, A. D. 1002, when he befieged, took, and deftroyed Dorchefter. This opinion is countenanced by its fituation, on an eminence, and oppofite to the caftle which lay eaft of it.

IT feems to derive its name of Pomery, from the latin Pomærium, which according to Livy was a fpace of ground, both within and without the walls of a city, which the Augurs, at its firft building, folemnly confecrated, and on which no edifices were fuffered to be raifed : the form is a parallelogram, but the fouth vallum fomewhat fhorter than the north. Its length 378 paces, the breadth 147 ; the vallum is pretty high ; on the north it is partly worn away, or was never raifed ; on the eaft there appears to have been a double one, part of which is difcontinued. The principal entrance is on the eaft, befides which there are three more ; one at the north eaft angle, another at the fouth weft, and a third on the fouth fide. In this field, and near this work, the Knights of the Shire are elected.

ON making the new way, a very little eaft of Segars Orchard, at the entrance into Dorchefter, the icening way was difcovered and croffed ; foundations of buildings were dug up, pieces of very thick glafs, and fragments of Roman brick of a bright red colour, from one to three inches thick, and none above fix inches long ; fome appeared by their concavity to have belonged to a Hypocauft.

THIS view, which fhews the eaft afpect, was drawn anno 1759.

Portland Castle Dorsetshire.

PORTLAND OLD CASTLE, DORSETSHIRE.

This building, which stands a little to the eastward of the old church, and fifty steps of stone above it, appears to have been the keep of the castle; it seems very ancient, its figure a pentagon; on its top are several machicolations and loop holes. The foundation of it was much above the top of the tower of the church, and it must have been almost impregnable before the invention of ordnance. It is vulgarly called the Bowe and Arrow Castle, and the Castle of Rufus, probably from a supposition, or some tradition, that it was built by that king. Anno 1142, it was taken by Robert Earl of Gloucester, from king Stephen, for the Empress Maud.

This view was drawn anno 1756.

Roman Amphitheatre Dorchester.

THE ROMAN AMPHITHEATRE NEAR DORCHESTER.

THIS earthen work is univerfally allowed to have been a Roman amphitheatre; it is, for what reafon is unknown, vulgarly called Maumbury. The following account of it is given in Hutchins's Hiftory of Dorfetfhire : " That in this parifh (Fording-ton) is fituated on a plain in the open fields, about a quarter of a mile, or 1500 feet fouth weft from the walls of Dorchefter, on a gentle afcent all the way to it, clofe by the Roman road which runs thence to Weymouth. From it you fee Poundbury, Marden Caftle, and the tops of the South Hills, as far as the eye can reach, covered with an incredible number of Celtic borrowes. It is raifed of folid chalk, upon a level, without any ditch about it. The jambs at the entrance are fomewhat worn away. On the top there is a walk of 8 feet broad, gradually afcending from the ends upon the longeft diameter to its greateft elevation in the middle, upon the fhort diameter, where it reaches half way up the whole feries of feats of the fpectators, who thence diftributed themfelves therein, from all fides, without hurry. On the top is a terrace of twelve feet broad at leaft, befides the parapet outwardly five feet broad, and four high, but fomewhat injured on the fide next the gallows, by the trampling of men and horfes at executions. There are three ways leading up to the terrace, one at the upper end over the cavea, and one on each fide upon the fhorteft diameter, going from the elevated part of the circular walk. Several horfes abreaft may go up this, afcending by the ruins of the cavea. This receptacle of the gladiators, wild beafts, &c. is fuppofed to have been at the upper end, under the afcent to the terrace, there being vaults under that part of the body of the work. The area is no doubt exceedingly elevated by manuring and plowing for many years, yet it ftill preferves a concavity, for the de-fcent from the entrance is very great, and you may go down as into a fhallow pit. The middle part of it is now 10 or 12 feet lower than the level of the field; and that, especially about the entrance is much lowered by plowing, because the end of the circular walk there, which should be even with the ground, is a good deal above it. On the outside of the upper end is a large round tumor, a considerable way beyond the exterior verge, and regular in figure, which certainly has been somewhat appertaining to the work. There are two rising square plots on the shortest diameter, four feet above the level of the walk or terrace, capable of holding 24 people each. Their side breadth is 15 feet, their length from north to south 20; and they stand somewhat near the upper end, not precisely on the shortest diameter. There is a seeming irregularity of the terrace on both sides at the lower end, for it is higher within than without, yet this produces no ill effect, but rather renders its appearance the more regular; for when you stand in the center within, the whole circuit of the terrace seems, and is really, of one level; but on the outside the verge of the north easterly part is sloped off gradually towards the entrance, where the declivity is conformable with it. Hence the exterior contour also appears of an equal height. The circular walks cut the whole breadth into two equal parts, upon the shortest diameter, probably making an equal number of seats above and under it. Dr. Stukeley says, it is computed to consist of about an acre of ground, and was originally about 140 feet diameter in the shortest way, and 220 the longest. The famous amphitheatre at Verona is but 233 and 136, and the vast colisæum at Rome but 263 and 165, reckoned by the French foot, a larger measure By an accurate admeasurement taken for this work, it was found that the greatest perpendicular height of the rampart above the level of the

	Feet	Inches.
Arena was - - - - - - - - - -	30	0
External longest diameter - - - -	343	6
External shortest diameter - - - -	339	6
Internal longest diameter - - - -	218	0
Internal shortest diameter - - - -	163	6
First ascent from the Arena to the greatest curve height -	50	0

The breadth of the side of the work, or solid, taken upon the ground plot, is equal to one half of the longest diameter of the area, or a fourth of the whole longest diameter. Its perpendicular altitude from the top of the terrace to the bottom of the area is a fourth of the longest diameter of the area. In the middle of each side is a cuneus, or parcel of seats, of near 30 feet broad, just over the more elevated part of the circular work, reaching up to the terrace, which swells out above the concavity of the whole, and answers to the rising ground in the middle of the terrace. Dr. Stukely computes it capable of containing 12,960 persons. At Mrs. Channing's execution (A. D. 1705) there were supposed to be 10,000 spectators present, who filled the sides, top, and area of this work, which is the compleatest of this kind in England. Some years ago a silver coin was ploughed up here, on the face of which was this inscription, IMP. M. IVL. PHILIPPVS, AVG. On the reverse LAVTIT. FENDAT. and a genius or fortune, with a garland in the right hand, and a helm of a ship in the left. This emperor reigned A. D. 240; but this work was probably made under the government of Agricola, who taught and encouraged the Britons to build temples, baths, and amphitheatres, &c. in order to introduce luxury, and soften the fierce and rough temper of that people.

THIS view was drawn anno 1755.

Winbourne Church, Dorsetshire.

WINBURNE, TWINBORN, OR WYMBURN MINSTER.

This plate gives a diſtant view of the ancient collegiate church of Winburne, called Wimburne Minſter. Of this church, Tanner gives the following Account:

" BEFORE A. D. 705, St. Cuthburga, daughter to Kenred, king of the Weſt Saxons, and ſiſter to king Ina, founded here an abbey of holy virgins, to the honour of the Bleſſed Virgin Mary, wherein ſeveral of the Saxon kings were buried. This nunnery being deſtroyed by the Danes, one of the Edwards kings of England, put in ſecular canons, ſo that it became a royal free chapel and collegiate, conſiſting of a dean, four prebendaries, three vicars, four deacons or ſecondaries, and five ſinging men; and ſince the ſuppreſſion, there is a ſort of choir preſerved, and ſome maintenance ſtill allowed to three vicars, (one of whom is ſtiled the official) four ſinging men, ſix boys, and an organiſt. This college, which was valued 26 Hen. VIII. at 131 l. 14 s. with moſt of the lands belonging to the ſame, was granted 1 Ed. VI. to Edward lord Clinton.

In this church was buried the body of St. Ethelred, king of the Weſt Saxons, ſlain by the Pagan Danes on the 23d of April, anno 872. His monument is ſtill ſhewn.

This town is ſuppoſed to have taken its name of Twinborn, from the rivers Stour and Allen, which meet near it."

This view was drawn A. D. 1784.

Beaurepaire, or Bearparke, Durham.
Pub. as Mar 1795 by I. Harper.

BEAUREPAIRE, OR BEARPARKE, DURHAM.

This was a villa or retreat for the priors of Durham, built by prior Bertram, who for that purpose obtained it of the Bishop of Durham, in exchange for an estate called Moorhouse, and accordingly erected a camera or lodge with a chapel. Prior Hugh of Darlington, who succeeded to that office about fourscore years after, in Bishop Stichill's time, enclosed the park, and as is said by the Monkish writers, built a camera here; by which they probably meant, that he made several additions to the buildings erected by Prior Bertram. When Bishop Beck persecuted the convent, he broke down the fences of the park, and drove out the came. In an extract from a Chronicle written in French by William de Pockyngton, clerk and treasurer to Prince Edward, son of Edward III. translated by Leland, and printed in his Collectanea, it is said, that when David King of Scotland made an irruption into these parts, before the battle of Nevil's-cross, he took up his quarters at Beau-repaire, the words are, "About this tyme, by the means of Philip Valoys King of Fraunce, David King of Scottes "enterid yn to the North Marches, spoiling and brenning, and toke by furce the Pyle of Lydelle, and causid "the noble Knight Walter Selby, captayne of it, to be slayne afore his own face, not suffering hym so much "as to be confessed. And after he cam to the coste of Dyrham, and laye there at a place caullid Beaurepaire, "a manor of the prior of Durefme, set in a parke, and thither resortid many of the cuntrey aboute, com- "pounding with hym to spare their grounds and manors. Then Wylliam Souche, archebishop of York, the "counte of Anegos, Mounsir John de Monbray, Mounsir Henry de Perey, Mounsir Rafe de Nevisle, "Mounsir Rafe de Haffinges, Mounsir Thomas de Rokeby, then Sherif of Yorkshir, and other knights "and good men of marched toward the Scottes, and first lay in Akeland Park, and in the morning encounterid "with Syr Wylliam Duglas, killing of his bond 500 menne. And he with much payne escaped to Beau- "repaire to King David, declaring the cumming of the Englishe hoste. Wher then King David issued, and "fought upon a more nere to Durefme towne, and ther was taken prisoner, and with hym Syr Wylliam

BEAR PARK.

Moiety de q. est en paroch. de Witton Paul Elvet.
Locus de bello rediva. Olim fuit vaccaria pertin. ad eleemosynam. Dat de qua excambium p. Moorhouse farm, p. B. priorem Dun. 4. Reg. de Cha. p. 1, & 41.
Bertramus Prior construxit cameram cum capello ibdm.
Hugo de Derlington prior inclusit Newpark.
Fuit rustica prior Dun sedes & John Fossour prior ibm. vixit & obiit. v. plus de eo. Rot. Bainbrigge, B. No. 64. & Cart. D. & Cha.
Custod. parci de Bearpark granted per les priors p. patent. p. vi. cum fœdo. Mickleton's MSS.

" Douglas, the Counte of Mouethe, and the Counte of Fyfe, and a great numbre of the communes of
" Scotland flayne. The King, becaufe he was wonded yn the face, he was carried to Werk, and ther he lyd,
" and thens brought to London."

As by this account Beaurepaire appears to have been the royal quarters, it feems reasonable to suppofe the
buildings were not materially damaged; the contrary is however afferted by fome writers, who fay, that among
other depredations committed in that inroad, the Scots pillaged and defaced this retreat, which, it is fuppofed,
were repaired by Prior Foffar, who acceded to his office in 1342, and took great pleafure in this place; and
it feems the more likely, as the architecture of the chapel points out the improvements of a refined age. As
authors are filent touching Beaurepaire from this period, it is probable nothing material happened to it till the
diffolution. The manor, with the houfe and park, were part of the poffeffions of the church reftored by the
royal endowment after the inftitution of the Dean and Chapter, by King Henry VIII. In the time of Dean
Grenvile, who was inftituted in 1683, an inquifition was taken of the deanry poffeffions, in which we find Beaurepaire thus defcribed. " Præter domos fic ædificat apud Dun fuit & eft fpectan. ad Decan. Decanat. Dun.
" & 40, 50, aut 60 annos ultimo elapf. & ultra nec non p. Tepus, cujus contry. memoria hora non exilit, fuit
" ftan. & exiften. apud Bear Parke infra Com. & Dioc. Dun quædam domus manfional. vocat. the manor
" houfe of Beare Parke, quæ quidem domus manfionalis diftans eft a Decnatu Dun. p. unu. miliare Anglicanu.
" vel eo circiter; ac infra eand. dom. manfionalem funt, feu faltem antiquitus & ab initio fuere ftan.
" & exiften. cameræ feu partitiones & cellæ particular. fequen. viz. a hall, two paffages near the hall, one
" large kitchen and an oven in it, a back room adjoining the weft end of the kitchen, a dining room, a great
" room leading to the chapel, called the dormitory, fome arches and two rooms above the arches, a chapel,
" and a room under it, three rooms or two at leaft, called the priors chamber, and the weftern room thereof
" called the priors lodgings, a little room adjoining the priors chamber, a ftair-cafe and vaults under all and
" every the lower floor rooms of the faid manfion houfe, excepting the hall and kitchen, and the room aforefaid
" adjoining the kitchen. And at Bear Parke aforefaid there formerly have been belonging to the faid manor
" houfe feveral courts and gardens that were walled about, and alfo fundry out-houfes, which are now wholly
" dilapidated, and nothing to be feen or perceived but the ruins thereof. Et etia. fedes locus fe villa de Bear
" Parke eft & ab antiquo fuit meneria. ac domus manfional. terrarq. dominical ejufd. manerij, & ædificia, &
" ftructure reliquæ reliquæ præmentionat. ad cond. dom. manfional fpectant. nec non tenementa & parcu
" ejufd. manerij aliuq. proficua & emolumenta infra præcinctus & terretoria dict. manerij annuatim emergen
" norie funt pars & parcella corporis Decanat. Dun. &c. Et terræ domineal & tenementa ac parcum
" manerij de Bearparke; aliaq. proficua infra territoria ejufd. manerij funt & pro 20 &c. annos ultimo elapfos et
" ultra fuere annuatim de claro valen. fumma 300l. 280l. aut 280l. legalis monetæ Angliæ ac præd. J. Sud-
" bury durante toto tepore, p. ad fint Decan. ac terris dominical & tenementis ac parcu aliiq. emolumentis
" manerij de Bearparke fumam 600l. &c. de claro legis monetæ Angliæ habebat poffeabat & in ufu fuo
" converrebat."

THE following defcription of the prefent ftate of this place was kindly communicated to me by Mr. Hutchin-
fon, from his valuable collections for the Hiftory of the Bifhoprick of Durham; to him I am alfo obliged for
moft of the other particulars.

THE fituation of this houfe is excellent, about two miles to the north-weft of Durham, on a lofty eminence
above the rivulet of Brune, in a dry foil, and furrounded with cultivated lands, having a long extended level
mead to the fouth; fine coppices are feattered over the fteep defcents on both fides of the river, and there is a
beautiful profpect to the north, rendered highly picturefque by the town and church of Witton Gilbert, and
the adjacent hamlets. Much deftruction has been made in the buildings fince Dean Grenville's time, and
nothing but naked and diftracted walls remain of this once beautiful place.

THE chapel (b) is thirteen paces long and eight wide, the eaft window confifts of three lights, circular at the
top and very plain, there are three windows on each fide, each divided by a mullion into two lights, their
framing on the outfide fquare. The wall is ftrengthened with a buttrefs of neat hewn ftone work between each
window, and a cornice runs round the building, of the zig zag figure. There is a door on the north fide of the
chapel from the court. The walls of the chapel in the infide are ornamented with a regular fucceffion of fmall
round columns or pilafters, belted in the midft, the capitals filled with a garland of open cut foliage of delicate
work, from whence fpring pointed arches; three pilafters and two arches between each pair of windows; the
weft end is equally finifhed with the pilafters and arches, and there is a fmall window in the center. At each fide
of the eaft window is a pedeftal for a ftatue of confiderable fize. The apartment under the chapel is lighted by
fmall fquare windows, but as the floor of the chapel is gone, it is not eafy to determine how it was conftructed.
Adjoining to the chapel on the weft is a long building, the two gabels of which are ftanding, having a large
window of fix lights to the fouth, this was moft probably the hall; on the north the remains of a building
twenty paces in length, lighted to the eaft, by three windows; this, I conjecture, was the dormitory; the other
remains are fo ruined and confufed as to render them totally indiftinct. There is a door-cafe ftanding, which
has been the entrance into the garden or fome chief court, with the arms of the fee in the center.

THIS view was drawn 1778.

(b) I MEET with the names of three chapels. 1ft. The chapel of St. Edmund in ædibus fuburbacii pr. & conv. Dun. Bellus
Redreus.

2d. THE chapel of St. Catherine in the manor, where fix days in the week fervice was performed by a chaplain.

3d. THE chapel of St. John in the park, where it is performed twice in the week. Hugh Whitehead, the laft prior and firft
dean of Durham, is faid to have repaired many hooks here which were fallen to decay.

The Chapel in Bearparke, Durham.

The CHAPEL of BEAUREPARE, or BEAR PARKE, DURHAM.

This view shews the inside of the chapel mentioned in the preceding description, as it appears when viewed from its north side.

BRANSPETH CASTLE, DURHAM.

O f this caſtle the following account and deſcription occurs in Leland'ɛ̃
Itinerary. " The village and caſtelle of Branſpeth ſtondith on a rocke among hilles
" higher then it.   On the ſouthe-weſt part of the caſtelle cummith dounc a
" litle bek out o the rokkes and hilles not afar off.   The caſtelle of Branſpeth is
" ſtrongly ſet and buildid, and hath two courtes of high building.   There is
" a litle mote that hemmith a great piece of the firſt court; in this court be
" three toures of logging, and three ſmaule *ad ornamentum*.   The pleaſure of the
" caſtelle is in the 2d court ; and entering into it by a great toure I ſaw in ſchochin
" in the fronte of it a lion rampant.

  " Sᴜᴍ ſay that Rafe Nevile, the firſt Erle of Weſtmorland, builded much of
" the howſe.   The Erle that is now hath ſet a new peace of worke to it."

OTHERS, among whom is Camden, attribute the building of this caftle to the Balmers, formerly a great family in thofe parts, who had their refidence there for feveral generations, till the male iffue failing in Bernard, or as Dugdale has it, in Bertram de Bulmer, it came to his only daughter Emma, who by a marriage with Geoffry Nevil, transferred it to that family, one of whom entering into a rebellion in the reign of Queen Elizabeth it efcheated to the crown.

SIR Nicholas Cole, created a Baronet by Charles I. anno 1640, refided here, as did fome of his defcendants, of them it was purchafed by Mr. Bellafis, and in 1774 was advertifed for fale.

THE following defcription of the prefent ftate of this building was by permiffion of Thomas Pennont, Efq; extracted from his notes.

" BRANCEPETH caftle confifts of a large tower, now modernized, and a habi-
" table houfe, which impends over a fteep and woody Dell; the reft, which is
" the wall of the church-yard, with one or two fquare towers, is on a flat; the
" part of the wall that is quite entire, has fmall fquare towers on the fummit,
" with corbal truffes for pouring down hot water, &c. on the affailants."

THIS view was taken anno 1775.

CITY of DURHAM.

DRAWN BY PAUL SANDBY, Esq. R. A.

ENGRAVED by Mr. CHESHAM.

DURHAM has but one weekly market on Saturday; neverthelefs, all forts of provifions, as well as other neceffaries for the conveniencies of life, are very cheap, as well as good. It is governed by a mayor, aldermen, recorder, and fheriffs. It has a confiderable manufacture of fhalloons, tammies, ftripes, and callimancoes.

The antiquity of Durham is not to be boafted of; fince the building of it was owing to the monks of Lindisfarne being difquieted by the Danes in their wars with the Englifh; and, wandering up and down with the religious of St. Cuthbert, they were at laft admonifhed by an oracle, as they tell us, to fettle here. This was about the year 995. The cathedral was erected out of the offerings which were made by the fuperftitious multitude at the fhrine of the abovenamed St. Cuthbert. And yet, notwithftanding the refidence of fo many dignified proteftant clergy, it is faid there are ftill great numbers of Roman Catholics in this city.

I need not tell you, that the bifhop of Durham is a temporal prince; that he keeps a court of equity, and alfo courts of juftice in ordinary caufes, within himfelf. He is ftiled earl of Sandberg, and takes place as bifhop immediately after the bifhop of London. As the country about Rome is called St. Peter's patrimony, fo that about Durham is called St. Cuthbert's, to whom the church is dedicated. David king of Scots laying all wafte with fire and fword, while king Edward III. was at Calais, Zouch, the valiant archbifhop of York, then governor of thofe northern parts, fought the Scots at Nevil's Crofs, where they were cut in pieces, and their king taken prifoner. St. Cuthbert was the fixth bifhop of Lindisfarne, or Holy Ifland, from whence the fee was removed hither.

The bifhoprick of Durham is efteemed one of the beft in England; and the prebends, and other church livings in the gift of the bifhop, are the richeft in the kingdom.

One of the old bifhops of Durham purchafed, for a round fum of money, all the rights of the palatinate, and other jurifdiction in this county, from Richard I. and, by his laft will, left them to the fucceeding bifhops. But Henry VIII. by act of parliament, greatly abridged the temporal power and jurifdiction of this bifhoprick; and king Edward VI. (or rather his uncle Somerfet) by act of parliament, diffolved the bifhoprick entirely; but it was reftored by queen Mary. Neither city or county ever fent four members to the houfe of commons, till the vacancy of the fee by the death of bifhop Cofins, anno 1672, and fince they return each of them two, which is all that the county fend.

Gretham Hospital.

GRETHAM HOSPITAL, DURHAM.

THIS hofpital is fituated near the eaftern extremity of the county, about four miles fouth of Hartlepool, and two weft from the fea, its foundation is faid by Godwin to have originated from the following caufe: King Henry III. having flain Simon de Montfort, who had rebelled againft him, feized on all his eftates, whereupon Robert Stichel, bifhop of Durham, as a prince palatine, feized on thofe within his jurifdiction as efcheats to him, thefe being alfo claimed by the king, the caufe was tried and determined in favour of the bifhop, who with the lands adjudged to him, founded this hofpital in honour of God, St. Mary, and St. Cuthbert, for a mafter and brethren, and for the relief of fuch poor and needy perfons as fhould refort thither; for which pur- pofe he endowed it with the manor of Gretham, and other lands. He alfo granted to the mafter and brethren of this houfe, an exemption from all tolls, aids, and tallages, and to all their benefactors, being contrite and confeffed, he releafed forty days pennance: this deed which is confirmed by Hugh, Prior of Durham, and the convent there, bears date, A. D. 1262. Its revenues were valued, 26th Henry VIII. at 100l. os. 3d. ob. in the whole, and 97l. 6s. 3½d. clear. Tanner fays, it feems to be yet in being, and the mafterfhip of it to be in the gift of the bifhop of Durham. This view was drawn anno 1778.

Monks Weremouth, Durham.

MONKS WEREMOUTH, DURHAM.

Monks Weremouth stands at the north mouth of the river Were, opposite to Sunderland.

King Egfrid gave this town to the famous Benedict Biscopius, who A. D. 674 founded a monastery here, and dedicated it to St. Peter. It suffered in the Danish wars, and was burned in the inroad made by Malcolm king of Scotland, A. D. 1070; but was afterwards begun to be re-edified by Walcher, bishop of Durham, to which Weremouth became a cell for three or four benedictine monks. It was valued, 26 Hen. VIII. at 25l. 8s. 4d. per ann. Dugd. 261. Speed; and was granted 37 Hen. VIII. to Tho. Whitehead.

This church, which has long served for parochial uses, is said to have belonged to the monastery. It had some resemblance to the church at Jarrow, and has of late been repaired.

This drawing, which was made in the year 1779, shews the most ancient part of the building.

The Bartlow Hills, raised over the Slain after the Victory obtained here by Canute King of
Denmark over King Edmund Ironside in the Year 1016.

Roman Sepulchral Monument
or Quietorium

Horsley Brit: Rom: p.331.   Vrna Lapidea: *Penes F. Gower, M.D.*

Found at Chesterford now in the poss:.n
of Dr. Gower at
Chelmsford

N.W. View of Little Dunmow Priory Church, Essex.

THE PRIORY OF LITTLE DUNMOW, ESSEX.

This monastery was founded A. D. 1104, by the Lady Juga, sister of Ralph Baynard, who built here a church dedicated to the honor of the Blessed Virgin Mary, which was consecrated by Maurice, Bishop of London: two years afterwards her son Jeffry placed therein canons, who shortly after their introduction observed the rule of St. Augustine.

The Priory consisted of a prior and ten or eleven religious, whose annual income at the suppression was estimated at 150l. 3s. 4d. Dugdale, 1731. 2s. 4d. Speed. The list of the priors may be seen in Newcourt. The site and manor of this priory were at the dissolution granted to Robert Earl of Sussex, and was sold by Earl Edward to Sir Henry Mildmay of Moulsham, Knt. who held it in 1640: it afterwards belonged to Sir William Wylde, Knt. and Bart. Recorder of London, and one of the Justices of the King's Bench, who dying 23d of November, 1769, his sister and heir Anne brought it in marriage to John Cochman, M. D. whose only daughter marrying Nicholas Tooke, Esq; it came into that family.

The monastery is now entirely razed; it was pleasantly situated on a rising ground. The foundations of the old building are visible on the south-west side of the church. The present manor-house stands on the site of the offices of the priory.

The collegiate church was a large and stately fabrick, the roof sustained with rows of columns, whose capitals are ornamented with oak leaves elegantly carved; some of them remain. The part which now makes the parish church, was the east end of the choir, with the north aisle. This church, dedicated to St. Mary, served for the parish as well as the convent. The Prior and canons presented one of their body to the bishop to serve the cure; but he was not instituted as in a rectory or vicarage. Since the suppression it is only a donative or curacy, in the gift of the Lord of the Manor, and now of James Hallet, Esq.

Here, under an arch in the south wall, is an ancient chest-like tomb, supposed to contain the body of the foundress Lady Juga. Near the same spot is a monument said to have been that of Walter Fitz-Walter, the first of that name, who died anno 1198, and was buried with one of his wives in the middle of the choir, whence it has been removed to its present situation; at least the alabaster figures of Sir Walter and his lady, who are now laid on an altar tomb, considerably too short for them. These figures are well executed for the time in which they were done, but are much defaced, probably by the removal, particularly the man whose legs are broken off at the knees. The lady has on a tiara, or mitre-like head-dress, ornamented with lace, ear-rings, and a necklace; at her feet on that side next her husband, is a small dog, so much defaced, as to be scarce distinguishable. Sir Walter is represented in plate armour, under it a shirt of mail, which appears at his collar and below the skirts of his armour. There is something remarkable in the appearance of his hair, which feems to radiate from a center fomewhat like the caul of a wig, but curling inwards. This fashion of hair or wig (for it appears doubtful which was intended) is obfervable on diverfe monuments of the fame age, as is alfo the head-drefs of the lady.

Opposite this monument, between two pillars, on the north fide of the choir, is the tomb of the fair Matilda, daughter of the fecond Walter Fitz-Walter, who according to the monkifh ftory, unfupported by hiftory, is pretended to have been poifoned by the contrivance of King John, for refufing to gratify his illicit paffion. Her figure is in alabafter, and by no means a defpicable piece of workmanfhip. Her fingers are ftained with a red colour, which according to the Ciceroni of the place, was done to reprefent the effects of the poifon, but in all likelihood is the remains of a former painting. Both this figure, and that of the Lady Fitz-Walter, afford accurate fpecimens of the necklaces, ear-rings, and other ornaments worn by the ladies of thofe days.

Among the fecular tenures of England, none have been more talked of than the bacon of Dunmow: by whom, or at what period this cuftom was inftituted, is not certain, but it is generally afcribed to one of the family of Fitz-Walter. A fimilar cuftom is obferved at the Manor of Wichenor, in Staffordfhire, where corn as well as bacon was given to the happy pair. By the ceremonial inftituted for this occafion at Dunmow, the party claiming the bacon, therein ftiled the pilgrim, was to take the following oath kneeling on two fharp pointed ftones in the church-yard, the convent attending, and ufing many ceremonies, and much finging, in order to lengthen out the time of his painful fituation.

> You fhall fwear by cuftom of confeffion,
> That you never made nuptial tranfgreffion;
> Nor fince you were married man and wife,
> By houfhold brawls or contentious ftrife,
> Or otherwife in bed or at board,
> Offended each other in deed or in word,
> Or fince the parifh clerk faid amen,
> You wifhed yourfelves unmarried again,
> But in a twelvemonth and a day,
> Repented not in thought any way,
> But continued true in thought and defire,
> As when you joined hands in holy quire.
> If to thefe conditions, without all fear,
> Of your own accord you will freely fwear,
> A whole gammon of bacon you fhall receive,
> And bear it hence with love and good leave;
> For this is our cuftom at Dunmow, well known,
> Tho' the pleafure be ours, the bacon's your own.

Then the pilgrim was taken on mens fhoulders, and carried firft about the priory church-yard, and afterwards through the town, attended by the convent, the bacon being borne in triumph before him. This is the form given by Mr. Morant, but from the words of the oath, it feems as if it fhould be taken by both man and wife.

The fharp ftones on which the party was to kneel, are now removed and loft.

The following lift of perfons who have demanded and received the bacon, is recorded in a M.S. in the college of arms, marked L. 14, page 226, anno 23d Hen. VI. Richard Wright of Bradbourghe, near the city of Norwich, in Co. Norfolk, demanded the bacon on the 17th of April in the faid year, and being duly fworn before John Canren, prior of this place, and the whole convent, and many neighbours, there was delivered to him one flitch of bacon.

Stephen Samuell, of Little Ayfton, in Co. Effex, hufbandman, came to the priory on Lady-Day in Lent, 7th of Edw. IV. and having taken the oath preferibed before Roger Bulcott, then prior, and the neighbours then affembled, had a gammon of bacon.

Anno 2d Hen. VIII. 1510, Thomas Lefuller, of Coggfhall, in Co. Effex, taking the ufual oath on the 8th of September, before John Tils, then Prior, there was delivered to him a gammon of bacon. From their entries it appears that fome of the claimants had a flitch, and others only a gammon of bacon; by what rule thefe deliveries were regulated is not mentioned.

To thefe Mr. Morant adds the following: At a Court Baron of Sir Thomas May, Kt. holder, 7th June 1701, before Thomas Wheeler, Gent. Steward, the homage Jury being five Cir ladies, fpinfters, namely, Elizabeth, Henrietta, Annabella, and Jane Beaumont, and Mary Wheeler, they found that John Reynolds, or Harold Brodoke, Gent. and Anne his wife, and William Parfley, of Much Eafton, butcher, and Jane his wife, by means of their peaceable, tender, and loving cohabitation, for the fpace of three years laft paft and upwards, were fit and qualified perfons to be admitted by the court to receive the ancient and accuftomed oath, whereby to entitle themfelves to have the bacon of Dunmow delivered unto them, according to the cuftom of the Manor; and they having taken the oath kneeling on two great ftones near the church door, the bacon was delivered to each couple.

The laft that received it were John Shakefhanks, woolcomber, and Anne his wife, of Wethersfield, 20 June, 1751. Since which fome perfons having demanded it, it has, as is faid, been refufed, probably from conjugal affection not being now fo rare as heretofore, or becaufe qualification oaths are now fuppofed to be held lefs facred. This view was drawn anno 1775.

EASTBURY HOUSE,

In the parish of Barking, Essex, stands on the edge of the
Marshes about a mile toward the east of the town, in the
road from Barking to Dagenham, by Ripple side. The
farm belonging to it, was, in the reign of Edw. VI, in the
possession of Sir William Denham, Knt. who also had other
estates in this neighbourhood. By him, probably, this
house was built, as its appearance shews it to be a building
of that age; and there is a date, 1573, on a leaden spout
on the south side of the house.

THE estate, possessed by Sir William Denham, is now divided among several proprietors; this house, with the farm belonging to it, is the property of a family of the name of Weldon.

A TRADITION prevails in this neighbourhood, that the discovery of the powder-plot was owing to an error in delivering a letter, designed for Lord Monteagle, to a person of the name of Montague, who is said to have been, at that time, an inhabitant of this house. It may be sufficient to refute this tradition, by observing that, the letter was not mis-delivered, but was received by Lord Monteagle, and by him communicated to the Earl of Salisbury. Historians mention, as an instance of the King's sagacity, that he conjectured this expression, that THE DANGER IS PAST SO SOON AS YOU BURNE THIS LETTER, must mean a danger from gun-powder; and directed those searches in the neighbourhood of the parliament house, by which the plot was discovered.

The drawing, which shews the S. W. view of the house, was made 1777.

LATTON PRIORY, ESSEX,

Stands about three miles nearly fouth of the parifh church,
and about half a mile weft of the prefent road from Epping
to Harlow: the priory church of which the fouth view is here
given, is now ufed as a barn; it confifts of a nave and crofs
aile, and the infide of the building is of the lighter ftile of
Gothic with the pointed arch, the materials of which it is
compofed are flint ftones, mortar and the old flat bricks ufually
called Roman; a fmall quantity of the fame materials was
found in the fouth wall of the farm-houfe which was lately
pulled down, and is now re-built.

What appears to have been the fite of the priory is furrounded with a moat, without which, fouth of the prefent
buildings, human bones are frequently found, this circumftance points out the ancient burial place; in digging fome
years ago in the orchard a pavement or path of old bricks
was found, of which there are now no remains. Eaft of the
church, without the moat, there appears a fmall rifing with

an hollow without it, like the remains of an intrenchment, the interval between this rife and the moat, the prefent inhabitants, from it appearance, call the Monks Bowling-green.

It appears by Domefday book, that St. Edmund's Bury abbey held lands in the parifh of Lattuna; and it is conjectered, that thefe lands were afterwards the endowment of Latton Priory, though when or by whom it was founded is not known: its foundation, fays Morant, but I known not on what authority, was before 1270; Tanner fays before 20 Ed. I, becaufe mentioned in the Lincoln taxation; its canons were Auguftine, and it was dedicated to St. John the Baptift. John Taylor, the laft prior, held the fite of the priory of Thomas Shaa in pure and perpetual alms, with 200 acres of arable, 200 of pafture, 50 of meadow 10 of wood, and 5l. rent, alfo the advowfon and parfonage of Latton, the whole then valued at 10l. yearly.

This priory is not mentioned by Dugdale, and the hiftory of few religious foundations is lefs known; one is led to conjecture that the fociety was never very numerous, or the revenue confiderable, as the Bifhop of London often appointed the prior, for want of a ftatuable number of canons to elect.

At the diffolution the fite of this priory was granted to Sir Henry Parker, to be held by the twentieth part of a knight's fee, he fold it to William Morris. It was afterwards in the poffeffion of John Kethe, who in 1556 fold it to John Titley, who in the 4th of Elizabeth conveyed it to James Altham, whofe defcendant and heir lately fold it to William Lufhington, Efq. the prefent poffeffor, who by his mother, is nearly related to the Altham family.

This drawing was made in 1776.

The GATE-HOUSE *or* TOWER *of* LADER-MARNEY-HALL.

Underneath
is interred
the Body of
John Ray
A.M.
Born the [...]
Died April 17[...]

This Monument was Erected in Black Notley Church Essex,
at the Sole Cost & Charge of the Right Revd Henry Compton
Lord Bishop of London. Vide Biographia Britannica.

PLASHEY CASTLE, ESSEX.

This castle is situated in the western side of the county, and in the hundred of Dunmow; it is mentioned in history and records by the various names of Placy, Plaisy, Plashe, Pleizet, Plesinchou, Plesheter, Plessys, Pleycie, Belhous, Bowels; and Leland in his Itinerary says, it was called Tumbleftoun; part of these appellations are supposed to be derivatives from the French word Plaisir, on account of its pleasant situation; Belhouse, or beautiful mansion, perhaps respected the building. It was the seat of the High Constables of England from the earliest times of that office to the year 1400.

Morant, in his history of Essex, supposes it was originally a Roman fortress; "But it " seems," says he, " to have been a considerable place long before the Conquest, and " even in the Roman times to have been a fortress or villa, for there is a ditch or en- " trenchment encompassing the west, north, and east parts of the present village, i. e. all " that is north of the road; and having the remains of another corresponding on the " south side, I have often traced it myself; it begins in a field across the road, north of " the church; on the same side of the way in a field about a quarter of a mile from the " church, in the road leading to High Estre, was found a fine glass urn, with some burnt " bones in it, which Samuel Tuffnell, Esq. shewed to the Society of Antiquaries."

In Mr. Holmes' MS. and N. Salmon's account of this place, Camden's authority is alledged for William de Magnaville, or Mandaville, being the founder of the castle here; but Mr. Morant says, he could not find where Mr. Camden says so, and adds, " it is " certainly much ancienter."

In Domesday Book it is called Plesinchou, and appears to have been part of the lands of Eustace, Earl of Boulogne; an encroachment is recorded, as made here upon the King, of one hide of land, by Humfrey *Aurei Testiculi.*

By the marriage of Maud, grand-daughter of Eustace, Earl of Boulogne, to King Stephen,

PLASHEY CASTLE, ESSEX.

Plethy became vefted in the crown, and was by that King beftowed on Geffery de Mandeville, when he created him Earl of Effex, and on his defection in favour of the Emprefs Maud, when he was feized and imprifoned by the King, he, to obtain his liberty, furrendered this and his caftle of Walden.

King Henry II. reftored to Geffery de Mandeville, fon of the above-named Earl, all the lands and honours that had ever belonged to his father or grandfather, to which William, his brother and heir fucceeding, here folemnized his marriage with Hardewife, daughter and heirefs of William le Gros, Earl of Albemarle, January 12, 1180. Henry II. gave him leave to fortify this caftle ; he died the 14th of November 1190, without iffue, and was fucceeded by Beatrix de Say, grand-daughter of his aunt Beatrix, wife of William de Say.

Beatrix de Say married Geffery Fitz Piers of Ludgerfhall Caftle, who was in her right made Earl of Effex, and his fons took on them the furname of Mandeville ; but the male line failing, Maud de Mandeville, anno 1199, marrying Henry de Bohun, Earl of Hereford, and Conftable of England, fhe carried the caftle into that family, and it was by Henry III. confirmed to his fon Humphrey, furnamed The Good, and continued in his defcendents till the reign of Edward III. when, for default of male heirs, it came to Eleanor, who married Thomas of Woodftock, Duke of Gloucefter, the fixth fon of that King, who in her right became Earl of Effex and Northampton, and Conftable of England ; he chiefly refided in this caftle.

At the acceffion of Richard II. this Duke prefuming on the authority of an uncle, and being a man of rigid virtue, interfered too much in the government, and rebuked his nephew's failings with fo much afperity, that he refolved to get rid of him ; for which purpofe Richard paid him a vifit at his caftle of Plefhy, on a fummer's evening, and perfuaded him to accompany him to London that night, to affift him with his advice in council. Thomas not fufpecting any ill intent, confented, and fet out flightly attended ; when they came near Stratford, the King riding off, a party of armed men, placed ready for that purpofe, feized the Duke, carried him on fhip-board, and conveyed him to Calais, where he was kept clofe prifoner till the 8th of September 1397, and then ftifled between two featherbeds. In the enfuing parliament, being declared a traitor, all his eftates efcheated to the crown, but his wife Eleanor was fuffered to enjoy this caftle, and moft of the lands of her anceftors till her death, 3d October 1399. On her demife this caftle and manor in a divifion of the eftates of that Duke came to Henry V. when they were valued at 106l. 8s. from which time they were united to the Duchy of Lancafter.

Anno 1215, in the difpute between King John and his Barons, this caftle was befieged by Savarike de Maulon, a Poictovian, who commanded part of the King's army. It then belonged to Geffery de Mandeville.

The manor of Plafhy, and the two Parks, were by Edward VI. granted to Sir John Gate, to hold in capite, by the 26th part of a Knight's fee ; but he taking part with Lady Jane Grey, it reverted to the crown, and there remained. The Little Park was granted to Sir John Clarke, One of the Barons of the Exchequer, whofe fon probably built the houfe called The Lodge, out of the materials of the caftle.

At prefent nothing remains of this edifice but a high mount, whereon probably the keep of the caftle ftood, having on the weft fide a brick bridge over it, and part of a gate here fhewn ; this mount is of an oval form, 45 paces in length, and 25 in width, and is furrounded by an area, called The Caftle-yard ; alfo bounded by a high rampart and ditch : this area contains about two acres. The foundations of buildings may be traced in many places.

This view, reprefenting the north fide, was drawn anno 1777.

CHARLES (Lord) MAYNARD,
of Thaxted,
Contributor to this Plate,
that elegant Structure
respectfully inscribed.

The Castle at Saffron Walden Essex
Drawn & etched in 1784.
by
W. Robinson.

This Castle was built in the Reign of William
the Conqueror by his follower Geoffrey de
Mandeville, who fixed his residence here.
The Keep & some of the earth work were in
being in 1763, & appears in 1784, as drawn
above, the Walls are now about 30 feet high.
And still call'd the Bury, adjoining to the
Castle, was the site of the Mansion House
to the Castle — The above is the East View
of the Church, & the Temple on the Western
Ring appears at the End of the Castle, this
Temple was built by Griffin Lord Howard
of Walden in Memory of the Victory obtained
in the Reign of George the 2.

Walden Castle Essex.

WALDEN CASTLE, ESSEX.

THIS castle, (Morant says), was begun by Geffrey de Mandeville, who came over with the Conqueror, and so distinguished himself, that William rewarded him with no less than an hundred and eighteen lordships, forty of which were in this county; Walden was one of them.

IT became afterwards the head of the barony, and descended to his son William de Mandeville, who joining with the Empress Maud, King Stephen caused him to be arrested at court, then A. D. 1143, held at St. Alban's. In order to obtain his liberty, he surrendered up his castles of Walden and Plasiz; but after his release again appeared under arms against the king, and committed many outrages: among others he seized and plundered the abbey of Ramsey in Huntingdonshire, for which he was excommunicated: at length, besieging the king's castle at Burwell, he received a wound in the head, of which he died 14th Sept. 1144. Some of the Knights Templars having got his body, caused the brain and bowels to be taken out, the body to be salted, and sewed up in a hide, and afterwards to be put up in a leaden coffin, which they hung on a crooked tree in their orchard, at the Old Temple, London; but the excommunication being afterwards taken off, they buried it privately in the churchyard of the New Temple. Geffery, his second son, had his father's estates restored to him, and they remained in the family till the extinction of the male line. The earldom of Effex, with thefe lands and caftle, were by King John, A. D. 1199, granted to Jeffry Fitz-Piers; after which, by default of iffue-male, they came to Maude, wife of Henry de Bohun, earl of Hereford, lord high-conftable of England, and continued in that family for many defcents. Humphry de Bohun, A. D. 1347, had licence to embattel his manor-houfe of Walden; his fon dying A. D. 1372, and leaving only two daughters, one of whom, named **Mary,** marrying Henry earl of Derby, afterwards king, by the title of Henry IV. the manor and caftle of Walden came to the Crown, and in right of his mother, defcended to King Henry V. It remained in the Crown till granted by King Henry VIII. to Thomas Lord Audeley.

From the Lord Audeley this caftle, manor, and other great eftates hereabouts, devolved to the noble family of Howard earls of Suffolk; and in 1777, when this drawing was made, the manor of Walden and caftle belonged to Sir John Griffin Griffin, having defcended to him from a female of that family.

The keep of this caftle ftripped of its outfide ftones, is ftill remaining, as fhewn in the drawing. Morant fays, there are alfo fome earthen works, and fome of the walls about thirty feet high on the infide. "An hill called the Bury, adjoining to the caftle, was the manfion-houfe of the caftle;" by this probably he means the manfion which Humphry de Bohun had leave to embattel.

Tiltey Abbey Essex.
Pub. 26 Feb. 1784 by J. Hooper.

TILTEY ABBEY, ESSEX.

THIS abbey is situated in the north-west part of the county, a few miles south of Thaxtead, and in the hundred of Dunmow.

ACCORDING to Tanner, it was founded about the year 1152, by Robert Earl of Derby, and Maurice Fitz Jeffery, for white monks, to the honour of the blessed Virgin Mary. Morant places this foundation in the year 1133, on the 20th of May, and says it was endowed by Maurice Fitz Geffery, who granted to it all his lands of Tileteia, without any exception: and that the said grant was confirmed by Robert Earl of Derby, as lord paramount of the fee. He adds, that their church was consecrated anno 1221, at which time several grants were made to them.

ABOUT the time of the dissolution here were only seven monks; the yearly revenues of the house were valued at 167l. 2s. 6d. Dugdale; 177l. 9s. 4d. Speed.

THE site was granted, says Morant, in 1542, by King Henry VIII. to Sir Thomas Audeley, Lord Audeley of Walden, and his heirs, under the following description. The site of the monastery, and the church, belfrey, and chapel; a mansion called the founder's lodging, and the guest hall; Tiltey Grange, and the manor of Tiltey; the rectory, with a chapel belonging to the same; lands and tenements called Rycrofts, Bingemones meadow in Tiltey, Charwreth, Plesdon Greene, and Boxtede, &c. to be holden in capite by the twentieth part of a knight's fee. He died 8th May 1544, possessed of this manor of Tiltye, with the advowson of the church and grange there, and two hundred acres of arable, sixty of meadow, three hundred of pasture in Easton, Broxtede, Chaurothe, Henham, and Plesdon. Margaret his eldest daughter, and at length sole heir, brought this, with the rest of his vast inheritance, to her two husbands, Henry Dudley, who was slain at St. Quintin's in 1557, and Thomas Howard Duke of Norfolk; by this last she had Thomas, afterwards created Earl of Suffolk, and three other children. She died 9th January 1565. Thomas Howard, Esq. her eldest son and heir, enjoyed it after her: but by licence, dated 2d March 1587, he sold the premises 1st April following for the sum of 5000l. to Henry Maynard, Esq; and in his family it hath continued ever since, being now in the Right Honourable Charles Lord Maynard.

THE names of the abbots, as given by Morant, are: anno 1370, Thomas Chisull; 1407, John Leighs; 1437, Simon Pabenham; 1520, John Oxford, John Browne. John Palmer, the last abbot, who signed the surrender.

OF this abbey little remains, except the building here shewn, now the parish church, said to have been the chapel to the hospital for strangers at the abbey gate, perhaps the building stiled in the grant the Guest Hall: and at a small distance north-eastward, part of the cloister walls, in which are marks of circular arches.

A GENTLEMAN of Thaxtead, living in 1777, when this drawing was made, remembered part of the lodgings of the monastery standing, inhabited by a farmer; these have been pulled down by Lord Maynard. The same gentleman said he had seen a survey of no very ancient date, in which the tower of the abbey church was represented as extant: it is now levelled with the ground, but the foundations might be easily traced out.

NORTH-WEST of the cloysters is a mill; a small distance from which, towards the north-east, are the beds of several fish-ponds, formerly stocked for the supply of the convent.

IN this chapel, besides the great window, which is well worthy observation, there are several ancient brasses and inscriptions, of which two are here given; the first is in old French and in the Saxon character, cut on the edges of a coffin-shaped stone, ornamented on its centre with a cross fleury.

Mahud de Mortimer gist Icy Jesu pur sa seeue pite e mesericorde de sa alme
eit mercy.

THE other on abbot named Thomas, who, according to tradition, is said to have governed the abbey, anno 1402.

Abbas famosus, bonus & vivendo pobatus
In Thakley natus qui jacet hic tumulatus
Thomas dictatus cum Christo sit sociatus,
Rite gubernavit istuq. locu pamavit.

THIS parish, says Morant, is rated to the land tax at 52 8l. The church, dedicated to the Virgin Mary, is of one pace with the chancel, tyled; a small belfrey belonging to it contains only one bell. This church was appropriated to the abbot and convent, who enjoyed all the tythes, great and small, till their suppression; after which it became a donative or perpetual curacy in the gift of the noble owner of the site of the abbey and manor. The Right Honourable Charles Lord Maynard hath settled a house with the appurtenances on the church clerk of this parish, and his successors in that office for ever, in the same manner as he hath done at both the Eastons.

WALTHAM ABBEY, ESSEX.

The first religious foundation here, was a church for two priests, built by Tovy, Stalhere, or Standard-bearer to King Canute, who laid the first foundation of a town in this place, on account of its neighbourhood to the forest, and its convenient situation for hunting.

But the present abbey was founded by Harold, son of Earl Godwin, in consequence of a grant from Edward the Confessor, upon condition that he should build a monastery in the place prescribed, in memory of him and his queen Editha; and moreover should adorn it with the relics of many holy apostles, martyrs and confessors evangelical books, vestments, and other proper ornaments; and also there institute a small society of brethren, subjected to canonical rules, according to the authority of the holy father.

Harold, in 1062, dedicated this monastery to the honour of a certain holy cross, found, as the legend says, by a carpenter somewhere in the West, and miraculously brought here, where it continued to possess its miraculous powers recorded in a manuscript mentioned by Mr. Morant as in the Cotton Library, Julius D. vi. 2. "De miraculis crucis in monteacuto "per fabrum inventæ tempore Canuti, et de ejus deductione ad Waltham."

Harold endowed his new founded abbey amply for the maintenance of a dean, and eleven secular black canons. After the battle of Hastings his body was here buried, being with some difficulty obtained from the conqueror by the intercession of his mother, and two of the monks of this abbey. His two brothers, who were killed in the same battle, were also buried here.

Maud, first queen to Henry I, gave to the abbey the mill at Waltham; his second queen Adelza, and other persons also increased the wealth of the abbey by considerable donations.

Henry II, to appease the Pope's anger on account of the death of Becket, had promised to erect an abbey for canons regular, to the honour of God and St. Thomas, and for the expiation of his sin. In consequence of which, in 1177, he changed this foundation from a society of seculars, to a monastery of regulars, for an abbot and sixteen monks of the order of St. Augustin, which seems to have satisfied the Pope, who was endeavouring to introduce regulars instead of seculars into all convents, because, as Henry's charter says, the secular canons had given much offence by their irregular and carnal lives: the truth perhaps was that the seculars were less attentive to the injunctions of the see of Rome, and were frequently married; it seemed however good to the King, Pope Alexander approving viros sanctæ conversationis substituere, et opiniona laudabiles.

By the charter of Henry II, great privileges and extensive territories were given to the abbey, which gifts were fully confirmed by a charter by his son Richard I, who also granted them other lands, the particulars of which, and the history of the property of the abbey may be seen in Fuller, Farmer and Morant.

Henry III, is said to have passed much time at this abbey, he granted it a weekly market and a fair. In his reign a dispute happened between the inhabitants of the town and the abbey, concerning a right of pasture in the town marsh, which ended in the submission of the townsmen: this dispute was followed by another between the abbot and the lord of the manor of Cheshunt, concerning the boundaries of their lands, which was determined in favour of the abbot; but the dispute was revived, and continued till the dissolution.

Very great privileges were granted by Edward III; two fairs at Waltham, and a market and fair at Epping-heath and at Takely.

The revenue of the abbey at its suppression was, according to Dugdale, annually 1079l. 12s. 1d; according to Speed 900l. 4s. 3d.

The site of the monastry was granted by Edward VI, to Sir Anthony Denny; and by purchase, and grant from Henry VIII, he had acquired most of its extensive possessions: his heirs, in the reign of Charles II, sold the abbey house and lands to Sir Sam. Jones of Northamptonshire, who gave this estate to Samuel, fifth son of Sir William Wake of Clevedon, in Somersetshire, in whose family it still continues.

The abbot of Waltham was one of the mitred abbots, and the abbey, from the time of its foundation, was free from all jurisdiction but that of the bishop of Rome and the King.

The church seems always to have been used as a parish church, and though originally dedicated to the Holy Cross, is said at some later period, to have been dedicated to St. Laurence.

The present parish church, which is only the western part of the ancient church, is a very venerable specimen of that stile of building usually called Saxon; the measures of it, as given by Farmer, are from west to east, in the inside of the body of the church 76 feet and a half; and from the body of the church to the east wall, where the communion table stands, 34 feet and a half, in all 111 feet; and from north to south 55 feet and a half. In the reign of Charles I, a figure of Harold, in one of the north windows of the church, was destroyed by the Puritans. The present tower, at the west end of the church, was erected in the reign of Philip and Mary, partly by the contributions of the inhabitants, and partly by the sale of the plate and vestments of the monastery, and of the bells. Its height is 89 feet from the foundation to the battlements, the workmanship of each foot (besides materials) in the lower part of the building, cost thirty-three shillings and four pence, and near the top forty shillings each foot. In 1668, a brief was granted to collect for the repair of the church, which producing but a small sum, the rest of the repair was made at the expence of the parish, and by the voluntary contributions of some of the parishioners.

Adjoining to the south side of the church is a chaple dedicated to our Lady, which has been used since the reformation for a school; under it is a charnel house, containing a large quantity of human bones laid up in great order. Some of them have lain there long, but there is no reason to believe the tradition of the place, that they are the bones of those who fell in Harold's cause, at the battle of Hastings.

A gate into the abbey yard, a bridge which leads to it, some ruinous walls, and an arched vault, are, with the church, now the only remains of this rich foundation: the stile of building of the church proves it antiquity, though there dos not appear any circumstances to determine positively whether it was built by Harold at the first foundation, or by Henry II, at the time of his refounding the abbey, as the Saxon or Roman stile prevailed to his time. The gate is evidently not older than Edward III, as there is yet to be discerned, on a shield on the west side of it, the arms of England quartered with the fleur de lis.

The abbey house, which had been repaired and rebuilt by its different possessors, was entirely pulled down in 1770. A tulip-tree, for which the gardens were known, and referred to, is still standing in full vigour.

The drawing, which was made in 1771, shews the gate, some ruined walls of the abbey, the north side of the church, and the mill.

Walton, at the Naze. Essex.

THE CHURCH OF WALTON ON THE NAIZE, ESSEX.

THE following account of this parish and church, is given by Morant in his History of Essex.

WALTON is the farthest of the three Sokens, bounded on the east by the German Ocean; part of it is a long slip of earth, running from south to north; about three miles in length, and one or less in breadth. The flowing in of the tide makes it a peninsula.

THE wall thrown up on this shore to keep out the sea, is what gave name to this town or village. It extended considerably farther east than it does now, but hath been devoured by the sea. Some have affirmed, that ruins of buildings have been discovered under water at a considerable distance. About five miles off from this shore, lies a shole of rocks, called West Rocks, which on a great ebb are left dry: A spot amongst them is called the town. The raging sea daily keeps undermining and encroaching upon this parish, so that the hall will soon be in an island.

THE Naize is a point of land in the east part of this parish jutting into the sea, well known to sailors. Near it the Trinity-house have erected a tower, or light-house, of brick, about eighty feet high from the foundation; for the direction and safeguard of ships passing that way. The most northern part or point of the peninsula in this parish, is called Walton Stone, and Goldman's Gap, is near the neck of land in the south part of the same. There is only one manor in this parish. Walton Hall is the mansion-house. This manor belonged, as the two other Sokens, to the Dean and Chapter of St. Paul's, and have passed from them to Thomas lord Darcey, earl Rivers, and the right honourable the earl of Rochford. The other estates of this parish, are; Walton Ashes; and another good farm, belonging to Philip Bennet, esq.—A considerable estate in Walton and Kirby belongs to Shaw King, esq.—John Kirby, esq. hath also an estate here—and Mr. John Wheely or Wheeler.

A FARM in this parish was purchased in 1739 by the governors of queen Anne's bounty, for the augmentation of the rectory of the Holy Trinity in Colchester. It consists of 55 acres, 3 roods, and 20 perches of freehold land, and about 34 acres of copyhold; but it is too near the sea, which undermines some part of it often. Mr. John Bernard, William Stone, &c. have also some lands in this parish.—Here was formerly the endowment, or corps of one of the prebends of St. Paul's, London, but the sea hath consumed or devoured it long ago. Therefore it is stiled *Præbenda Consumpta per mare*. It has the thirteenth stall on the left side of the choir, and is rated at one mark.

BETWEEN the church and the sea, near half a mile from the sea, lie two parcels of land, about half a mile asunder, one let for 15 l. a year, and the other for 4 l. 10 s. supposed to be let for the use of the poor that do not take collection. Here is a famous copperas-house. A fair is kept in this place, July 2d. The church which is now in ruins, consisted of a body and two ailes; and the chancel only of one pace. It is united to that of Kirkby. This parish is rated in the land-tax at 605 l. 2 s.

THIS view was drawn A. D. 1777.

Rodmarton Place Gloucestershire.
Pub. Nov.1.1814 by J. Storer.

THE ABBOT OF CIRENCESTER'S VILLA, AT RODMARTON, GLOUCESTERSHIRE.

THIS view ſhews the ancient manorial houſe at Rodmarton, in Gloucesterſhire, 6 miles ſouth-weſt of Cirenceſter, and 3 north-eaſt of Tetbury, ſaid to have been the villa of the abbot of Cirenceſter ; but of this, no evidence appears, either in the liſt of the poſſeſſions of that monaſtery, or in ſir Robert Atkins's account of the manor of Rodmarton. If then the abbot of Cirenceſter ever reſided here, he muſt have only rented the manſion, as it certainly never belonged to his abby; which Sir Robert Atkins, indeed ſays, had lands in this place.

VILLA AT RODMARTON, GLOUCESTERSHIRE.

THE houfe ftands a fmall diftance fouth-eaft of the church ;
it forms three fides of a quadrangle, and feems very ancient ;
and according to the ftile of thofe times, even magnificent.
The grand entrance was on the north fide, by a flight of
fteps, covered over with tiling, and leading to a large room
up one pair of ftairs, which feems to have been a great
hall. The building is of ftone, and has feveral ancient
church-like windows, with carved mullions ; it was not long
fince inhabited by a farmer, but at prefent is ufed for a
granary. It is the property of Charles Cocks, efq. lord of
the manor.

THIS view was drawn anno 1785.

Beverstone Castle.

BEVERSTONE CASTLE, GLOUCESTERSHIRE.

THIS castle takes its name from the parish wherein it stands, which is situated in the hundred of Berkeley, one mile distant west from Tetbury, three miles south from Hampton, and 12 miles south from Gloucester. It was anciently called Bureſtan, from the blue ſtones found in and near it.

THIS caſtle is ſaid by ſir Robert Atkyns, to be very ancient. The earls Godwin, Swegen, and Harold, (ſays he) met at this place, under pretence to aſſiſt king Edward the confeſſor, againſt the Welch; but they entered into conſpiracy againſt him, for which they were forced to fly the kingdom.

KING Hen. II. gave the manor of Beverſtone to Robert Fitz Harding, anceſtor of the Berkeley family; he ſettled it on Robert, his ſecond ſon, in marriage with Alice, daughter heir of Robert de Gaunt; Maurice, the produce of this marriage, took upon himſelf the family name of his mother, and was called Maurice de

Gaunt. This Maurice seems to have done great repairs to this castle, and was probably the first who converted it from a simple mansion to a place of strength : as it is said by sir Robert Atkyns, in his account of this manor, that in 11th of Hen. III. he was prosecuted for fortifying his castle of Beverstone without licence, but that two years afterwards he obtained one for that purpose ; no authority is cited in proof of this assertion. He dying without issue, 14th Hen. III. the manor and castle descended to Anselm de Gourney, who had married his sister Eve.

In this family it remained for several descents, till on the failure of issue male, it came to John ap Adam, who had married Elizabeth, the sole daughter and heiress of John Gourney, the last possessor of that name. Thomas ap Adam, son of the above-named John, sold the manor to Thomas lord Berkeley, 4th of Edw. III. and he was seised of the castle in the 35th of that reign, when he beautified and greatly enlarged it, by the ransom of prisoners taken at the battle of Poictiers. Leland makes him the builder of it. It was a square, and moated on all sides, and had a tower at every corner ; one of the towers is still remaining. It continued in this family till sold by sir John Berkeley, soon after the 20th of Elizabeth, to sir John Pointz. Henry Fleetwood, esq. was lord thereof in the year 1608. In a few years after that date it was purchased by sir Michael Hicks, to one of whose descendants it at present belongs.

During the civil wars under Charles I. this castle was occupied as a garrison by both parties.

Part of this castle has been fitted up for a farm-house. The gate, or chief entrance, was on the east side, flanked by two towers, part only of one remains.

A market and fair was granted to this place in the reign of Edw. I. but they have been long disused.

This view, which shews the west side of the castle, was drawn anno 1785.

Cross in Iron Acton Church Yard, Gloucestershire.

THE CROSS AT IRON ACTON, GLOUCESTERSHIRE.

THIS beautiful crofs ftands in the church-yard of Iron Acton, on the north fide of the church : Sir Robert Atkins calls it "a very antient large crofs with arches," but gives no account when, or by whom it was erected ; probably it was intended like the crofs of the black friars, Hereford, that at St. Paul's, Cheapfide, &c. to ferve as a kind of pulpit for the preaching friars.

IRON Acton church, fays Sir Robert Atkins, is in the Deanry of Hawkfbury. It is a rectory worth 120l. yearly. Mr. Shute is patron, and the prefent incumbent.

THE church hath a fouth ifle, and a large tower with pinnacles at the weft end, and a chancel on the fouth-fide of the other belonging to the manor-houfe, where is an infcription for the Pointz's, and two old ftatues of ftone.

IRON Acton lies about 12 miles north eaft of Briftol, and in the hundred of Thornbury ; it obtained the appellation of Iron Acton from the great quantity of iron ore and cinders digged up, indicating, that here were formerly great iron works.

THIS view was drawn anno 1786.

Priory & Kitchen, of Stanley St. Leonard, near Stroud, Gloucestershire.

THE PRIORY OF STANLEY ST. LEONARD'S, GLOUCESTERSHIRE.

STANLEY St. Leonard lies within the Hundred of Whitstone,. about four miles west from Stroud, six north-east from Durfley, and eleven south from Gloucester. Here was a small monastry, supposed to have been founded by Roger de Berkeley, who endowed it with the advowsons of the several churches of Ozleworth, Cowley, Erlingham, Uley, Slimbridge, and in the year 1146, with the consent of Sabrith, or Sabrath, then prior, and the rest of the religious, and also with the approbation of Simon, bishop of Worcester, made it a cell to the abbey of Gloucester, a house of benedictine monks. In the year 1156, he further added to his benefactors by bestowing on it the church of Cam, with the appurtenances, and a grove called Fyshere; these gifts were afterwards confirmed by K. Henry III. A difficulty occours in the account of the foundation, as mentioned by Tanner and others, who say, this monastry, consisting of a prior and canons, was founded in the church of St. Leonard, which seems to express that it was founded in a church then extant, and dedicated. to St. Leonard; this by no means appears, the parish church being dedicated to St. Swithin; and neither history nor tradition mention any other near that fpot. This priory was diffolved, with the abbey of Gloucefter; but, before that event took place, there being only two monks in the priory, King Henry VIII. by a letter dated June 11th, in the 30th year of his reign, defired that thofe monks might be recalled to the abbey, and that the abbot and convent would grant a leafe of this cell for ninety-nine years to Sir William King-fton, knight, which was done accordingly, at the yearly rent of 36l. 13s. 4d. with fome few refervations, as appears by abbot Malvern's manufcript. The annual revenues of the priory, at the diffolution, amounted to 126l. 0s. 8d. according to Speed; a table of valuation in Stevens's fupplement makes its clear value 106l. 17s. The fcite of this cell, and all the lands in England belonging to it, were granted to Sir Anthony Kingfton, 36th of Henry VIII. referving a rent of 40s. per annum. In the 2d year of Edward VI. Sir Anthony conveyed thefe premifes by licence of alienation to Anthony Boucher, Efq. who the next year conveyed them to John Sandford, Efq. anceftor of the prefent proprietor.

THIS view fhews the old kitchen, and fome other parts of that monaftry. Rudder, in his hiftory of Gloucefterfhire, fays, the old piory houfe was taken down "about 30 years ago, and the outward " walls of a good houfe were built on the very fpot of ground whereon " it ftood; but the infide is not yet finifhed." Rudder's hiftory was printed in 1779, fo that the houfe muft have been pulled down about the year 1749.

THE church, part of which appears in this view, is built in the form of a crofs, and has a large tower, once crowned with a high fpire in the midft. This tower is of a very fingular conftruction, having a double wall, with a paffage and recefles between them.

THIS view was drawn 1786.

Stanley St Leonards Church, Gloucestershire.

ST. SWITHEN's CHURCH, NEAR THE PRIORY OF STANLEY, ST. LEONARD, GLOUCESTERSHIRE.

THIS view shews the church of St. Swithen's, with some of the offices of the ancient priory. The peculiarity in the construction of this church has been noticed in the account of the kitchen of the priory.

THIS view was drawn anno 1786.

BEAULIEU ABBEY, HAMPSHIRE.

(PLATE I.)

In the year 1204 King John founded an Abbey in the New Forest called Bello Loco, Fine Place, or Beaulieu, and placed therein thirty monks, brought from other Cistertian houses. The history of the foundation of this house is given in the Monasticon, nearly in the following words:

In the sixth year of the reign of King John, that King built a certain monastery of the Cistertian order in England, and named it Beaulieu; it is said this house owed its origin to the following occasion: King John having taken an unjust prejudice against the Abbots, and other persons of the Cistertian order, and by his Ministers not a little aggrieved them; these Abbots, desirous of removing this dislike, and if possible of obtaining the royal favour, repaired to Lincoln, where the King then held a parliament, when coming into his presence he was so enraged at them, that he ordered his attendants to trample them under their horses feet; but no one being found who would obey so cruel and so unheard-of a command from a Christian prince, the Abbots, despairing of acquiring the King's favour, retreated hastily to their inn. The night following the King sleeping in his bed dreamed he was brought before a Judge, the said Abbots being present, who were commanded to scourge him on the back with whips and rods; waking in the morning he asserted he had felt that scourging. This dream he related to an Ecclesiastic of his court, who told him God had been uncommonly merciful to him in thus clemently and paternally deigning to admonish him, and to reveal his mysteries to him; he therefore counselled the King to send immediately for these Abbots, and humbly to ask their pardons for his cruel order. The King consenting, they were sent for, and on receiving the message, feared they were to be expelled the kingdom, but God who had not left them, had disposed otherwise, coming into the King's presence he dismissed that hatred he had entertained against them.

THE King afterwards granted them his charter for the foundation of this house, which he endowed royally with diverse estates, whose boundaries are therein described. It is to be observed that he had the year before given to the same Monks his manor of Farendon, so that there was some time elapsed between what they would call his conversion and the foundation of the monastery; and indeed it appears from Mathew Paris, that the church was not finished and confecrated till the year 1246.

THE King further bestowed on them an hundred marks towards building their Abbey, and wrote circular letters to the Abbots of the Cistertian order to assist them in completing and furnishing the same.

THIS abbey was, like most of the houses of that order, dedicated to the Virgin Mary: at the dissolution its yearly revenue amounted to 326l. 13s. 2d. Ob. q. Dugdale—428l. 6s. 8d. Speed. The site was granted 30th Henry VIII. to Thomas Wriothesley, Esq. and is at present the property of his Grace the Duke of Montague.

BROWNE WILLIS has the following particulars respecting this abbey:

HUGH was the first Abbot; the next that occurs was another Hugh, and then I meet with Arius de Gisortio; he sent a convert to build an abbey at Newnham, Devonshire: the next that occurs is Dionisius; he charged the first convert, and sent a second to Newnham. He died anno 1280, as the annals of Worcester tells us, and was succeeded by William Gisortio, elected the 9th cal. of May 1281. After him I meet with only the bare names of some of his successors, and these were Robert de Bockland, Peter de Chicheftre, William de Hamilton, and John. Tidemanus de Winchecombe, Abbot of this place, was, anno 1343, made Bishop of Landaff, and afterwards of Worcester; Thomas Sheffington, made anno 1509 Bishop of Bangor, held this Abbey in commendam.

THOMAS STEPHENS was last Abbot, and with nineteen Monks surrendered this convent the 17th of April 1538, and had a pension of 66l. 13s. and 4d. per ann assigned him.

ANNO 1553 here remained in charge 5l. in fees, 15l. 18s. 8d. in annuities, and these pensions, viz.

To William Bascavile 5l. Herman Hawpton 5l. Alexander Aleyn 5l. John Kizzie 5l. Thomas White 5l. Robert Pinkeston 4l. John Somerfelde 4l. and to Thomas Gaulb'e 4l.

THE appellation of Beaulieu, or Fine Place, was very justly given to the spot where this abbey stands, and its environs, as it still possesses every requisite to form a beautiful situation.

THE remains of this monastery at present consist of the church, fitted up for a parochial one, repaired about the year 1743, as appears by a date on the great buttress at the east end; the priors lodgings converted into a dwelling house, or ruined building. perhaps the dormitory, and the gatehouse or porter's lodge. The dwelling-house or prior's lodging is surrounded by a mote with a draw-bridge; in it is an elegant vaulted hall, and on the front of the house a handsome Gothick canopy with a niche; the figure, probably the Virgin Mary, it is said, fell down a little while ago. The abbey walls extended a great way, enclosing an area of sixteen or seventeen acres well wooded and watered, and full of the foundations of ruined buildings. About three miles south-west from this abbey, and one from Sowley Pond, are large ruins of the grange or farmhouse belonging to this monastery, a chapel, and particularly a monstrous barn, measuring upwards of 225 feet in length, and 75 in breadth, built chiefly with stone.

THIS view was drawn anno 1776.

THE GREAT HALL OF BEAULIEU ABBEY, HAMPSHIRE.

THE building here delineated was the Great Hall, or Refectory of the Abbey, and is now converted into the parish church of the village of Beaulieu; notwithstanding its alteration, traces of the original destination still remain. On the great buttress at the end of this edifice in a square compartment, is the date 1734, probably the time when it was repaired, or altered and accommodated to its present form and use.

This View was drawn anno 1776.

CALSHOT CASTLE.

DRAWN by PAUL SANDBY, Esq. *R. A.*

Engraved by Mr. RIDER.

THIS Castle is in the county of Hants, pleasantly situated on a promontory on the west side of the mouth of that arm of the sea, called, improperly, Southampton river. It was built by Henry the Eighth, to defend that town. This, though intended chiefly for defence, is a handsome fortress, with a moat on the side next the land, over which is a draw-bridge. A garrison is constantly kept here, commanded by the governor of the castle.

In the passage from Southampton to the Isle of Wight, it appears to be floating in the water. It has lately received very considerable improvements. About a mile behind it, the Hon. Temple Lutterel has erected a very lofty tower, which commands an extensive prospect, and affords a very fine object for the Isle of Wight.

CHRIST's CHURCH CASTLE, HAMPSHIRE.

This castle is situated a small distance north of the once famous monastery of Christ Church, Twinham, and seems never to have been of any great extent, if one may judge from the keep and the ruined walls of its east and west sides still standing, which inclose an area of only twenty-eight by twenty-four feet. These walls are ten feet thick, and about twenty-six feet high, and stand on an artificial mount raised about twenty feet. About an hundred yards east of this keep, and close to the west side of a small creek, serving for a mill-stream, which appears to have been once walled in, stands a building that from several circumstances seems to have belonged to the castle, and probably to have been the state apartments of the constable or governor.

Its figure is a right-angled parallelogram, the length from north to south measuring nearly twenty-four yards, its breadth eight at the south end of the east side, but separated by a wall; there is a small projecting tower, calculated for a flank, under which the water runs; it has loop-holes both on the north and east fronts; these walls are extremely thick.

On the ground-floor are a number of loop-holes, which plainly shew it was a place designed for defence, and not part of the monastery, as is by some pretended, these loop-holes are formed by a large semicircular arch within, lessening by degrees, and terminating in a chink; of thefe there are two on the eaft fide, one at the north end, befides thofe in the tower already mentioned; there were likewife three doors, one to the weft, one at the fouth end, and another opening to the water, the laft has a flat arch, feemingly very handfomely ornamented, but it being clofe over the water, a near approach is impracticable, unlefs in a boat; the eaft fide is almoft covered with ivy.

FROM the ground-floor there was an afcent to the upper apartments by a ftone ftair-cafe in the north-eaft angle, part of the ftairs are ftill remaining.

THE place for receiving the floor of the firft ftory is very vifible; it feems to have been one room only, lighted by three large windows on the eaft, and as many on the weft fide, they were all included in femicircular arches formed of ftones very neatly cut, and divided in two by a fmall pillar in their centre.

IN the eaft fide, and fomewhat north of the centre, was a very large fireplace, worked circularly into the main wall, having alfo a high cylindrical ftone chimney, feemingly the only one in the building.

AT the north end there appears to have been a large arched window, the columns, and part of the internal arch, are ftill remaining, and anfwer to a handfome femicircular arch on the outfide, decorated with zigzag ornaments. This has been ftopped up, and two brick fire-places, one over the other, with a chimney of the fame materials, built up in it, feemingly of no antiquity; from whence it is evident that this building has been converted to a dwelling; whether there were originally rooms over this ftory is doubtful; over the fouth end, near the top, there is a circular window, which feems to have been made for lighting fome upper apartment.

FROM what remains of the ornamental part of this building, it appears to have been elegantly finifhed, and cafed with fquared ftones, moft of which are however now taken away; by the ruins of feveral walls there were fome ancient buildings at right angles to this hall, ftretching away towards the keep.

VERY little occurs in hiftory refpecting this caftle, though feemingly a royal one; it is juft-mentioned by Peck, in his Defiderata Curiofa, among the reft of the caftles and houfes then belonging to the crown, where the falary of the conftable of the caftle is charged at 8l.-os. 9d.

SOME other fragments refpecting it occur in a furvey made October 1656, wherein relative to this caftle are thefe words, "To the which Sir Henry Wal-" lope, in his time, was high conftable, and had fee——of the game afforefaid."

" MEM. The conftable of the caftle, or his deputy, upon the apprehenfion of " any felon within the liberty of Weft Stowefing, to receive the faid felon, and " convey him to the juftice and to the faid jail, at his own proper cofts and " charges, and otherwife the tithingman to bring the faid felon, and chain him " to the caftle gate, and there to leave him. Cattle impounded in the caftle, " having hay and water for twenty-hours, to pay four pence per foot."

THIS caftle and the manor of Chrift Church are the property of J. Clerke, Efq.

THIS view fhews the eaft and north fide of the building, and on the right hand part of the keep of the caftle, was drawn anno 1776.

THE PRIORY OF TWYNHAM, OR CHRIST CHURCH, HAMPSHIRE.

(PLATE I.)

THIS priory was originally called The Church of Twynham or Twynhamburne, according to Camden, from its situation at the conflux of the rivers of Avon and Stour.

THE æra of its foundation is not ascertained. Camden says only in general, that it was built in the Saxon times ; Dugdale, Tanner, and other authorities mention it as existing as early as the reign of King Edward the Confessor ; accordingly a history of its foundation printed in the Monasticon, it is recorded in Doomsday Book, as a college of secular Canons. Their number in the reign of William Rufus was twenty-four, besides one Godric, a man of great piety, whom they obeyed as their patron and senior, the name of Dean, says the history before-mentioned, being as it were unknown among them.

RANULF FLAMBARD, Bishop of Durham, the favorite of William Rufus, having obtained this church of that King, determined, on account of many miracles performed here, to pull down the old building, and to erect a more magnificent one in its stead. It is said he had formerly been Dean or Superior of this community, and therefore retained a particular affection for it ; for this purpose he obtained from the Canons the whole of their income, except so much as was necessary for their immediate support, in which he was strenuously but unsuccessfully opposed by Godric, who for a while absented himself from the fraternity, but was afterwards re-instated.

RANULF then proceeded to put his plan into execution, and pulled down not only the old church, but nine houses which stood beyond the cemetery, with some others belonging to the Canons, and erected the present church, together with all the necessary offices and conveniencies for a monastery. The buildings being completed, he dedicated it to Christ, and proposed to have introduced regular Canons. Godric and ten of the Canons being dead, he allotted their Prebends for life to the remaining Canons for their support ; but falling into disgrace with King Henry I. he was imprisoned, and his new foundation stripped of all its wealth, and given to a clerk named Gilbert de Dousgunels, who went to Rome in order to procure leave to complete Flambard's intention of settling regular Canons there, but died in his return. At this time there remained five Canons only.

RICHARD DE REDVERS having obtained of King Henry I. this town, the adjacent lands, and also the church, placed in the latter one Peter de Oglander, a Priest, and confirmed to it all its former possessions and immunities, adding divers lands, particularly in the Isle of Wight, and one of his baronies called Abbam; the parishioners likewise endowed it with their tithes. The church nevertheless did not flourish under this Peter, who appears to have been a dishonest and selfish man.

ABOUT the year 1150 Henry Bishop of Winchester, and Hilarius the Dean, at the request of the Earl Baldwin, son of Richard de Redvers, brought hither Canons regular of the order of St. Augustine, and constituted a Prior, ordaining that the secular canons should hold their benefices during their lives, serving as before, but subject to the regulars, by whom after their deaths their places were to be filled up. Earl Baldwin confirmed to this house all the grants made by his father, and added benefactions of his own, which were ratified by his son Richard, who allowed them likewise the free election of their own Prior.

THE yearly revenues of this priory were valued the 26th Henry VIII. at 312l. 7s. 9d. Dug.—544l. 6s. Speed. And the site of it was granted 32d Henry VIII. to the inhabitants of the town, and 37th Henry VIII. to Stephen Kirton. At present it belongs to the Honourable Mr. Coventry.

BROWN WILLIS, in his History of Abbies, has the following particulars respecting this priory:

" JOHN DRAPER, last Prior, suffragan Bishop by the title of Neapolitanus, surrendered this convent 28th " November 1540, 31st Henry VIII. and had a pension of 133l. 6s. 8d. per annum assigned him anno " 1553; here remained in charge 25l. 6s. 8d. in fees, 21l. 6s. 8d. in annuities, and these following " pensions, viz. to Richard South 6l. 13s. 4d. William Clerke 6l. 13s. 4d. Robert Merisfelde 6l. 13s. 4d. " Thomas Hancock 6l. 13s. 4d. Walter Churche 6l. John Pepet 6l. William Martyn 6l. Walter Na- " thewe 6l. John Stone 6l. Thomas Andrews 6l. John Tolf 6l. John Dover 6l. Thomas Cook 6l. and " and to Anthony Pitman 3l. 6s. 8d."

AND the same author gives the following list of names from the register of Worcester:

" RICHARD MAURI was admitted Prior Id. Maii 1286; he died anno 1302, and was succeeded by Wil- " liam Quintin, admitted 3 Id. April 1302; his successor as I guess was Edmued, who dying anno 1337, " Richard Butesthorne was nominated to succeed him, and confirmed in this office March 28 following; " he governed not long, for anno 1340 Ralph de Legh was admitted Prior 21st August 1340; he died " anno 1348, and was succeeded by Henry Eyre, on whose decease John Woodenham became Prior 21st " July 1377; he died anno 1397, and had for his successor

JOHN BORARD, confirmed 8th November 1397; after him I meet with no more till John Dorchester, on whose death, which happened on 1477, John Draper was substituted in his stead December 16, 1477, who, as my accounts suggest, was the last Prior, which, if so, he must have possessed this office about 62 years.

ON divers grave-stones in the church there are still legible the names of the under-mentioned dignitaries of this priory, with some almost obliterated inscriptions, wherein the word prior only is distinguishable.

RICHARD x the tenth Prior; John Doland the nineteenth; William Eyre the twenty-fifth, Thomas Trill the twenty——th; and Robert Say, Sub Prior.

THIS view, which was drawn in 1776, shews the south view of the church, with the very ancient transept, undoubtedly the original building erected by Bishop Flambard; the tower and other parts of this structure are probably of a much later date.

THE PRIORY OF TWYNHAM, OR CHRIST CHURCH, HAMPSHIRE.

This view reprefents the fouth fide of the church together with the tranfept, as feen from the garden of Guftavus Brander, Efquire. The former plate was by an error of the prefs called the fouth fide inftead of the north.

Of the ruins of this once rich and magnificent monaftery, little remains but the church, a part of the refectory fouth of it, and fome ruinous walls to the weft; a mill and the miller's houfe, once perhaps the porter's lodge, or the dwelling of fome inferior domeftic. It was probably built or repaired by Draper the laft prior, the initials of his name, neatly carved in ftone, being placed on one of the window frames; Mr. Brander, well known for his proficiency in natural hiftory, and other branches of polite literature, has built a handfome houfe on the fouth fide of the church, on a fpot called the Place, or Palace Court; in digging the foundation the workmen found fome very ancient ftone coffins of different forms, the fides of fome of them compofed of different pieces, but all without lids or bottoms.

The refectory, now converted into a hot-houfe, afforded fomething ftill more extraordinary, for in the year 1774 the workmen found a ftone cramped down with lead, it meafured 2 feet by 20 inches, under it in a cavity inclofed with ftones on each fide, having a bottom like a veffel or cheft, was found near half a bufhel of fowl's bones, the greateft part of them cocks legs with long fpurs, there were alfo many belonging to the hern or bittern.

THE PRIORY OF TWYNHAM, HAMPSHIRE.

A BRANCH of the river, which runs close under the east end of the church to the mill, seems to have been walled round, with here and there some small turrets; in the meadow called the Convent Garden, on the south-east side of the river, are the traces of several fish ponds and stews for keeping fish.

THE church is built in the shape of a cross, having a handsome and lofty tower at the west end, which, with the east end, seems more modern than the rest of the building.

THE tower is built with Purbeck stone, the rest with Cane and Quarrer stone, some masons from Purbeck, who lately viewed this tower, pointed out and named the different veins from whence it was digged.

HIGH up, on the west side of this tower, in a nich under a Gothic canopy, is the figure of Christ crowned with thorns, holding in his left hand a cross, his right raised as in the act of benediction, under his right breast is a triangular mark, seemingly intended for the wound made by the spear; on each side the west door are escutcheons with the arms of the Montagues.

THE inside of this church is very handsome, but the body is much disfigured by some high pews; the whole measures in length 302 feet, and from wall to wall, including the aisles, in breadth 60.

THE transepts are each 23 feet from north to south, by 24.

THE area is divided into a body and two aisles, each aisle being about 13 feet wide, and only about 18 high, having a handsome fretted ceiling formed by the interfections of the ribs of the aisles.

THEY are divided from the body by a double row of solid square piers, ornamented with columns, supporting three stories of arches, the first and second circular, the third, in which are windows, pointed; round these in the body only, is a triforium or passage.

THE aisles now terminate some yards short of the east end of the body, though it is probable they were once continued to the end, from the circumstance of a tomb, of no very ancient form, part of which appears on the outside of the north wall beyond the termination of the aisles, which tomb seems as if it had been originally placed in the interval, between the body of the church and the aisles, having a front open to both, it was only plaiftered up with mortar, the stone being broken on the outside, no bones were found.

BETWEEN the uppermost windows are columns, from which spring ribs of arches, now broken off, whence it seems that the roof was once vaulted, and the remains of some beams, adorned with painted leafwork, forming pointed arches close to the tiles, shew it was also once wainscoted; on examining the outside, it is evident here have been two roofs, the chasings of one higher than that which at present covers it being still remaining.

This View was drawn Anno 1776.

The Hofpital of S.t Crofs.

THE HOSPITAL OF ST. CROSS, NEAR WINCHESTER, HAMPSHIRE.

PLATE I.

This hofpital was founded in the year 1132 by Henry de Blois, Bifhop of Winchefter, for the health of his own foul and the fouls of the kings of England. The original inftitution was for the maintenance of thirteen poor men, fo debilitated by age or infirmities as to be unable to maintain themfelves without charitable affiftance; thefe men were to be provided with proper clothing and beds fuitable to their infirmities, and alfo to have a daily allowance of good wheaten bread, good fmall beer, three meffes each for dinner, and one for fupper; but in cafe any of thefe fhould happen to recover a confiderable degree of ftrength; fo as to be judged able to maintain himfelf, he fhould be refpectfully difcharged, and another admitted in his place. Befides thefe thirteen poor brethren, one hundred poor men, of modeft behaviour, and the moft indigent that could be found, fhould be received daily at dinner, and have each a loaf of common bread, one mefs, and a proper allowance of beer, with leave to carry away with them the remains of their meat and drink left after dinner.

The founder alfo directed other charities to be diftributed among the poor in general, in fuch proportion as the revenues of the hofpital fhould be found able to allow, the whole of which was to be applied to charitable ufes.

The endowment of this hofpital was not altogether derived from the founder's own private fortune, but confifted in the donations of divers confiderable rectories belonging to his diocefe, or that were under his patronage, the greateft part of which, though granted to the hofpital by the exprefs terms of the charter of foundation, were neverthelefs only made fubject to the payment of certain annual penfions, except the churches of Hufborne, Whitchurch, Fareham and Twyford, with their chapels.

The revenues of this houfe appear by an old record of inquifition to have amounted originally to 250l. per annum; in Wykeham's time they were faid by him in his letters to the pope, to be above 300l. per annum; and were afterwards proved by one of the ftewards contemporary with that bifhop, as well as by feveral other perfons to have exceeded the yearly amount of 400l. the whole free from all deductions or taxes, either to the pope or king, as being entirely appropriated to the use and benefit of the poor, except 7l. 4s. 6d. per annum, which was the valuation of the master's portion.

THE particular allowances to the poor, according to the above-mentioned inquisition were as follows : each of the thirteen secular brethren were allowed daily, one loaf of good wheaten bread of five marks weight, that is, three pounds four ounces, one gallon and a half of good small beer, a sufficient quantity of pottage ; three messes at dinner, viz. one mess called mortrell, made of milk and white or wastle-bread, one mess of flesh or fish, and one pittance as the day should require ; and one mess for supper ; the whole of which was then valued at 17d. q. a week, and in Wykeham's time at 3d. a day. On six holidays in the year they had white bread and ale in the same quantities, and one of their messes was roast meat, or fish of a better sort ; and on the eves of those holidays, and that of the founder's obit, they had an extraordinary allowance of four gallons of ale among them. The hundred casual poor were fed in a place called *Hundred-meneshall* ; each of them had a loaf of inferior bread of five marks weight, three quarts of small beer, a sufficient quantity of pottage, or a mess of pulse, one herring, or two pilchards, two eggs, or a farthing-worth of cheese ; value 3d. per week. Of these hundred poor, thirteen were taken from amongst the poorer scholars of the great grammar school at Winchester, sent by the school-master. On the anniversary of the founder's obit, August 9, being the eve of St. Lawrence, three hundred poor were received at the hospital ; to each of the first hundred were given one loaf and one mess of the same sort with those of the brethren's ordinary allowance, and three quarts of beer, the second hundred received the usual hundred men's allowance, and to each of the third hundred were given a loaf of the brethren's bread. On six holidays in the year, the hundred men had each a loaf of the better sort of bread, and a double mess. Besides these, there were maintained in the hospital, a steward, with his clerk, a porter, eleven servants, two saddle horses, two teams of six horses each, and two carters.

THE guardianship and direction of this hospital had by the founder, in the year 1157, been deputed to the master and brethren of the hospital of St. John of Jerusalem, saving to the bishop of Winchester his canonical jurisdiction. Some disputes arising between bishop Toclive, immediate successor to the founder, and the above-mentioned master and brethren, king Henry the Second interposed, and settled them in favor of the bishop, to whom and his successors was ceded the administration of this hospital, who thereupon bestowed on it the impropriation of the churches of Mordon and Hanniton, and procured them a discharge from an annual pension paid to the monks of St. Swithin.

SOON after this reconciliation, bishop Toclive out of regard to God, and for the health of his own and the king's souls, directed that over and above the number of poor directed to be fed daily, by the institution of the founder, one hundred additional poor should be added, who were to receive the same provisions as those ordered the other brethren, for which he found the revenues were fully sufficient. This regulation is dated April 10, 1185, and was made at Dover in the presence of the king, and attested by him. It does not however seem to have continued long in force, for it ceased long before the time of William of Wykeham, and instead of it, (by what authority is uncertain) an establishment was introduced consisting of four priests, thirteen secular clerks, and seven choristers, who were maintained out of the revenues of the hospital for the performance of divine service in the church. The four priests dined at the master's table, and had each a stipend of 13s. 4d. and the whole allowance to each was valued at 3l. 6s. 8d. per annum ; the thirteen clerks had each daily one loaf of bread, weight 61s. 8d. or 3lb. 1 oz. Three quarts of beer, and one mess of flesh or fish, the same as issued to the brethren, was allotted to two of them, value 10d. q. a week ; the seven choristers had each one loaf of common family bread, and one mess, or the fragments of the master's table and common hall, so as to have a sufficient provision, value 5d. per week, and they were taught at school in the hospital. THIS view was drawn anno 1780.

WINCHESTER ... CITY ... NEAR WINCHESTER

THE HOSPITAL OF ST. CROSS, NEAR WINCHESTER. Plate II.

The revenues of this hospital suffered much from the mal-administration and embezzlements of four of its masters; namely, Edyngton, Stowell, Lyntesford, and Cloune; but William of Wickham being elected bishop of Winchester, he with a most unremitting zeal, during a litigation of six years, followed them through all the labyrinths of chicanery, both at home and at Rome, and finally reinstated the charity in all its rights and property, and at his death left it in such order, that his successor Cardinal Beaufort, who had resolved to dispose of a considerable sum in some charitable foundation, chose rather to add to this hospital than to found a new one; and, therefore, made an additional endowment for the maintenance of two priests, thirty-five brethren, and three sisters, exclusive of those of the orginal foundation, and in the year 1444 built lodgings for them: this new establishment he seems to have designed for decayed gentlemen, as he entitled it the alms-house of noble poverty. This endowment consisted of lands and manors of the yearly value of 500l. granted by Henry VI. in consideration of the sum of 13350 marks paid him by the cardinal, who afterwards added the impropriations of Crundell and other churches in the diocese of Winchester.

The revenues of this hospital, though considerably diminished, still maintain a master and nine poor brethren, who enjoy their places during life. The office of master is a very lucrative appointment, generally held by some dignified clergyman. The allowance to the brethren is one pound of meat per day, three quarts of good small beer, and five loaves of wheaten bread, each loaf weighing twenty-four ounces, besides certain additional allowances of meat and drink on particular days, and sixpence weekly.

There are likewise four out-pensioners, who have each, during life, a stipend of 10l. per annum; the sum of 25s. is also distributed among the poor every year, being the remainder of the revenue formerly appropriated to the feeding of the poor in Hundred-mennethall. There is besides at this time, a daily allowance to the porter, of a certain quantity of bread and beer, for the refreshment of poor travellers, who are entitled to a piece of white bread and a cup of beer on demand.

The following description of this hospital is given in the history of Winchester.

The buildings belonging to this foundation consist of one extensive irregular court, which has a beautiful rural effect, and altogether exhibits a piece of venerable antiquity. The church, which is a curious remain of Saxon architecture, was built in the reign of King Stephen, by the first founder; it is in the form of a cross, and confits of three ifles, with a tranfept or crofs ifle. The roof is remarkably lofty, and is fupported by round maffive pillars, with round headed arches, ftronger than the Doric or Tufcan; and there are fome paintings upon the pillars and walls of the fame kind as thofe in the cathedral and in the chapel of St. Mary Magdalene. The ifles from the altar to the weft door are 150 feet in length, and the tranfept is 120. The chancel is exceedingly neat, and is paved with white marble, and on each fide of the altar are handfome fcreens of fpire work, carved in ftone, and neatly ornamented. Upon a defk on the left fide of the chancel are carved the names of all the officers belonging to the Hofpital about the year 1575, among which are thofe of a chanter of finging men, which formerly officiated in it, but at prefent there is no provifion for a choir.

THE great weft window of this church is built in a very ornamental ftyle, and was formerly an elegant one, as is obvious from the remains of fome curious painted glafs, with which it was once finifhed; there remains nothing in it at prefent legible, or at leaft intelligible except the word Nicholas Bedford. A window in the eaft fide of the north tranfept was formerly ornamented in the fame ftile, and ftill retains an Ave Maria, with fome fragments, under, which is, " Orate pro " anima Ricardi Butefhall. i. e. pray for the foul of Richard Butefhall." He was mafter of this hofpital in the year 1346; and in a fouth window of the crofs ifle are thefe arms, viz. Gules, three lions heads paffant, fleur de lis reverfed; Or, three eagles, quartering Barry, and a chief. On the roof of the nave are two chevrons between three rofes, the arms of Wykeham; alfo the arms of France and England quartered. There is a coat of arms between thefe two which is defaced.

THE lodging rooms of the poor people adjoin to the church, at the weft end of the fouth ifle, and, after forming an angle, extend from north to fouth and from the whole weftern fide of the court. The north fide confifts of the mafter's houfe, which is fpacious and elegant; the refectory, or brethrens hall; and the gateway. In the windows of the refectory are thefe arms, viz. Argent. a crofs pat. S. quartering France and England. A bord. Gobon. In the hall the brethren meet to fhare their allowance; and on fome certain days in the year, they dine and fup together in common. The gateway before mentioned is formed in a fquare ftately tower, over which is a room called the founder's chamber. The north front of the tower is embellifhed with three niches, in one of which remains the effigies of Cardinal Beaufort, in the act of adoration to another figure now deftroyed. Beneath thefe on each fide of the gateway, are the fame arms as laft mentioned, for the cardinal who is fuppofed to have built the gateway, the refectory, mafter's houfe, and all the lodgings on the weft fide of the court and the porter's lodge. The whole eaft fide of the court, from the porter's lodge to the north tranfept of the church, confifts of a cloifter, over which is a gallery, or range of decayed apartments, fuppofed to be part of the lodging rooms of the poor people on the original foundation of Henry de Blois, and who were probably in procefs of time forced out by the mafter and brethren of the latter foundation, or by the decay of their lodgings and revenues, which might have become no longer able to receive and fupport them. Againft the walls of the gallery is infcribed, Dilexi fapientiam, R. S. 1505. t. e. I have coveted wifdom. R. S. for Robert or Roger Sherborne, mafter of the hofpital; who was alfo preferred from hence to the bifhoprick of St. David's. He was afterwards bifhop of Chichefter, and founded in that cathedral church four prebends, for which place thofe only are qualified, who are, or have been fellows of New College, Oxford. On the outfide of the cloifter is this infcription, " Henricus " Compton, Epifcopus, i. e. Henry Compton, bifhop." He was alfo mafter of this hofpital, and from thence promoted, A. D. 1674, to the fee of Oxford, and afterwards to that of London.

In the church there are feveral ancient tombs, braffes, and epitaphs, chiefly of the mafters and brothers of this hofpital.

This view, which fhews the S. afpect, was drawn anno 1780.

Hyde Abbey

HYDE ABBEY NEAR WINCHESTER, HAMPSHIRE.

(PLATE I.)

ALLFRED King of the West Saxons having brought over from Flanders, the learned monk Grimbald, founded a house and chapel at Winchester for secular cannons, under his government, he afterwards projected a greater foundation, and by his will ordered a noble church and college to be erected on the north side of the cathedral, this was begun anno 901. and finished by his son Edward, who dedicated it to the Holy Trinity, the Virgin Mary, and St. Peter. It was called the New Minster, to distinguish it from the Cathedral, or Old Minster, within the Precincts of whose cemetary it stood. The building being completed, Edward placed therein secular cannons, who remained here till the year 963, when they were expelled by Ethelwould Bishop of Winchester, a great favorer of monks, on account as was pretended, of their scandalous lives, and an abbot and monks put in possession of the house: But many differences and inconveniences arising from the too near neighbourhood of those two great monasteries, their bells, singing, and other matters mutually interfering with each other; the monks of New Minster thought it proper to remove to a place called Hyde, on the north side of the city, and a small distance without its walls; where King Henry the first at the instance of William Gifford, bishop of Winchester, founded a stately abbey for them. St. Peter was generally accounted the patron, though it is sometimes called the Monastery of St. Grimbald, and some times of St. Barnabas, and in Anglia Sacra, said to have been dedicated to St. Peter, St. Paul, and St. Collumbanus. From this time the Monastery lost its title of the New Minster.   The

The monks of this houfe, were endowed with very confiderable lands, privileges, and immunities, not only by their founder King Edward, but alfo by feveral of his fucceffors Kings of England, namely, Athelftan, Edward, Edred, Edgar, Edmund Ironfide, Edward the Confeffor, William the Conqueror, and particularly Henry the firft, and Maud his Queen, as may be feen in their charter, in the Monafticon. It was likewife, not without its misfortunes, for William the Conqueror at his firft coming, finding the abbot and twelve of his monks in arms againft him, feized on their eftates, and held them above two years; and in the reign of King Stephen, they were fo plundered, and oppreffed by Stephen de Blois his brother, then bifhop of Winchefter, that their number was reduced from forty to ten monks; this partly arofe from his jealoufy of their encreafing wealth and power, and partly from a defign of making them fubfervient to his intended project, of raifing the fee of Winchefter to an archbifhoprick, and the abbey of Hyde to a bifhoprick, which with the diocefe of Chichefter were to be fubordinate to Winchefter.

This abbey was the burial-place of diverfe Princes, and great perfonages, viz. King Edmund and his fon Elfred, St. Eadburgh daughter of King Edward, Aelfred fon of King Edulf: King Aelfred, and as fome fay, King Edred, notwithftanding there is an infcription for him in the cathedral of Winchefter.

Before the diffolution, this Monaftery was valued at 865 _l._ 18 _s._ ob. q. per. ann. Dugdale 865 _l._ 1 _s._ 6 _d._ ob. q. Speed. the fite was granted 37th of Henry 8th to Richard Bethell.

That this building was demolifhed very foon after the reformation, appears from Leland, who fpeaking of it, fays, " in the fuburb ftood the great abbey of Hide, " and hath yet a paroche church. This abbey was called Newenminfter, and " ftood in the clofe hard by St. Swithin's, otherwife, called Ealdenminfter, but " when it was tranflated thence to Hide, it bore the the name of Hide. The " bones of Alfredas, King of the Weft Saxons, and of King Edward his fon " and kind were tranflated from Newenminfter, and laid in a tomb before the " high altar at Hide. In which tomb, was of late found two little tables of lead, " infcribed with their names; and here lay alfo the bones of St. Grimbald and Indoce."

Of this once noble edifice very little remains, except part of the precinct wall, fome out buildings towards the ftreet, and a gateway, the mouldings of which exhibit on each fide the head of a King; the fame head occurs on a wall towards the fouth. The church which was built with flint cafed with fquared ftone, appears from traces of its walls to have confifted of three aifles, and to have been at leaft two hundred and forty feet long, moft of the buildings hereabout, feem to have fome materials of the abbey about them, and the tower of St. Bartholomew is fuppofed to have been erected with ftones collected from its ruins.

This View was drawn 1780.

HYDE ABBEY, PLATE II, &c.

HYDE ABBEY, NEAR WINCHESTER. PLATE II.

THIS view shews the North aspect of the remains of this abbey, with the church of St. Bartholomew, supposed to have been originally built soon after the conquest, but repaired and its tower erected about the year 1541, out of the ruins of the said abbey, which according to the history of Winchester had been then destroyed near two years. It is thought here was formerly another isle.

LIST of the abbots of this abbey, chiefly taken from Brown Willis. Galfridus was abbot of Newminster, Anno 1121; in whose time the monks of that abbey were removed to Hyde, where he began the building of the church, but died in the year 1124, before it was compleated. He was succeeded by Osbertus, who died Anno 1135. After which this monastery was much oppressed by Henry de Blois, bishop of Winchester.

HUGH Schorchevyleyn, called in the annals of Winchester, Hugh de Lens, was the next abbot; he was much disliked by the monks, who complained and appealed against him, as likewise against the bishop, who, as it is said, endeavour'd to pervert the state of the abbey; and about the year 1143, tried to prevail with the pope to make his see an archbishoprick, and this abbey a bishoprick, subject with the see of Chichester, to his jurisdiction. These controversies between the abbot and his monks, ended Anno 1149, in his being deposed. after him Salidus was made abbot; upon whose death, which it is said happened Anno 1171, Thomas, prior of Montacute, was elected, tho' it does not appear he was consecrated before the year 1174. He resigned Anno 1180, and was succeeded by John, prior of Cluny, who died 1222. Walter de Astone was next elected, and dying Anno 1249, was succeeded the same year by Roger de St. Walerick, who died Anno 1263. His successor was William de Wigornia; he dying Anno 1282, was succeeded by Robert de Popham; whose successor Anno 1292, was Simon de Caninges; he dying Anno 1304, had for successor Geffry de Feringes, who resigned Anno 1317.

WILLIAM de Odiham, was elected in his ſtead, whoſe ſucceſſor was Walter de Fiſhyde, the time of whoſe incumbency is uncertain. Anno 1362, Thomas Peithy occurs abbot; upon whoſe death or reſignation, John Eyneſham was elected, who died Anno 1394. His ſucceſſor was John Letcombe, or Lattecombe; after whom John London, appears abbot Anno 1407; he died Anno 1415, and was ſucceeded by Nicholas Strode; after whom is found Thomas Bromele, who is mentioned as abbot Anno 1440; he continued till about the year 1460, and then Henry Bonvile, occurs abbot, who was ſucceeded on the firſt day of December, Anno 1471, by Thomas Wyrcetur. When he died is uncertain, but he is mentioned Anno 1480, in which year the ſeries of the abbots in the regiſter leaves off. It is however probable that he continued till the year 1485, when Thomas Forte was elected, who did not hold that office long; for Anno 1489, Richard Hall, was choſen abbot, and is recorded as ſuch Anno 1500, and in all probability remained ſo for near forty years; for after him, no other abbot is mentioned before the year 1528, about which time John Salcot, alias Capon, a doctor of divinity of Cambridge, was tranſlated from the abbey of Huſm, in Norfolk, to this place. He was the laſt abbot, and (as a reward for having been very inſtrumental in procuring in his own univerſity the king's divorce) on the 19th of April, Anno 1534, he obtained licence to hold the biſhoprick of Bangor, in commendam with this abbey; and for his good ſervices at the diſſolution, Anno 1539, and his ready yielding of the abbey to the king; in the ſurrender of which he procured his monks, 21 in number to join; he was promoted to the biſhoprick of Saliſbury, which he held till the year 1559.

AMONG the manuſcripts of the Cotton Library, mark'd Cleopatra E. 4. is a letter containing orders to this abbey a ſhort time before the deſſolution, corrected as is ſaid, in the Catalogue by Cromwell's own hand. Theſe corrections are ſuppoſed to be the marginal notes.

"Firſt, it is releaſed and permitted to the Reverend Father in God John
" Biſhop of Bangor, Abbot of the Monaſtry of Hide, that he ſhall goo or
" ride at his libertie whither he will, and take 3 or 4 of his bretheren with him,
" and kepe them as long as he ſhall thinke mete, or remitting them or any of
" them home, to ſend for other in their ſtedes.

The ſame honeſt-tie and modeſtie in faſon as beſemeth men of Religion.

Item, that ſuch Officers as have been accuſtomed to ride abrode to ſee the work of the Mon, or to keep their Courts, ſhall have the ſame libertie therein with the Abbot's licence, they were wont to have, ſo as they be only occupied in overſight of the ſaid worke and keepinge of Courts.

So that they reſort to no light or ſuſpect place, and that they uſe themſelves in their recreations as otherwiſe therein ſhall appertayne to honeſtie and their profeſſion.

" Item, that the ſaid Abbot may give the Prior, Subprior and
" other Officers, being ſuch as he ſhall think of Diſcreaton,
" licence thre or foure tymes at the moſte in the yeare, to goo
" abroad for their refreſhe and recreacon, taking with him or
" them ſo having licence, thre or foure other bretheren at the
" leaſte.

" Item, whereas the ſaid Mon, is charged by the King's highneſs in his gracious
" viſitation to fynd three ſcollers ſtudents at oon of the Univerſities in England.
" It ſhall be lawfull for the ſaid Abbot, during his life, to appoint and gyve
" exhibicon to oone ſcoller and ſtudent, to be accompted in the ſame nombere,
" beinge he an Engliſhman, or borne within ſome of the King's Dommnons.
" which ſhall applie his ſtudy and lerning in the pties of beyond the ſee
" within any univerſitie there, ſoe as by color thereof the King's revennue
" herein be not fruſtrated or deceyved."

This view was drawn Anno 1780.

King John's House
Published 1 Nov. 1785. As A Harper

KING JOHN's HOUSE AT WARNFORD, HAMPSHIRE.

THIS venerable ruin, which has so long remained unnoticed by the curious, stands in the garden of the Earl of Clanricarde, at Warnford, in the county of Southampton, on the high road from London to Gosport. It is known by the title of King John's House, an appellation common to many ancient structures, in which that king had no concern; King John and the devil being the founders, to whom the vulgar impute most of the ancient buildings, mounds, or entrenchments, for which they cannot assign any other constructor, with this distinction, that to the king are given most of the mansions, castles, and other buildings, whilst the devil is supposed to have amused himself chiefly in earthen works, such as his Ditch at Newmarket, Punch Bowl at Hind Head, with diverse others too numerous to mention.

IN a map of Hampshire, engraved by Norden, about the year 1610, this building is marked as a ruin; and in some writings of a more ancient date belonging to the Clanricarde family, it is conveyed with the manor and present mansion, by the denomination of the Old House.

WHAT it originally was, can only be conjectured—two ancient inscriptions on the parish church; the first on the north, and second on the south side within the porch, seem to afford some grounds to suppose it the ancient church built by Wilfrid, bishop of York, between the years 679, when he took refuge among the South Saxons, and 685, when he returned to his see.

The Inscription on the North is as follows:

Adæ hic de portu, solis benedicat ab ortu,
Gens cruce signata, per quem sic sum renovata.
May all christian people, even from the rising of the sun,
Bless Adam de Port, by whom I am thus renovated.

On

KING JOHN's HOUSE AT WARNFORD, HAMPSHIRE.

On the South Side.

Fratres Orate
Preces veftra fanctificate,
Templi Factores
Seniores et Juniores
Wilfrid fundavit,
Bonus Adam fic renovavit.

Brethren both young and old, pray, and with your prayers hallow,
The builders of this church, which Wilfrid founded, and good Adam
thus renovated.

THE whole of this conjecture refts on the word renovavit which is not always confined to repairing or rebuilding the identical edifice, on the very fpot,
on which it ftood ; but is often ufed to exprefs a different building, appropriated to the fame purpofes or fraternity, to which the former was devoted, and in
the prefent inftance, the erection of a new parifh church, when the former from
age or accident became ufelefs, might without any great impropriety be ftiled
a renovation, and indeed this conjecture receives fome fmall fupport from the
vicinity of the prefent church, there being only the diftance of about twenty
yards between the two buildings, fo that they might poffibly both ftand in the
fame churchyard. Adam de Port poffeffed Warnford, in the reign of Henry
IId, Richard the IId, and John.

THIS ruin meafures on the outfide eighty feet, from eaft to weft, and fifty-
four from north to fouth, its walls are four feet thick, and conftructed of flint,
fet in grout work : It is divided into two unequal rooms, the largeft or eaftern-
moft 46 feet by 48, it has two windows on the north, and two on the fouth,
as alfo two doors in the north and fouth walls, near the weftern extremity, and
another in the weft fide leading to the leffer room. At about eighteen feet from
the eaft and weft walls, and ten from the north and fouth, ftand four columns,
which with four half columns, let into the eaft and weft walls, once probably
fupported a vaulted roof. Thefe columns, which are of two different forts,
fhaft and capital included, meafure nearly 25 feet, or eight diameters ; they
are of a ftone as compact and durable as marble, their bafes octagonal ; moft of
the arches of the doors and windows are circular.

WEST of the large room is one meafuring about eighteen feet from
eaft to weft, and occupying the whole breadth of the building from north to
fouth, this room is lighted by two windows, one on its north, and the other
on its fouth fide, and on the north fide of its weftern end are four fmall chinks
widening outward.

WHEN this building was firft taken notice of, it was ufed as a barn, and covered with a modern roof, this has fince been taken off, and it now forms a
very ftriking ornament to the garden.

THE door feen in this view is evidently of more modern date than the oldeft
part of the parifh church, which fhews it has been repaired fince the erection
of that building, probably for a chapel to the manfion.

Mr. WINDHAM has given two views, and a defcription of this ruin in the
Archialogia, from whence many particulars of this account are taken.

THE view which fhews the fouth afpect was drawn Anno 1779.

Merdon Castle, Hants.

MERDON CASTLE, HANTS.

MERDON castle is in the parish of Hursley, about four miles south West of Winchester. It was one of the Episcopal Castles, or Palaces of the See of Winchester. It was built by Bishop Henry de Blois, king Stephen's brother, about the year 1138. He fortified it with strong intrenchments soon afterwards; at the time that he and his brother the king besieged the empress Maud, in Winchester castle, who had taken post there with Robert earl of Gloucester. It was in being, and in a state of habitation, at least as late as 1266. For in the Computus of Bishop Gervasy, of that year, there is an entry for repairing and furnishing the hall; however, I believe that in the next century it became ruinous, and almost entirely dilapidated. It was alienated, with the Manor of Merdon, from the See of Winchester, in queen Elizabeth's time, and is now the property of Sir Thomas Heathcote, Baronet. Only a fragment of a Flinty tower, a shapeless mass remains, surrounded by two very considerable concentric circumvallations. In the central area, where this ruin stands, is also a modern farm house. There seems to have been some other trench-work. The old original well of the castle remains, of extraordinary depth and diameter. I suppose the ruin to be part of the Keep. A park adjoins, now Sir Thomas Heathcote's, in which is his house, called Hursley Lodge, anciently a lodge in the Episcopal part. The whole extensive parish of Hursley, is called the Manor of Merdon. This view, which shews the north aspect, with part of the ruined building, was drawn 1733.

For the ANTIQUARIAN REPERTORY.

PORTCHESTER CASTLE, HAMPSHIRE.

THE annexed Plate exhibits the north aspect of the inner court of Portchester Castle, which takes its name from the village wherein it stands, and is five miles north-west of Portsmouth. It was once a town of note, then called Caer-Peris. Stow, from Roufe, says it was built by Gurgunftus, son of Beline, who lived three hundred and seventy-five years before Chrift; it was likewife, according to tradition, the place where Vefpafian landed: it had then a famous harbour; but the sea retiring, the inhabitants left the place and removed to the ifland of Portfey. Both the founder, and the time when this caftle was built, are unknown; but it is univerfally acknowledged to be of great antiquity.

The caftle is a fquare, whofe internal-fide is four hundred and forty feet; its area contains four acres; four chains, and feven perches.

The walls are fix feet thick and about fifteen high, having in many places a paffage round them, covered with a parapet. It has eighteen towers of various fhapes and magnitudes, including thofe of the keep, and is furrounded on the north, weft and fouth fides by a ditch of different breadths, fifteen feet deep; on the eaft it has been filled up by the fea. The entrance is, on the weft fide, through a gate, thirty feet deep and fourteen wide, under a fquare tower. On the infide, over the gate, are two projecting figures, fomewhat refembling Egyptian fphinxes. In the eaft wall, directly oppofite this gate, is another of like dimenfions. There are likewife two fally-ports.

The keep encompaffes a parallelogram of fixty-five by one hundred and fifteen feet. It has four towers, three of them ftanding on the outfide wall; one of which, much larger than the reft, forms the north-weft angle of the fquare; the fourth ftands at the fouth-eaft corner of this building. Here are many rooms, feveral very large, and fome arched with ftone; among them, one which appears to have been a chapel. The entrance is through a gate, on the fouth fide, only eight feet wide. Several of thefe towers, as well as part of the walls, are now in ruins.

Toward:

Towards the south-east part of the area of the square stands St. Mary's, or the parish-church of Portchester. Here King Henry the First, in the year 1133, founded a priory of cannons of the order of St. Augustine, which was not long after removed to Southwicke, where it continued till the Dissolution, when it was valued at two hundred and fifty-seven pounds, four shillings and four pence per annum, according to both Dugdale and Speed. The site was granted, the thirtieth of Henry the Eighth, to John White. The living of Portchester is a vicarage, of which the king is patron, and according to Ecton it is discharged. The clear yearly value is estimated at thirty pounds per annum, and the yearly tenths is twelve shillings.

This church has manifest marks of great antiquity; and by a moulding on the south side of the tower, formerly serving to cover the extremity of the roof, it appears it had once a south aisle, answering to that now standing on the north, which compleated the form of the cross. The east end has been likewise rebuilt, as is visible by a similar circumstance, which shews it was formerly of the same height as the west part of the body of the church. The arches over the doors and windows of the ancient part, are all circular, and at the west end are richly decorated with those indented ornaments which characterise the stile of Saxon architecture. It was last repaired, in the year 1710, by Queen Ann. In it is a curious font, and also the monument of Sir Thomas Cornwallis, knight, groom-porter to Queen Elizabeth and King James the First.

The castle formerly belonged to the family of the Nortons, and afterwards to that of the Whiteheads, who conveyed it to Alexander, father of Robert Thistlethwaite, Esq. the present proprietor.

In the last and two preceding wars it was rented by the government, for the keeping of the Spanish and French prisoners. Of the latter there were, in the year 1761, upwards of four thousand confined in this place. This occasioned several temporary buildings and conveniencies to be erected; the pulling of these down, together with the breaches made by the prisoners in attempting to escape, has not a little co-operated with Time in his depredations on this antient structure.

The Drawing was made July the 18th, 1779.

GATE TO PORCHESTER CASTLE, HANTS.

THIS view shews the strong interior gate, leading from the outer to the inner ballium or court of Portchester castle, wherein were the keep, chapel, and state apartments; some of the latter, from their stile of building, seem to have been either erected or greatly repaired as late as the reign of King Henry VIII. or Queen Elizabeth, whilst other parts, particularly the great tower or keep, bear evident marks of more remote antiquity.

THIS view was drawn anno 1782.

PORTCHESTER CHURCH, HANTS

THE CHURCH IN PORTCHESTER CASTLE, HAMPSHIRE.

THIS church, which is a very picturesque object as well as a piece of great antiquity, was, as has been observed in the account of the castle, originally much larger than it is at present, and also of a different form. A great number of circumstances evidently shew that it has undergone a variety of repairs at very different periods; the most modern are chiefly of brick. The particulars respecting the foundation of the priory here by Henry the Third, and its removal to Southwicke, are given in the description of the castle; they serve however to prove the antiquity of its first construction, did the stile of its architecture and appearance want any additional evidence.

THIS view was drawn anno 1761.

SOMERFORD GRANGE, HAMPSHIRE.

SOMERFORD GRANGE ſtands about two miles eaſt of Chriſt Church, and was formerly a farm or grange of the monaſtery of that name; at the diſſolution it was, with the manor, granted to John Draper the laſt prior. It conſiſts of a ruined brick houſe, apparently not older than the reign of Charles I. but probably erected on the ſite of a more ancient building. At the eaſt end of this houſe is an ancient chapel, which by the initials J. D. cut on a ſquare ſtone window block, ſeems as if it was built or repaired by John Draper the prior above-mentioned; the roof of this chapel is handſomely arched with wood; the building itſelf is of ſtone; in it is a place for keeping the holy water.

This farm is held by ―――― Dagge, eſquire, under a leaſe from the dean and chapter of Wincheſter, together with the great tithes of Chriſt Church, the barns and granary (a ſtone building) being appropriated for their reception.

Here are alſo ſeveral large fiſh-ponds, whence the priory was formerly ſupplied with fiſh.

This view was drawn anno 1777.

Portsea Castle, Hants.

SOUTH SEA CASTLE, HAMPSHIRE.

SOUTH Sea castle stands about a mile south of the town of Portsmouth, near the sea beach. This fort, in its present state, consists of work of three different reigns. The interior part is a block house, evidently built about the time of Henry VIII. surrounded by a kind of star fort erected in the reign of Charles II. as appears from the following inscription, on a tablet placed between two stone balls near the steps, on the south side of the block house above mentioned.

CAROLUS II. REX.

A. REG. XXXIIII.

An̅o̅. DOMI. 1683.

THE whole has been repaired and modernized since the accession of the present royal family. This their arms over the chief gate of the castle seem to point out.

THE taking of this castle by the parliamentary forces in the year 1642 is thus related in a book entitled Jehovah---Ieh. God in the Mount, or England's Parliamentarie Chronicle, printed 1644, p. 161.

" On Saturday September the third, in the night, the parliament forces took Sousey castle, which lies a mile from the towne upon the sea, and the way thither is on the sea sands. The captain of the castle his name was Challiner, who on Saturday had been at Portsmouth, and in the evening went home to the castle, and his souldiers tooke horse loads of provision, bisket, meal, and other necessaries with them. They reported he had more drinke in his head than was befitting such a time and service, and the townsmen gave out that he had been bribed with money to yield up the castle, but 'twas false, though the first may be true, yet was not that neither any furtherance to the taking of it, for thus it was, there were about eighty musqueteers and others that came that night to the walls of the castle, and under their ordnance, and had with them a very good engineer, and thirty-five scaling ladders, and the whole company in the castle were but twelve, officers or commanders, who all were not able to deal with ours in such a disadvantage, wherefore ours having suddenly and silently scaled the walls, called unto them, avised them what to doe, shewing the advantage we had over them, and therefore their danger, if they resisted, who seeing the same, immediately yielded the castle to us, whereupon our triumph at our taking it, was plainly heard, about two of the clock in the morning into the town ; and so soon as they were masters of the castle, they discharged two pieces of the castle ordnance against the town. The town of Portsmouth capitulated the next day."

South west of this fort or castle is a battery faced with stone almost adjoining to it, and communicating with it by a bridge. South Sea castle has been lately repaired, and still continues one of the national garrisons. Anno 1782, Francis Leshe, Esq; was Deputy Governor of it, with a salary of 91l. 5s. It is subordinate to the garrison of Portsmouth.

In Peck's Desiderata Curiosa is a list of the garrisons belonging to the crown in the reign of Elizabeth, where the following state is given of this garrison:

SOUTH SEA CASTLE, PORTSMOUTH.

	£.	s.	d.
Captaine fee per diem	0	2	0
Under Captaine fee per diem	0	1	0
Porters 2, the one per diem	0	0	8
The other	0	0	6
Master gunner fee per diem	0	0	8
Gunners 14, soldiers 11, one day watch, fee a piece per diem	0	0	6

This view, which shews the north aspect, was drawn anno 1782.

TICHFIELD HOUSE, CHAPEL.

THE CHAPEL OF TICHFIELD HOUSE, HAMPSHIRE.

SEVERAL perfons of approved tafte, and eminent for their knowledge in Antiquarian refearches, having pointed out the remains of the Chapel and Great Hall of this manfion, as fubjects worthy of notice; the firft of them is here prefented to the publick : concerning its hiftory very little information could be procured, at leaft fuch as might be depended upon, neither does tradition afcertain whether this was the chapel of the monaftery, or only that of the manfion erected out of its ruins. It is faid, that it was partly ftanding within the memory of perfons now living, and was demolifhed for the fake of the materials. Its remains fhew it was an elegant, though not a very extenfive building. Since its defecration, it has been ufed as a dove-houfe. No traces of any fepulchral monuments are to be feen, if there ever were any, they are now levelled and covered over with the rubbifh, by which the ground hereabouts feems to have been much raifed.

This view was drawn anno 1782.

WARBLINGTON CASTLE. HANTS.

WARBLINGTON CASTLE, HAMPSHIRE.

WHETHER the ruin here represented is a fragment of the ancient mansion of the family of the De Warblington's, (who resided here in the reigns of Edward I. II. and III. during which they were several times sheriffs and members for Hampshire) or the remains of a seat which afterwards belonged to the earls of Salisbury, is not certain; although most probably the latter, both from the stile of the building and part of the materials, which are bricks seemingly much of the same form and proportion as those now made. In the reign of queen Elizabeth, this seat belonged to the family of the Cottons, of which was Dr. Henry Cotton, the son of sir Richard Cotton, knight, to whom that queen had been god-mother, and on making him bishop of Salisbury, merrily observed, that " formerly she had blessed many of her " god-sons, but never before had a god-son who could bless her." With this bishop, doctor William Cotton, who was of another family, was consecrated bishop of Exeter, whereupon the queen (as Dr. Fuller tells us) made this pun, " that she had now well Cotton'd the west."

THE above scanty portion of information is all I have been able to collect respecting the ancient history of this edifice; but by the favour of an ingenious correspondent, I am enabled to give an ample description of its present state; this I shall communicate in his own words :

WARBLINGTON castle is situate about half a mile to the eastward of Havant. It appears to have been built with brick, faced on the outside with hewn stone. It's form was nearly square, surrounded with a deep foſſe. The front was probably toward the ſouth-weſt, where the gate-way and tower now are ſtanding, as repreſented in the drawing. The tower, I apprehend, to have been a ſtair-caſe; but the ſtairs, which were I conjecture of wood, are gone; the tower at preſent is become a pigeon houſe; there is a ladder to aſcend it, but it was ſo bad that I did not chuſe to go up. The extent of the front was about equal to the ſpace repreſented in the drawing. The ditch ſtill extends through that diſtance. The ſtone with which it was faced, muſt have been brought thither by ſea, for this country for a great diſtance affords none of that kind. The farm-houſe, which appears in perſpective in the drawing, might have been part of the old caſtle, or may have been built from the ruins of it: but the former is the moſt likely to have been the caſe, as the ſtone ſeems well jointed, and the maſonry much of the ſame kind with the gate-way and tower, and it ſtands on the edge of the foſſe on the north eaſt. Toward the ſouth eaſt, part of a wall is ſtanding on the brink of the foſſe, covered with ivy; but I did not perceive any thing very curious or beautiful in it; from the ſtation I made the drawing, it was concealed by the elm trees; there may be other points of view, from which I might form a pleaſing addition to the other objects, but I did not happen to ſtumble upon them. From the form of the arch on the great gate-way, I ſhould conjecture it to have been built in the time of Hen. VII.

The idea of the vulgar is, "that a king lived there at the time when there were ſo many kings in Eng- " land, and that it was knocked down by Oliver Cromwell, when he deſtroyed ſo many other ſuch " places." I give you their own expreſſions as near as I can recollect. Clarendon mentions no ſiege of it as far as I can remember; it is marked in the map of Hampſhire in Camden's Britannia, but not as a caſtle. Perhaps it might not be large enough to deſerve that title: though certainly it was a place of ſome ſtrength, and may merit the appellation of ſtrong houſe, uſed by Clarendon for ſome houſes capable of ſuſtaining a military aſſault. I do not underſtand the word uſed in explanation of the mark in the map in Camden.

The original building and fortreſs included within the foſſe, might be near an acre of ground, as near as I, who am not accuſtomed to meaſuring ground, can gueſs. The foſſe muſt have been at leaſt ten feet deep. Perhaps the buildings might have formed an hollow ſquare, or quadrangle within it. The north eaſt and north weſt ſides of the caſtle, are covered by a field, which I was told by the very hoſpitable tenant, farmer King, is about five acres. That field is ſurrounded by a mound and a foſſe as deep as that of the caſtle. The mound is thick, and at leaſt eight feet high from the level of the field, but it is a mere curtain, without any baſtions to flank it. The whole of it is now overgrown with high coppice wood. The ground is marſhy on the north eaſt and ſouth eaſt ſides of this field.

As the caſtle ſtood within little more than a muſket-ſhot of the beach, and was near the ford into Haling iſland from the main, paſſable at low water, it might perhaps have been built by ſome lord who poſſeſſed that iſland and the adjacent eſtates; and as it was placed near the ſhore of that arm of the ſea which connects the harbours of Langſtone and Emſworth, it was well ſituated for protecting traders who might chuſe to traffic in either of thoſe ports. Perhaps the entrenched field I have deſcribed, may have been a place for holding markets and fairs, under the juriſdiction of the lord of the caſtle: to military purpoſes I think it ill adapted from its want of baſtions.

The preſent owner is Mr. Panton, who lives in Piccadilly. I underſtood that it came into his family by marriage from the Lumley family.

The pariſh church is near the ruins of the caſtle, to the ſouth eaſt. I apprehend it was the chapel. As I happened to ſay ſo to the farmer, he obſerved to me that he thought " the church had been " built after the caſtle was finiſhed, with the refuſe ſtone, for that there was very little good ſtone in " it." He further told me, that the ſtory went in the neighbourhood that the church was built by two maiden ladies, ſiſters, and that the pillars on one ſide were fluted, and on the other not ſo. I wiſhed to have inſpected it, but found that the key was two miles off. Its outward appearance did not tempt me to draw it. This view was drawn anno 1785.

The Castle or County Hall, Winchester, Hants.

WINCHESTER CASTLE, HANTS.

This once strong and stately castle, vulgar tradition reports to have been built by King Arthur about the year 523; perhaps there might have been some ancient Saxon fortress on that spot, but most probably it was greatly repaired, if not rebuilt, by the Normans.

By a plan drawn of it anno 1630, it appears to have been quadrangular, with a tower on each angle; and a view of it in Speed, shews that the entrance from the west was over a bridge leading to a gateway, contiguous to the south-west angle of the building. According to the same authority it had outworks flanked with towers on the south. Heylin styles it "a gallant but not a great castle, bravely mounted on a hill for defence and prospect."

During the troubles of the reign of King Charles I. it was seized, anno 1642, by Sir William Waller for the parliament, being assisted by Oliver Cromwell; it was afterwards taken by the Royalists, and the Lord Ogle made governor thereof: he for a while defended it in 1645 against Oliver Cromwell, who after its surrender, brought his cannon close to it and battered it down, except the chapel, the building here represented, which now serves for the county hall for trials at the assizes. Indeed it is said by the Winchester Annalist, that the assizes for the county were held here, at least, as early as the year 1272, and he frequently remarks that the royal family quitted their residence at this place in order to make room for the judges. This chapel was, and still is, a magnificent edifice, consisting of three ailes, and is 110 feet in length and 45 in breadth; the roof supported by elegant gothic pillars of marble of excellent workmanship. A chantry belonged to it, as appears by its dissolution at the reformation.

OVER the court of Nisi Prius, above the judge's seat, hangs what is commonly called King Arthur's round table, which is 18 feet diameter; round it, in the ancient character, are inscribed the names of several of King Arthur's Knights, spoken of in old romances, such as Sir Launcelot de Lake, Sir Tristram, Sir Pelleas, Sir Gewain, Sir Gereth, &c. &c. Although this table is certainly not of the age pretended, it is nevertheless a piece of antiquity, and was probably made and used for some great festival, wherein those fabulous knights were represented; a matter by no means uncommon on those occasions; one instance of which occurs in the entertainment of Queen Elizabeth at Kenilworth Castle. Paulus Jovius, who wrote above 200 years ago, relates that this table was shewn to the Emperor Charles V. and at that time many marks of its antiquity had been destroyed, the names of the knights being then just written afresh, and the table, with its whole ornaments, newly repaired.

THIS castle was not only a royal residence, but here also parliaments were assembled and important causes tried. It was besides the scene of divers other remarkable events, a chronological account of some of which here follow:

IN this castle, about the year 1066, Archbishop Stigand, when degraded, was confined by William the Conqueror, where he remained during his life. And in 1072, in this chapel was tried a famous cause, concerning the superiority of the See of Canterbury over that of York, before Hubert the pope's legate, King William, and all the bishops and abbots of the kingdom.

IN the year 1075, Waltheof Earl of Northumberland, being accused and convicted of high treason, was beheaded before the gates of this castle.

IN the year 1141 this castle was occupied, victualled, garrisoned and defended, by the Empress Maud for several weeks against the wife of King Stephen, but the supply of water being cut off, Maud escaped to Oxford, and the castle was surrendered.

SEVERAL parliaments were held here in the reign of Henry II. When King Richard I. went to the holy war in 1184, he committed this castle to the keeping of Hugh bishop of Durham, as one of the most important places in his dominions; but there being some grounds of suspicion that the king's brother intended to usurp the throne, Gilbert Lacy secured this castle for the king, who returning from the holy land was here crowned again, though he had been before crowned at Canterbury by Baldwin Archbishop of Canterbury in 1189.

ANNO 1216, when Lewis the Dauphin invaded this kingdom, he attempted, but in vain, to make himself master of this castle, which was defended by the citizens.

IN this castle Henry III. sat as judge, and himself tried many prisoners; here too, during the same reign, the citizens found a refuge from the cruelties of the army of the barons, commanded by the Earl of Leicester, who in vain attempted to reduce it by force.

ANNO 1302, here King Edward confined the bishop of St. Andrew's, whom he found in arms against him in Scotland; allowing him six-pence per day for his diet and expences, three-pence for his servant, and for a chaplain and a boy three-half-pence.

THIS view, which shews the north-east aspect, was drawn A. D. 1781.

Cathedral Church of Winchester.

WINCHESTER OLD MINSTER, NOW THE CATHEDRAL, HAMPSHIRE.

THE account given by Tanner of this foundation, is related in these words: Here is said to have been a monastery very early, founded by king Lucius for monks following the rule of St. Mark, which was destroyed in Diocletian's persecution, A. D. 266, but restored under Deodatus the abbat, in honour of St. Amphibalus, about the year 300; after which it continued about two hundred years, till the monks were killed, and their church turned into a Pagan temple, for the idolatrous worship of Dagon, by Cerdic king of the West-Saxons. These and other matters relating to religious men in this city, being so particularly and positively asserted by Rudburn and the Winchester Annalist, could not well be here omitted, though they seem to be very fabulous. It is more likely that Kynegilse, the first christian king of the West Saxons, began a cathedral church here, which might be finished by his successor Kinewaleus, and monks placed herein by bishop Birin, in the year 646. These were destroyed by the Danes, A. D. 867, and in the next year secular priests took possession of this church and the lands belonging to it, and kept the same till A. D. 963, when bishop Ethelwold, by the command of king Edgar, expelled them, and placed here monks of the order of St. Benedict, brought from Abendon. This church was anciently dedicated to the Holy Trinity, or to St. Peter, as others to St. Birin, St. Swithin, and St. Ethelwold ; but in later times, St. Swithin the bifhop, was chiefly accounted the tutelar faint of this priory, which was generally diftinguifhed by his name. It was endowed, at the general fuppreffion, with 1507l. 17s. 2d. per ann. Dugd. Speed; after which, the fite and great part of the revenues, were fettled by king Henry VIII. anno regni 32, on a dean and twelve prebendaries, for whom and fix minor canons, ten lay-clerks, eight choirifters and other members, this cathedral was then re-founded and dedicated to the holy and undivided Trinity.

THE prefent edifice was, according to the Hiftory of Winchefter, begun by bifhop Walkelyn, a Norman, in the reign of William the Conqueror, A. D. 1079. He finifhed the tower, the choir, the tranfept, and probably the weft end ; and on St. Swithin's day, A. D. 1093, the monks, in the prefence of almoft all the bifhops and abbats in the kingdom, paffed with much folemnity from the old monaftery into the new one, tranflating the fhrine of that faint to the new church. The whole was afterwards repaired and improved by William of Wickham, and finifhed as now appears by bifhop Fox, who died A. D. 1528, and was a great contributor and benefactor to it. Great part of the monaftery and out-buildings have been demolifhed fince the new foundation, as ufelefs.

THE length of this venerable pile from eaft to weft is five hundred and forty-five feet ; of thefe, our lady's chapel includes fifty-four, and the choir about one hundred and thirty-fix. The length, from the iron door near the entrance of the choir to the porch at the weft end, is three hundred and fifty-one feet ; the length of the tranfepts is an hundred and eighty-fix feet ; the breadth of the body, below the tranfepts, is eighty-feven feet, and of the choir, forty. The vaulting in the infide is twenty-fix feet high ; the exact height of the tower is one hundred and thirty-eight feet and a half ; and its area, fifty feet by forty-eight. This tower is carried up a very little height above the roof, not more than twenty-fix feet, and has no proper finifhing, but is covered in as if the building had been left off ; which very probably might be the cafe, for there is ftrength enough below to fupport a higher fteeple than that of Salifbury.

THIS view, which fhews the fouth-eaft afpect of the cathedral, was drawn from Dr. Lowth's garden in the year 1781. The building feen on the fouth fide, is his prebendal houfe.

Wolvesley Castle.
Publiched Aug.t 20 1783 by A.Hooper

WOLVESLEY CASTLE, HAMPSHIRE.

WOLVESLEY Castle was a palace belonging to the Bishops of Winchester, situated a small distance south-east of the cathedral, on a pleasant spot, watered by a branch of the river Itching, and by some supposed to be that, where the Saxon Kings held their residence. Its appellation of Wolvesley is said to be formed from the Wolphian Kings and the word *Eye*, signifying the corner of a meadow.

THIS castle was erected A. D. 1138, by Henry de Blois, Bishop of Winchester, brother to King Stephen, a great builder in these parts, its ruins shew it was a structure of considerable extent, and from the known magnificence of its founder, demonstrated in his other erections, there is every reason to believe, it was also very elegant, though at present its remains scarcely exhibit the least vestige of ornament, consisting mostly of the inner, or groutwork part of the walls, stripped of the squared stones with which they were faced, clearly evincing that the hand of man has contributed more to its demolition, than both the tooth of time and injuries of weather.

WOLVESLEY CASTLE, HAMPSHIRE.

Leland in his Itinerary defcribes it in the following words: "Wolvefley Caftle is well towered and for the moft part watered about:" and Camden fays, it was very fpacious and furrounded with many towers.

It remained entire till the civil wars in the reign of King Charles II. when it was plundered and demolifhed by the Parliamentary army, under Sir William Waller, who fold the lead and other faleable materials. The chapel efcaped the demolition, and is ftill remaining; from its ftile it feems more modern than the time of Henry de Blois.

After the Reftoration, anno 1684, Bifhop Morley laid out 2300l. in erecting an epifcopal palace here, a very fmall diftance fouth of the former building, but dying before it was completed, he left by his will 500l. to finifh it.

Through a gate eaftward of the cathedral there was a communication between it and the palace, this gate was lately, if not at prefent, ftanding, on it were the arms and name of Bifhop Fox.

THIS View was drawn anno 1780.

The Chapel of Wolvesley Castle, Hants.
Published &c.

THE CHAPEL OF WOLVESLEY CASTLE,
WINCHESTER, HANTS.

This was the chapel of the ancient palace of the bishops of Winchester, called
Wolvesley castle; it is said to be of more modern construction than that edifice,
the time of its erection is unknown; but pretty high up on the north side, a little to the eastward of the center buttress, there is carved in alto relievo, the head
of a bishop with his mitre, this most probably was meant to represent the builder.
That this chapel was part of the ancient structure is evidently apparent, two circular arches in a ruined stone wall with which it is connected, are seen over the
roof of a modern shed built up against it.

This chapel measures in length thirty-seven feet by thirty broad, and is lighted by three windows on the south side, and one on the east, but has neither
painted glass, ancient monuments, nor inscriptions, if ever there were any of these
articles, they in all likelihood did not escape the fury and mistaken zeal of the
demolishers of the castle: and indeed the inside of this building seems to have
undergone divers modern repairs, perhaps in consequence of some depredations
committed on it at that time; among which is, being paved with black and
white marble, done in all probability by bishop Morley, when he built the present palace, which has given occasion to the vulgar opinion, that this chapel was
erected by that prelate. Its communication with the palace is by a long gallery
of sixty-eight feet by sixteen on the first story; out of which a door opens into
a gallery, containing the episcopal seat.

This being the private chapel of the palace, divine service is not performed
there except when the bishop is resident. Many marriages have been solemnized
here before the passing of the marriage act.

This view was drawn anno 1780.

St. Albans Abbey, Hertfordshire

ST. ALBAN's ABBEY, HERTFORDSHIRE.

This abbey stands near the ancient Roman city of Verulam, in Saxon times called Verlam Ceafter or Watling Ceafter, in a place at the time of its erection named Holmhurft, said to be the fpot whereon St. Alban fuffered martyrdom, in a perfecution of the chriftians, by the emperor Dioclefian.

Ten years after this perfecution had ceafed, the furviving chriftians built a church to his memory; but that having been deftroyed in the wars between the Britains, Picts and Saxons, Offa the Great, king of Mercia, repaired the old church, and about the year 793 founded a noble abbey for Benedictine monks, and tranflated hither the relics of St. Alban and placed them in a fhrine, having firft obtained his canonization from pope Adrian. To this monaftery he gave great endowments and revenues, and in a council at Colcyth made conftitutions for their government and fecurity.

In the year 1154, Nicholas bifhop of Alba (an Englifhman, born near this monaftery) being chofen pope, affumed the name of Adrian IV. He granted many privileges to this abbey: among them were thefe.—1. That as St. Alban was the firft Britifh martyr, this abbat fhould be the firft abbat in England, and take place of all others. 2. That the abbat or monk whom he fhould appoint archdeacon, fhould have a pontifical jurifdiction over the priefts and laymen in all the poffeffions belonging to this church. 3. That no archbifhop, bifhop nor legate, fhould vifit or interfere with the affairs of this monaftery, which might be regulated only by the pope himfelf. 4. That the abbat fhould collect and receive the Romefcot or Peter-pence, through all the county of Hertford ; privileges then enjoyed by no other prior or abbat in the realm.

KING Offa, when he firft founded this monaftery, alfo erected many houfes near it for the reception of ftrangers and travellers, and the necellary lodgings of the fervants and officers. They in procefs of time encreafed to a town, which was called St. Alban's after the faint to whom the houfe was dedicated.   At the diffolution, 26 Hen. VIII. this abbey was, according to Dugdale, valued at 2102l. 7s. 1d. ob. q. per annum. Speed gave it at 2510l. 6s. 1d. ob. q.   The church fince made ufe of as parochial, and a great part of its fite were 7 Ed. VI. granted to the mayor and burgeffes.

THE hiftory of the abbats of this houfe is given in Browne Willis's Mitred Abbies, wherein we meet with many particulars refpecting different repairs and erections on this venerable pile.   The following account of the ftate of the abbat of this houfe, taken from a MS. paper in the library of Thomas Aftle, Efq. will give the reader a good idea of the riches and magnificence of the convent.   This paper is in the hand-writing of Elias Afhmole, and dated 26 Auguft, 1668.

MR. Robert Shrimpton, grandfather by the mother's fide to Mrs. Simpfon of St. Alban's, was four times mayor of that town ; he died about 60 years fince, being then about 103 years of age.   He lived when the abbey of St. Alban's flourifhed before the diffolution, and remembered moft things relating to the buildings of the abbey, the regimen of the houfe, the ceremonies of the church, and grand proceffions ; of all which he would often difcourfe in his life-time.   Among other things, that in the great hall there was an afcent of fifteen fteps to the abbat's table, to which the monks brought up the fervice in plate, and ftaying at every fifth ftep, which was a landing-place, on every of which they fung a fhort hymn.   The abbat ufually fat alone in the middle of the table, and when any nobleman or ambaffador, or ftranger of eminent quality, came thither, they fat at his table, towards the ends thereof.   After the monks had waited awhile on the abbat, they fat down at two other tables, placed on the fides of the hall, and had their fervices brought in by the novices, who when the monks had dined, fat down to their own dinner.   This Mr. Shrimpton remembered that when the news came to St. Alban's of Queen Mary's death, the late abbat, for grief, took to his chamber, and died in a fortnight.

HE alfo remembered the hollow image erected near St. Alban's fhrine, wherein one being placed to govern the wires, the eyes would move and head nod, according as he liked or difliked the offering ; and being young, he had many times crept into the hollow part thereof.   In the grand proceffions through the town, where the image of St. Alban was carried, it was ufually borne by two monks, and after it had been fet down awhile at the market crofs, and the monks effaying to take it up again, they pretended they could not ftir it, and then the abbat coming and laying his crofier upon the image, and faying thefe words, Arife, arife, St. Alban, and get thee home to thy fanctuary ; it then forthwith yielded to be borne by the monks.   In the abbey there was a large room, having beds fet on either fide for the receipt of ftrangers and pilgrims, where they had lodging and diet for three days, without queftion made whence they came or whither they went ; but after that time, they ftayed not, without rendering an account of both.

THIS view, which was taken from the upper room of the parfonage houfe, A. D. 1787, fhews the fouth-weft afpect of the building.

Gate of S.ᵗ Albans Abbey, Hertfordshire.

THE GOAL OF ST. ALBAN's, HERTFORDSHIRE.

THIS gate was built about the year 1090, by Paul or Paulinus, the fourteenth abbat; who, as Willis relates, rebuilt the church and all the other structures, but the bakehouse and pantry, out of the stones, tiles, and wooden materials of Verulam, which his predecessors had reserved.

MATTHEW Paris says, that when he had finished the church, he built a dark prison for disobedient monks; and it is said there was a communication from the great church to the goal, though long since broken down.

THIS gate is chiefly of stone, and though not elegant or ornamented, is strong, and well proportioned: the groin-work of the inside of the gate, is at this time in perfect repair. There are on each side the arch, three rooms: these are likewise arched or groined, and still perfect and strong, so as to be used for the confinement of prisoners; this building at present serving for the goal of this liberty or district. The small erections adjoining to it, have been lately added, and are the house for the goaler and other necessary offices.

THIS view, which shews the south front, was drawn A. D. 1787.

Berkhamsted Castle, Hertfordshire.

BERGHAMSTED CASTLE, HERTFORDSHIRE.

BERGHAMSTED Castle is supposed to have been the palace of the kings of Mercia; among whom, Withred, king of Kent and Mercia, A. D. 697 held a great council at this place, and probably in this castle, whereat Birtwald archbishop of Canterbury, presided; Gybmund bishop of Rochester, and divers other prelates and great personages, were also present. Here divers laws, printed in Chauncey's History of Hertfordshire, were enacted.

AFTER the battle of Hastings, William the Conqueror here halted for some days with his army, in order to meet archbishop Lanfranc, with the great lords and nobles of England; and here he received their oaths of allegiance, on his solemn engagement by oath to observe and keep inviolable the ancient laws of the kingdom, which the preceding kings of England, especially king Edward, had ordained.

NOTWITHSTANDING this engagement, he seized the estates of many of the great English land-holders, and gave them to his Norman followers. Among these donations was the town of Berghamsted, which he gave to his half-brother, Robert earl of Moreton, who fortified the castle with a double trench and rampart. On William earl of Moreton, his son, engaging in a rebellion against Henry I. in Normandy, all his estates in England were seized, and his castle razed to the ground, by which this town and manor came to the crown, where it remained till the year 1206, 7th of John, when that king granted the castle and honour of Berghamsted to Jeoffry Fitzpiers earl of Essex, with the knight's fee thereto belonging, in fee farm for an hundred pounds per annum, to hold to him and the heirs of his body, by Aveline then his wife. Anno 1215, 16 John, this castle and town were again in the crown; for when the barons lay still, king John possessed himself of the castle, and appointed Ranulph the German, to have the custody thereof. When Lewis the dauphin of France, invaded this realm, A. D. 1216, he laid siege to this castle; the garrison, taking advantage of the negligence of the besiegers, made two successful sallies, taking divers chariots, provisions, and a banner of William earl of Mandeville; but after a long siege, the king commanded them to yield it up to the dauphin.

IN the second year of the reign of Henry III. this castle was again in the crown, and by that king given to Richard his younger brother, for his good services at the siege of the castle of Riole in France; but he shortly after took it away from him, on account of a dispute;

but by the interpofition of the earls of Pembroke and Chefter, it was reftored to him, and was held by Edmund, his fon, earl of Cornwall. He dying without iffue, in the year 1300, at the college of Bonhomes, which he had founded, this caftle and honour reverted to the crown, and was A. D. 1308, 1ft of Edward II. granted to Piers Gavefton, created earl of Cornwall. He being executed, the caftle, &c. came back to the crown, and was in the year 1311, 4th of Edward III. granted with the town, honer, and divers other manors, valued at 2000 marks per annum, to John of Eltham, earl of Cornwall, fecond fon to king Edward II. in tail general. He dying without iffue, king Edward advanced Edward his eldeft fon, called the black prince, to the dukedom of Cornwall, and gave him among the other eftates belonging to the title, this caftle and honour, to be held by him and his heirs, and the eldeft fons of the heirs of the kings of England. A. D. 1388, 11 Rich. II. when Robert de Veer was advanced to the title and dignity of marquis of Dublin, and afterwards duke of Ireland, that king gave him liberty to refide at this caftle, which was one of his own royal palaces, allowing him wood and fuel to be taken out of his woods and park for his firing.

A. D. 1400, Henry of Monmouth, afterwards king by the title of Henry V. poffeff'd this caftle, honour and town; as did, in 1422, Henry of Windfor his eldeft fon; to whofe eldeft fon, Edward of Weftminfter, it was granted in the year 1454; but when Henry VI. his father, was depofed, they came into the poffeffion of Edward IV. who granted the ftewardfhip of this caftle and lordfhip, anno 1461, the firft year of his reign, to John lord Wenlock, one of his privy-councellors.

RICHARD III. is faid to have been born at this caftle; and here died Cicely, daughter of Ralph Nevil, earl of Weftmoreland, mother of king Edward IV. Since this time, this caftle and honor have been annexed to the dukedom of Cornwall, and appropriated to the princes of Wales fucceffively.

A. D. 1560, queen Elizabeth demifed the fite of the caftle, circuit and precinct, to fir Edward Carey, for a term of years, under the yearly rent of a red rofe, payable to the queen at the feaft of St. John the Baptift, and by other letters patent demifed to him two water-mills in this town and lordfhip, under the yearly rent of 7 l. 8 s. and the fame queen did grant by her letters patent, the manfion-houfe, with the lodge and park, to this fir Edward Carey and the lady Paget his wife, and to the heirs male of their bodies for ever, to hold of the queen, her heirs and fucceffors, as of this lordfhip, by fealty only in free focage and not in capite, rendering a fee farm rent of 8 l. 6 s. 8 d.

AND the faid queen, by letters patent in the fecond year of her reign, conftituted this fir Edward Carey, high-fteward of this honor and manor. This fir Edward Carey obtained a leafe of this caftle and manor, and from him they came to fir Adolph Carey; who dying the 10th of April 1609, it defcended to fir Edward Carey, who fucceeded him; and two third parts of the manor-houfe being burned down about thirty years fince, he repaired the houfe; but not above a third part, or a little more, remains now ftanding, and yet is a very fair large building; but he face fold the fame to John Sayer, efq. who held it fometime, and died poffeffed thereof on the 11th of Feb. 1682, leaving iffue three fons, John, Edward, and Jofeph; whereof John and Jofeph are dead, and Edward is now the prefent poffeffor. It has fince this account given by Chauncey, been purchafed by one of the family of Roper, in whofe defcendant it ftill remains.

THIS caftle was of an oval form, furrounded by a double ditch and ramparts of earth; thefe are ftill remaining. The whole fite, ditches included, according to the prefent occupier, meafures about eleven acres. A few fragments of the furrounding walls, are ftanding here and there, but none that retain any marks of ornament. South-eaft of the area of the caftle, is a high artificial mount on which the keep formerly ftood: it is called the Tower-hill, and meafures about 40 feet diameter on the top. A wall, now overgrown with trees, fhrubs and brambles, runs up to the top of it: there is another mount, much fmaller, near the weftern fide or extremity. There has been a good deal of building here at different times. On digging within the area of the caftle, two brick floors or pavements, one a few feet under the other, were difcovered. A fmall cottage has been built out of the ruins, wherein the tenant refides.

IT is worthy obfervation, that this caftle, like many others of ancient date, is commanded by a hill at a very fmall diftance from it, which feems to prove that the ranges of the machines ufed formerly in fieges, were very fmall.

THIS view was drawn A. D. 1787, and fhews the north-eaft afpect.

THE RYE HOUSE, HERTFODSHIRE.

PLATE I.

THE Rye House is situated near the bank of the river Lea, in the parish of Stansted Abbot, Hertfordshire, on the side of the road, which passes from London through Hoddesdon.

HENRY VI, granted licence to Andrew Ogard (whose arms are on the spandrills of the door) and others, to impark the manor of Rye, which was then called the Isle of Rye, and to erect a castle with battlements and loopholes. This manor was possessed by Edward Baesh, Esq. descended from a person of the same name, who, as appears by his epitaph in Stansted church; had been General Surveyor for the victuals of the Navy-Royal of the Marine Establishment, under Henry VIII, Edward VI, Mary and Elizabeth. Edward, the first of the family who possessed this estate, died 1653, without issue, and his brother Ralph inherited it; who for his zeal in the royal cause, was made a Knight of the Bath: he was succeeded by his son Edward, who was knighted; and in 1676, sold this manor to Edmund Field, who was Burgess for Hertford, in the twenty-third of Charles II. It is now in the possession of Paul Field, Esq. one of the Burgesses for the town of Hertford. The building here represented, has both battlements and loopholes, and was probably the gate of the castle, which Andrew Ogard had liberty to erect; and if so, is among the earliest of those brick buildings, raised after the form of the bricks was changed, from the ancient flat and broad, to the modern shape; but what has brought this house into public notice, is its being confidered as the fpot fixed on for the intended affaffination of Charles the fecond, in his return from Newmarket, in 1683. The house was then tenanted by one Rumbold, who had ferved in Cromwel's army; he being once or twice at a meeting of fome difcontented perfons, who in the courfe of their converfation, talked of many fchemes for changing the government; and among others of killing the King and his brother as the fureft: Rumbold informed them of the fituation of the Rye House, which he then inhabited; that there was a moat round the houfe, through which the King fometimes paffed in his way to Newmarket; that once the coach had gone through without the guards attending it, and if he had placed any thing in the way to have ftopt the coach for the fhorteft time, he could have fhot both the King and his brother, and might have efcaped through the grounds by a way in which he could not have been followed. This converfation furnifhed Rymfey and Weft with an opportunity of framing the moft probable part of the evidence they gave againft the perfons who were brought to trial, for a fuppofed intention to murder the King and the Duke of York, which from their having fixed on this houfe as the fcene of action, was called the Rye Houfe plot. Burnet fays he had feen Weft's narrative of this matter, which was fo improbable, that it was not fuffered to be printed.

THERE is a vulgar tradition, that after Rumbold's execution, his head was placed on an iron fpike, ftill remaining on the top of a twifted chimney on the houfe, and his limbs on the branches of a large elm which ftood on the oppofite fide of the road, but has been lately cut down. The grounds of this tradition are unknown; Rumbold was certainly not executed till two years after the plot, when being taken on the defeat of the Duke of Argyle in Scotland, he was condemned as a rebel. At his death he poffitively denied the knowledge of any plot; he admitted his having mentioned how eafily he could have killed the King and Duke, but declared no fcheme had ever been formed, or agreement entered into to attempt their death.

This View was drawn anno 1777.

THE RYE HOUSE, HERTFORDSHIRE.

(PLATE II.)

THIS plate gives a more diftinct view of the houfe, together with that of the barn, from which it was faid the
confpirators were to have fired at the King as he paffed by
the road feen on the left. The elm on which the limbs
of Rumbold are reported to have been fufpended, is alfo
fhewn as it was ftanding in the year 1772, when this
drawing was made.

THE gate is now ufed as a work-houfe to the parifh of
Stanfted Abbot.

Sopewell Nunnery, near St. Albans, Herts.

SOPEWELL NUNNERY, NEAR ST. ALBAN's, HERTS.

THIS nunnery, which is situated a small distance south-west of the town of St. Alban's, according to tradition, owes its origin to the following circumstance: Two religious women, whose names are forgotten, having made themselves a kind of hermitage with branches of trees, and covered it with leaves and bark, near Eywood, by the river side, dwelt there a considerable time, leading lives of such abstinence, chastity, charity, and piety, that the fame thereof reached the ears of Jeffery, the 16th abbat of St. Alban's; who, about the year 1140, built them a cell, and caused them to be cloathed like nuns, and to assume the rules of St. Benedict. For their support he gave them certain lands and rents; and to preserve their fame from the assaults of scandal, he ordered they should always be locked up in their house, and that their number should not exceed thirteen, all select virgins; though at the dissolution there were only nine. He also allotted them a burying ground, which he caused to be consecrated, but with a restriction that none but the nuns of that house should be buried there; probably to prevent his abbey from being deprived of the advantages arising from the sepulture of great or rich personages. This house was subject to the abbey of St. Alban's, and dedicated to the honour of the Blessed Virgin.

HENRY de Albancio and Ciceley his wife, with Roger his brother and Robert his son, gave two hides and one virgate of land in their manor of Cotes, and Richard de Taney his land called Blackhide in the foke of Tidehang, to God, Mary the mother of Chrift, and the maidens of this cell. Upon the diffolution, king Henry VIII. in the 30th year of his reign, granted it to fir Richard Leigh, knt. from whofe family it paffed by a daughter to Edward Sadler, fecond fon of fir Ralph Sadler, made a bannerett for his gallant behaviour at the battle of Muffelborough, 1ft Ed. VI. In his defcendants it remained, till on the failure of iffue male, it went in marriage to Thomas Saunders of Flamfted, efq. who fold it to fir Harbottle Grimfton, bart. from whom it devolved to the lord Grimfton, the prefent proprietor.

FROM the ftile of thefe ruins, as well as from their being chiefly built with brick, they cannot be of much elder date than the reign of Henry VII. or VIII. and poffibly may be the remains of a manfion built by fir Richard Leigh with fome of the materials, and on the fite of the nunnery. When Chauncey's Hiftory of Hertford-fhire was written, this houfe was entire, or at leaft is fo reprefented in the plan, and is in fome old furveys called Sopewell Hall and Sopewell Houfe. It is faid that about fifty or fixty years ago, the buildings here were in fuch a ftate as to make lord Grim-fton doubtful which of the two, this manfion or that of Gorehambury, he fhould fit up for his refidence. On one of the walls of the garden are two fquare tablets of ftone, on each of which is carved a dexter hand and arm completely armed, holding a fword engrailed, with fomething like a fcrawl under it. As thefe are enclofed, and only to be viewed at a diftance, there may poffibly be fome minute parts or members of this piece of fculpture left out in the defcription.

THE yearly value of this houfe at the diffolution, is eftimated by Dugdale at 40 l. 7 s. 10 d. Speed makes it 68 l. 8 s.

IT is faid that Henry VIII. was married to Anne Boleyn at this place.

THIS view was drawn A. D. 1787.

Chapel in St Augustin's Monastry, Canterbury Kent.

RUIN'D OFFICES IN ST. AUGUSTINE's MONASTERY, CANTERBURY.

THE buildings here reprefented, ftand within the walls of the Monaftery, North of the Church ; the gate is of brick, and has over the center of its arch, two Quatre Feuilles, a Fleur de Lis, and a Rofe moulded in brick earth before burning, and after-wards burned ; thefe ftand fingly one above the other, with three fmall Efcutcheons of the fame material and workmanfhip, beneath the whole. This Gate, from its ftile and bricks, feems to have been built about the time of Henry the Eighth, or Elizabeth.

Adjoining to its South-fide is a fmall neat Building, probably before the diffolution a Chapel, or fome other Office of the Monaftery ; but when this Drawing was taken, A. D. 1750, was converted to an Ouft or Kiln for drying Hops. Between two windows near its North end, was carved on a fquare ftone Tablet, the figure of a Mitre and a Ton, poffibly a Rebus of the Name of the Builder, Founder, or fome Benefactor.

PLAN OF DOVER CASTLE. KENT.

St Gregory's Canterbury, Kent.

ST. GREGORY's PRIORY, CANTERBURY, KENT.

MR. GOSTHING in his walk, gives the following account of this Priory. St. Gregory's was a large handsome house of stone, built by Archbishop Lanfranc, in 1084, who added to it several dwellings, well contrived for the wants and conveniencies of those who should live there, with a spacious court adjoining. This Palace, for so Edmer calls it, he divided into two parts, one for men labouring under various distempers, the other for women who had ill health; providing them with food and cloathing at his own expence, appointing also officers and servants, who should by all means take care that nothing should be wanting, and that the men and women should be kept from communication with each other. He built also on the opposite side of the way, a Church, to the honour of St. Gregory, where he placed canons regular, who should administer spiritual comfort and assistance to the infirm people above mentioned, and take the care of their funerals, for which he provided them with such an income as was thought sufficient.

PART of this Priory is now standing, but not a great deal, only one large room, unless the buildings of the street may be looked upon as the lodging of the poor and fick, who were provided for there ; the ground belonging to its precinct is almoft tirely laid out in gardens for our market.

TANNER thus records the foundation of this houfe. In the North-gate ftreet, (fays he,) over againft the hofpital of St. John, Archbifhop Lanfranc alfo founded an houfe for fecular Priefts, A. D. 1084, to the honour of St. Gregory, but Archbifhop William Temp. Hen. I. made it a priory of Black Canons. About the time of the diffolution here, were thirteen religious, who were endowed with the yearly revenue of 121l. 15s. 1d. Dug. 1661. 4s. 5d. Ob. Speed. The fcite was granted 28 Hen. VIII. to the Lord Archbifhop of Canterbury, in exchange for Wimbledon, &c.

THIS view was drawn, 1758.

Gundulph's Tower
Cathedral 1 Nov. 1783. By T. Hogan

GUNDULPH's TOWER, ROCHESTER.

THIS Tower, which ftands on the north fide of the cathedral church of Ro-
cheſter, is generally fuppoſed to have been built by the biſhop whoſe name it
bears, as a place of fecurity for the treaſure and archives of that church and
fee. Some fuppoſe it to have been intended for a bell tower, and others for
an eccleſiaſtical priſon, but whatever might be its deſtination, its machicolations,
its loop-hole windows, and the thickneſs of its walls ſhew that ſtrength and defence were confidered as neceſſary.

THIS Tower was originally in height about ſixty feet, four or five of which
have either fallen, or been taken down, its walls are ſix feet thick and contain
within them an area of about twenty feet ſquare, it was divided into five floors
or ſtories of unequal height, and had a communication with the upper part of
the church by means of an arch or bridge, the ſteps of which are ſtill viſible.
The common report is, that this was the only entrance into it; but on exa-
mination there were two other doors, one on the north fide, at the baſe of the tower, and another on the third ſtory. From diverfe circumſtances in the church,
there are fome grounds to ſuppoſe this tower was erected after that edifice was
completed.

This view was drawn anno 1781.

Maidstone Bridge Kent.

MAIDSTONE BRIDGE. (PLATE I).

It is uncertain at what time this bridge was built. Newton, in his Antiquities of Maidstone, says, " At the bottom of the high street, is a fair stone bridge, built across the Medway, of seven arches; it is supposed with great probability, that it was first built by some of the Archbishops of Canterbury, who, as we have seen, were Lords of the Manor; however, I don't find any evidence, at what time it was erected, or by whom. It was in the reign of King James I. repaired by an assessment on the town and parish."

This view, which shews the north side of the bridge, was drawn anno 1760.

Maidstone Bridge, Kent. Pl. 2.

MAIDSTONE BRIDGE. (PLATE II.)

The fouth-fide of this bridge is here exhibited: over it is feen the roof of a building, fituate on the weftern bank of the river, a fmall diftance north of the bridge, which building, from a crofs over its cafternmoft end, appears to have been a chapel or oratory. The river Medway rifes in Afhdowne foreft, in Suffex, and paffing through Kent difcharges itfelf near the Ifle of Shipey, by which it is divided into two branches, one called the caft, and the other the weft fwale. It is navigable for barges of fifty or fixty tons, as high as Maidftone, and is croffed by feveral bridges, the chief are thofe of Maidftone, Aylsford, and Rochefter.

THIS view was drawn anno 1760.

Queenborough Castle, Kent.

QUEENBOROUGH CASTLE, in the Isle of SHEPEY, KENT.

This view was taken from an undoubted original drawing made by Hollar, in the collection of the late Mr. Grose, of Richmond, in Surry. It is supposed to be that from which Hollar engraved the small view of this castle, a print extremely rare. On a comparison, it was found perfectly to agree with the traces and foundations of this edifice, now levelled with the ground. Of which Mr. Hasted, in his History of Kent, gives the following account :

The parish of Queenborough, which lies the next adjoining south westward from that of Minster, on the western shore of this island, was so called in honor of Philippa, Queen to King Edward III.

There was an ancient castle here, called the castle of Shepey, situate at the western mouth of the Swale, formerly, as has been already mentioned, accounted likewise the mouth of the river Thames, which was built for the defence both of the island and the passage on the water, the usual one then being between the main land of the county and this island.

This castle was begun to be new built by King Edward III, about the year 1361, being the 36th of his reign, and was finished about six years afterwards, being raised, as he himself says in his letters patent, dated May 10, in his 42d year, for the strength of the realm, and for the refuge of the inhabitants of this island.

This was undertaken under the inspection of William of Wickham, the King's chief architect, afterwards Bishop of Winchester, who, considering the difficulties arising from the nature of the ground and the lowness of the situation, acquitted himself in this task with his usual skill and abilities, and erected here a large, strong and magnificent building, fit equally for the defence of the island and the reception of his royal master. When it was finished, the king paid a visit to it, and remained here some days, during which time he made this place a free borough in honor of Philippa his Queen, naming it from thence Queenborough, and by charter bearing date anno 1366, he created it a corporation, making the townsmen burgesses, and giving them power to choose yearly a mayor and two bailiffs, who should make their oath of allegiance before the constable of the castle, and be justices within the liberties of the corporation, exclusive of all others, and endowing them with cognizance of pleas, with the liberty of two markets weekly, on Mondays and Thursdays, and two fairs yearly, one on the Eve of our Lady, and the other on the Feast of St. James; and benefiting them with freedom of tholle, and sundry other bountiful privileges, which might allure men to inhabit this place. Three years after which, as a further favor to it, he appointed a staple of wool at it.

King Henry VIII. repaired this castle in the year 1556, at the time he rebuilt several others in these parts, for the defence of the sea coasts; but even then it was become little more than a mansion for the residence of the constable of it, in which situation it continued till the death of King Charles I. in 1648; soon after which, the powers then in being seized on this castle, among the rest of the possessions of the Crown, and on the 16th of July following, passed an ordinance to vest the same in trustees, that they might be forthwith surveyed and sold, to supply the necessities of the state; accordingly this castle was surveyed in 1650, when it was returned, That it consisted of a capital messuage, called Queenborough Castle, lying within the common belonging to the town of Queenborough, called Queenborough Marsh, in the parish of Minster, and containing about twelve rooms of one range of buildings below stairs, and of about forty rooms from the first story upwards, being circular and built of stone, with six towers and certain out-offices thereto belonging; all the roof being covered with lead. Within the circumference of the castle was one little round court, paved with stone; and, in the middle of that, one great well; and without the castle was one great court surrounding it; both court and castle being surrounded with a great stone wall, and the outside of that moated round: the said castle abutting to the highway leading from the town of Queenborough to Eastchurch, south—and it contained three acres, one rood, and eleven perches of land. That the whole was much out of repair, and no ways defensive by the common-wealth, or the island on which it stood, being built in the time of bows and arrows. That as no platform for the planting of cannon could be erected on it, and it having no command of the sea, although near unto it, they adjudged it not fit to be kept, but demolished, and that the materials were worth, besides the charge of taking down, 1,792l. 12s. od. ½.

The above survey sufficiently points out the size and grandeur of this building which was soon after sold, with all its appurtenances, to Mr. John Wilkinson, who pulled the whole of it down and removed the materials.

The scite of the castle remained in his possession afterwards till the restoration of King Charles II. anno 1660, when the inheritance of it returned again to the crown, where it has continued ever since.

There are not any of the remains of the castle or walls to be seen at this time, only the moat continues still as such, and the ancient well in the middle of the scite, which long remained choaked up; but was, after several attempts made to restore it, anno 1723, opened by order of the Commissioners of the Navy. A full account of which was communicated to the Royal Society by Mr. Peter Collinson, and is entered in their Transactions.

The constables of this castle were men of considerable rank, as appears by the following list of them:

Anno 36 Edw. III. John Foxley was the first constable.
Anno 50 Edw. III. John of Gaunt, Duke of Lancaster.
Anno 8 Rich. II. Robert de Vere, Marquis of Dublin and Earl of Oxford, attainted anno 11 Rich. II.
Anno 16 Rich. II. Sir Arnold Savage, knight, obt. 12 Henry IV.
Anno 20 Rich. II. William Le Scroope, son of the Lord Scroope.
Anno 1 Hen. IV. William de Watterton.
Anno 4 Hen. IV. John Cornwall, Baron of Fanhope.
Anno 10 Hen. IV. Thomas Arundel, Archbishop of Canterbury.
Anno 1 Hen. V. Gilbert de Umfreville, obt. anno 9, Hen. V.
Anno 28 Hen. VI. Humphry Stafford, Duke of Buckingham, obt. 27 July, anno 38 Hen. VI.
Anno 1 { Edw. IV. John Northwood, Esq.
        { George Duke of Clarence, obt. 17 Edw. IV.
Anno 1 Rich. III. Thomas Wentworth.
      2 Ditto, Christopher Collyns.
Anno 1 { Hen. VII. William Chevney.
        { Sir Anthony Browne, knt. of the garter, obt. 22 Hen. VII.
Anno 2 Hen. VIII. Francis Cheney.
Anno 3 Hen. VIII. Sir Thomas Cheney, knt. of the garter, &c. obt. anno 1 Elizabeth.
Anno 1 { Eliz. Sir Richard Constable, knt.
        { Sir Edward Hoby, knt.
Temp. Jac. 1. Philip Earl of Pembroke and Montgomery, the last constable of this castle.

In the reign of Queen Elizabeth, the annual fee of the keeper of this castle was 29l. 2s. 6d.

From a book containing the grants of the 1st and 2d of Rich. III. preserved among the Harleian MSS. in the British Museum, and marked No. 433, there is an entry of a warrant for timber to be delivered to Christopher Collyns, for certain reparations at the castle o Queenborough; and, in another place in the same book, is a commission empowering him to take masons, stones, &c. necessary for the works in the said castle, whence it is evident that castle was then repaired.

Sandgate Castle, Kent.

SANDGATE CASTLE, KENT.

THIS is one of the caftles built by king Henry the eighth; in conftruction it much refembles thofe of Deal, Sandown, Walmer and Camber, or Winchelfea, and indeed moft of the caftles erected in that reign, all which confift of a combination of round towers. Thefe, from their form, are incapable of being completely flanked or defended by any adjacent work. It ftands a fmall diftance weft of Folkftone, on the beach or fand, whence probably it derives its name. It is overlooked by a high cliff, within gun fhot of it, as may be feen in the drawing.

HERE queen Elizabeth lodged in the year 1588, in her progrefs into Kent, in order to put the coaft in a ftate of defence againft an invafion, with which this kingdom was at that time threatened by the Spaniards.

THIS view was drawn A.D. 1762.

THE TEMPLE OR MANSION OF THE KNIGHTS TEMPLARS AT STROUD, KENT.

THE TEMPLE OR MANSION OF THE KNIGHTS TEMPLARS AT STROUD, KENT.

KING HENRY II. having granted to the knights templars the manor of Stroud, with the hundred of Shamell, they erected a mansion in the southern part of the parish near the banks of the river Medway, from which the manor has ever since been called the Temple Manor.

THIS gift was confirmed to them by King John and also by King Henry III. in the 2d year of his reign, but in the begining of the reign of King Edward II. the great wealth and power of this community, exciting the envy of the other orders and the avarice of diverse great men, they were accused of a variety of crimes, which were not however proved against them, they were neverthelefs, Tanner fays, at the instigation of the King of France, imprisoned, their goods and estates confiscated, and in the 6th year of that king, anno 1312, the whole order dissolved. Their estates were by Pope Clement V. granted to the knights hospitallers which grant was confirmed by the king, November 28, 1313, who ordered possession to be delivered to them, faving his own and his subjects rights, under which exception several manors and estates were granted away, and with-held from them.

POPE JOHN XXII. anno 1322, having confirmed the donation of his predeceffor Clement to thefe knights, and in a bull anathemized all thofe, as well ecclefiaftics as laymen, who againft right kept poffeffion of their lands, probably occafioned the act of parliament which paffed the next year, wherein it was ftated that the eftates of the templars having been given for pious ufes, the king and parliament granted that they fhould be affigned to other religious perfons, thereby to fulfil the intention of the donors, and they were accordingly granted to the hofpitallers, who held them till the 18th year of the fame reign, when the prior granted the fee of this manor to the king, who by writ commanded the fheriff of Kent to take it into his hands. It remained in the crown till the reign of Edward III. who firft granted it to Mary de St. Paul countefs of Pembroke for life, and in the 12th year of his reign to her and her heirs for ever, to be held by the accuftomed fervices. This lady at firft intended to have built a religious houfe here, but altering her mind, fhe in the 18th year of the fame reign, gave it to a monaftery fhe had lately founded at Denny in Cambridgefhire, where it remained till the general diffolution, when it was furrendered to King Henry VIII. who in the thirty-fecond year of his reign granted diverfe poffeffions of that houfe, among which was the manor of Stroud, to Edward Elrington Efq; who the fame year fold it to Sir George Brooke, Knt. Lord Cobham and his heirs, whofe grandfon in the 1ft year of king James I. being convicted of treafon, it efcheated to the crown, and was foon after granted to Robert Cecil, earl of Salifbury, whofe fon and heir William earl of Salifbury, fold it to Bernard Hyde, Efq; of London, by whom it was beqeathed to his third fon Mr. John Hyde, he in the reign of King Charles I. difpofed of it to James Stuart duke of Richmond, who fhortly after alienated it to —— Blague of Rochefter, one of whofe defcendants fold it to Mr. John Whitaker, who in 1780 was in poffeffion thereof.

VERY little remains of the ancient manfion, except a fpacious cellar, vaulted with chalk, and ftone groins; the walls were of an extraordinary thicknefs. The greateft part of the prefent building, from its ftile cannot be older than Elizabeth or James I. it is now a farm-houfe.

This view was drawn anno 1759.

UPNOR CASTLE, KENT.

UPNOR CASTLE, KENT.

THIS caftle ftands on the weftern bank of the river Medway, a fmall diftance below Chatham Dock, which is fituated on the oppofite fhore.

UPNOR Caftle was according to Kilburne, built by Queen Elizabeth, in the third year of her reign, for the defence of the river; it is chiefly of ftone, its external figure a parallelogram, much longer than broad, the longeft fide facing the water; it has two towers at its extremities, the fouthermoft is appropriated for the refidence of the Governor; the entrance is in the center of the weft fide.

ON the eaft fide next the water, are the remains of fome ftone walls, which feem to have formed a falient angle like a modern Ravelin; here probably was a platform and battery, this is now covered by high pallifadoes, with a crane for fhipping powder.

As a fort, this caftle was never of much confequence, efpecially as it was very injudicioufly placed, it has therefore very properly been converted into a powder magazine.

THE eftablifhment, according to Mr. Hafted, is a Governor, ftore-keeper, clerk of the cheque, a mafter gunner, and twelve other gunners; formerly all the forts between this caftle and Sheernefs, were fubordinate to it, and were under the command of its Governor. In the military establishment for the year 1659, the Governor's pay was only 5s. per diem, the remainder of the garrison consisted of a gunner, a servant, two corporals, one drum, and thirty soldiers, with an allowance of eight pence per diem for fire and candle.

On the top of the bank, a small distance south-west of the castle, is a modern built barrack capable of holding a company, where there is generally a subaltern's party of invalids, but when there is a camp on the opposite shore, or soldiers in the barracks at Chatham, this duty is done by a detachment from thence; the gunners are also lodged here; the store-keeper has a good house and garden close behind the castle. The present Governor is Major William Browne, whose salary is 10s. per diem.

The following gentlemen appear to have been Governors of this castle at the times specified.

Anno 1684.   Robert Minors, Esq; Governor and Captain.
       1703.   Colonel Rous.
       1735.   Lieutenant Colonel John Guise.
       1770.   Major General Deane.
       1775.   Lieutenant General James Murray.
       1782.   Major William Browne.

This view shews the west or land side of the castle, and was drawn anno 1757.

White Friars, Canterbury.

THE WHITE FRIARS, CANTERBURY.

THIS plate shews part of the remains of the first house of the Franciscan, or Minorite Friars, established in England. Nine in number of these brethren first arrived here from abroad, A. D. 1224, five of whom stayed at Canterbury, by the direction of King Henry III. and settled themselves on a piece of ground near the poor priests hospital; but about the year 1270, John Diggs, an alderman of that city, translated them to an island then called Bynnewith, on the west part of the city, where they continued till the dissolution, after which the Friery was granted 31st Henry VIII. to Thomas Spelman. At present scarce any thing of the buildings, except the part here represented, are remaining, the outer walls and foundations excepted.

SPEED and others erroneously make Henry VII. the first founder of this Friery, which was settled almost three hundred years before his time. He might (says Tanner) be a great benefactor, though Somner has not observed it, and might change the first conventual Francifcans into that reformed branch of their order called observants, but could not be the first founder. Weaver, p. 234, tells us, this house was valued, at 39l. 12s. 8d. ob. per ann. but there is no valuation of it in either Dugdale or Speed.

THIS view was drawn anno 1758.

Leicester Abbey.

THE ABBEY OF ST. MARY DE PRATIS, AT LEICESTER.
PLATE I.

THE following account of the foundation, and other particulars respecting this abbey, is given by Burton in his History of Leicestershire.

HE (Robert Bossue, earl of Leicester) founded also, in 1143, 9th of Stephen, the most sumptuous and elegant monastery of St. Mary de Pratis, without the walls, for canons regular of the order of St. Austin, so called from its situation upon the edge of the meadows, and having the delicious and pleasant prospect of them and the water; into which house the said lord Bossue became a canon regular professed, for the space of fifteen years, that so by repentance he might expiate his former treasons committed against his king and sovereign. This abbey had in this shire twenty-six parish churches appropriated unto it, which at the suppression thereof was valued yearly to dispend 1062l. os. 4d. ob. q: The abbey now is the inheritance of the right hon. William earl of Devonshire, baron Cavendish, of Hardwick, in the county of Derby. Of this house formerly was an abbot, that most learned Gilbert Foliot, who was afterwards made bishop of Hereford, A. D. 1149, and after that bishop of London, A. D. 1161, memorable for two things; the one, his allegiance and fidelity to his sovereign, being always faithful and true to King Henry II. in all those confusions between him and Thomas a Becket, archbishop of Canterbury. The other for a resolute answer made to an unknown voice heard by him; for, as Mathew Paris reports it, coming one night from the king, after a long conference he had had with him on these troubles with the said archbishop Becket, as he lay meditating and musing thereon in his bed, a terrible and unknown voice sounded these words in his ears, " *Dum revolvis tot & tot deus tuus est Astaroth.*" *i. e.* Whilst thou revolvest so many and so many times, thy God is Astaroth.—Which he taking to come from the devil; answered as boldly, " *Mentiris, dæmon, Deus meus est Deus Saboath.*"—Devil thou liest : My God is the God of Saboath.

To this account it is necessary to add, from Tanner, that the monastery was founded in honour of the assumption of the Blessed Virgin Mary, and endowed, according to Dugdale, with 951 l. 14 s. 5 d. ob. q.—Speed makes it 1062 l. 0 s. 4 d. ob. q.—and the site was granted 4 Ed. IV. to William, marquis of Northampton. It is said that the greatest part of the lands and tithes belonging to the collegiate church of prebends intra castrum, in the town of Leicester, was by Robert de Bossue alienated and annexed to this his new foundation.

Very little of the ancient abbey is remaining, except the gate and some of the outer walls; there are, indeed, ruins of a mansion, comparatively a modern building, erected out of the materials of the monastery, according to a manuscript account of the storming of Leicester, May 30, 1645, written by Richard Symonds, an officer in the royal army, and preserved in the British Museum. This house was then the residence of the countess of Devon, and was the quarters occupied by the king during the above-mentioned attack, and for some days afterwards. It was nevertheless burned by his troops, perhaps to prevent its being useful to the enemy. This particular we learn from a list of the marches made by King Charles I. from January 10, 1641, to the time of his death. It is entitled Iter Carolinum, published in Gutch's Collect. Curiosa.

This view, which shews some of the outer walls and towers of the abbey, at the back of the mansion, was drawn A. D. 1784.

N. View of Leicester Abbey. Pl. 2.

THE ABBEY OF ST. MARY DE PRATIS, LEICESTER.

PLATE II.

THIS plate fhews the ruins of the manfion of the duchefs of Devonfhire, fuppofed to have been built out of the materials of the abbey foon after the diffolution; and which, as has been before obferved, was burned by the Royalifts.

IN this monaftery died that eminent ftatefman and magnificent prelate, Cardinal Wolfey, A. D. 1531, in his way to London, after his difgrace. His laft words are faid to have been, "Had I ferved the God of heaven, as faithfully as I did my mafter on earth, he had not forfaken me in my old age, as the other hath done."

Names of the Abbats out of the Regifters of Lincoln and the Collections of the Rev. Mr. Samuel Carte, of Leicefter:

1. RICHARD, who was the firft abbat, became admitted to this dignity, an. 1144, an. 9th of king Stephen. He prefided 24 years, and was fucceeded by, 2. William de Katewyke, elected abbat an. 1167, 14 Hen. II. He governed 10 years, and was fucceeded by, 3. William de Broke, elected abbat an. 1177, 23 Hen. II. He fat there nine years, and was, an. 1186, made abbat of the Ciftertians, and fucceeded in this abbacy by, 4. Paul, elected abbat the fame year, viz. an. 1186, an. 8 Rich. I. He governed 19 years, and was fucceeded by, 5. William Pepyn, an. 1205, 15th of king John. He continued abbat 19 years, and had for his fucceffor, 6. Ofbert, elected an. 1224, 8 Hen. III. He prefided 5 years, and was fucceeded by, 7. Mathias, an. 1229, 13 Hen. III. He governed 6 years, and refigning an. 1235, was fucceeded by, 8. Alan de Ceftreham, on the 5th of the cal. of Nov. 1235, 19 Hen. III. He fat 9 years, and was fucceeded by, 9. Robert Fuernetyn, admitted abbat the 4th of the nones of Nov. 1244, 28 Hen. III. He prefided three years, and was fucceeded by, 10. Henry Rothely, on the cal. of Aug. 1247, 31 Hen. III. He prefided 23 years and then refigned, an. 1269, to 11. William Schepefheved, who was admitted abbat the 2d of the nones of Oct. 1270, 54 Hen. III. He governed 21 years, and then dying, was fucceeded by, 12. William Malverne, elected on the 5th of the id. of Sept. 1291, 19th Ed. I. He fat 26 years, and on his death, which happened an. 1317, was fucceeded by, 13.

Richard Towers, elected abbat the 13th of the cal. of June 1317, 11 Ed. II. He was abbat 28 years, viz. till the time of his death, and was succeeded by, 14. William de Cloune, the 12th of the cal. of Nov. 1345, 19 Ed. III. He procured himself and succeffors to be exempt from being fummoned to parliament, as may be feen by the patent exhibited in Selden's Titles of Honour, p. 604. He prefided 32 years, and then dying, was fucceeded, an. 1377 by, 15. William Kerby, on the 3d of the nones of Feb. an. 1 Rich. II. He prefided 16 years, and died an. 1393; whereupon, 16. Philip Repyngdon was admitted abbat the 28th of June 1394, 17 Rich. II. He governed 11 years, and then being preferred to the fee of Lincoln, was fucceeded in this abbacy by, 17. Richard Rothele, the 5th of the cal. of May 1405, 6 Hen. IV. He fat 16 years, and was fucceeded by, 18. William Sadington, the 13th of the cal. of Nov. 1420, 8 Hen. V. He continued here 22 years, and dying an. 1442, was fucceeded by, 19. John Pomery, the 16th of the cal. of June 1442, 21 Hen. VI. He prefided 32 years, and was fucceeded by, 20. John Shepefhed, elected abbat the 11th of the cal. of Sept. 1474, 14 Ed. IV. He prefided 11 years, and was fucceeded by, 21. Gilbert Manchefter, elected the 2d of the cal. of Oct. 1485, 1 Hen. VII. He continued 11 years, and was fucceeded by, 22. John Penny, admitted abbat on the 7th of the cal. of July 1496, 11 Hen. VII. He fat 13 years, and being, an. 1504, made bifhop of Bangor, obtained leave to hold this abbey in commendam; which he did till the year 1509, when he was tranflated from Bangor to Carlifle. However he feems to have ended his days in this abbey, by his burial in St. Margaret's church, in the town of Leicefter; to the building of which, I prefume, he was a good benefactor; where his effigies yet remain, at the upper end of the north aifle, being handfomely carved in alabafter in his epifcopal habit. On his refignation, 23. Richard Pexal was admitted March 31, 1509, 1 Hen. VIII. He occurs abbat in a deed dated July 10, 1520, 12 Hen. VIII. and as fuch, fubfcribed by proxy, at the convocation holden April 5, 1533; at the latter end of which year, or the beginning of the next, he was fucceeded by, 24. John Bowchier or Bouchier, the laft abbat. In Aug. 11, 1534, he fubfcribed to the king's fupremacy; however, he afterwards withftood the diffolution with fuch refolution that the vifitors threatened him and his canons with adultery and buggery, unlefs they would fubmit and furrender their monaftery, as we are informed in Collier's Eccl. Hift. vol. II. and Dr. Tanner's Preface to his Notitia Monaftica.

Anno 1553, here remained in charge 3l. 6s. 8d. in fees, and 32l. 19s. 4d. in annuities, and the following penfions, viz.

To John Bowchier, laft abbat, 200l. Richard Duckett 10l. John Buckefhame 6l. Richard Webbe 6l. John Lacye 6l. Hugh Sheppey 5l. 1s. 8d. John Revell 5l. 6s. 8d. George King 5l. 6s. 8d. William Parmoter 5l. James Lawe 5l. and to Thomas Weftus 5l.

That this conventual church was demolifhed very foon after the furrender, may be eafily furmifed from the following letter, written by one of the commiffioners to Crumwell.

My moft bounden dutye remembryd, this is to advertis youre good lordfhippe of the hole eftate of the late monaftery of Leicefter, in the wiche we have taken the furrender and feyne of th' abbot and convent, and the writinges therof be in my cuftodye. By your lordfhippes goodnes towardes me I now ame in the poffeffion of the houfe, and all the demefnes wiche was unlett at the tyme of our repare thether. We alfo founde the houfe was indettyd to the kynges heyghnes, wherof we make no reconinge of; and for the difcharge therof we have made a fale of the ftoke and ftore withe the houfehold ftuffe and ornaments of the churche, wiche amounte unto 228l. The plate is onfolde, wiche maifter Freman taketh the charge of, and is valuyd at, by weyght, 190 pounds. The lead by eftymacion is valuyd at 1000l. The bells at 88l.—For the difchargeynge of th' abbot, convent and fervants of the faide monaftery, there haithe beyne payde, as dothe apere more particularly by the bouks we fend your lordfhippe, 149l. And for as moche as th' abbot hath not receyveyd of us in redy money, but 20l. he haithe requyride me to defyer your lordfhippe to be fo good lorde unto hym, as he may have 20 pounds or 20 marks. The churche and houfe remeynethe as yet undefacede, and in the churche be many thynges to be maide fale of. For wiche that may plefe your lordfhippe to let me knowe youre pleyfure, as well for the further fale to be made, as for the defafinge of the churche and other fuperfluus byldinges wiche be about the monaftery; a hundred marks yerly will not fufteyne the charges in repayringe this houfe; that all byldinges be lett ftande as your lordfhippe fhall knowe more hereafter. Thus I pray Jhefus long to preferve you in helthe withe muche honore.

Written at the late monafterye of Leycefter, the 29th day of Augufte, by your lordfhipes moft bownden fervante,

FRANCIS CAVE.

BISHOP's PALACE, LINCOLN.

THIS Palace, according to some writers, was began by
Remigius, the first Bishop and founder of the cathedral, but
demolished in the wars during the reign of King Stephen.
It was rebuilt by Robert de Chisney, or Chisneto, called
also de Querceto; the fourth Bishop, who was consecrated
in September 1147, and died January 8th, 1167; his
great expences in this building, as well as the purchase of
a house for the residence of himself and successors in
London, occasioned his leaving the fee indebted to one Aron

a Jew, the fum of three hundred pounds. St. - Hugh, the Burgundian, the feventh Bifhop of this fee, confecrated anno 1186, began a great and magnificent hall, which was finifhed by Hugh de Wells, the ninth Bifhop, who died anno 1234. The great tower and gate was built by Thomas de Bec, the feventeenth Bifhop, anno 1341, whofe arms are placed thereon. The kitchen had feven chimnies in it. This palace flood fouth of the Roman wall, upon the brow of the hill, and was a very elegant building, ornamented with many fine bow-windows. It commanded a moft extenfive profpect over the lower city into Nottinghamfhire. The ruinous ftate of this edifice is in a great means owing to the fury of the civil wars under the Kings Charles the Firft and Second.

This View was drawn Anno 1774.

THE NEW TEMPLE, LONDON.

THE NEW TEMPLE, LONDON.

THE origin, rules, and diffolution of the rich and powerful order of knights templers, has been already fully related in the preface to this work, and under the article of the Temple at Stroud, in Kent; it will therefore fuffice to fay, that this manfion was erected by the knights of that order in the reign of Henry II. and in the year 1185, dedicated to god and our bleffed lady, by Heraclius, patriarch of the church called the Holy Refurrection, in Jerufalem. It was ftiled the New Temple in reference to a former principal houfe of the order, fituated in Holbourn and denominated the Temple.

THE New Temple and its offices, contained all that fpace of ground from White Friars eaftward to Effex houfe without Temple Bar, and at a part of that alfo as appears by the firft grant thereof to Sir William Paget, Knt. fecretary of ftate to king Henry VIII. Pat. 2d, Ed. 6. This Temple was again dedicated in 1240, as alfo about the fame time re-edified.

AFTER the condemnation of this order, their diffolution and the confifcation of their eftates, Edward II. in the year 1313, gave to Etimer de Valence, Earl of Pembroke, the whole place and houfe called the New Temple, at London, with the ground called Fiquet's Croft, and all the tenements and rents, with the appurtenances, that belonged to the Templers, in the city of London and fuburbs thereof; alfo the land called Fletecroft, part of the poffeffions of the faid New Temple. After Aimer de Valence, it is faid, Hugh Spencer ufurping thefe eftates, held them during his life, but by his attainder they reverted to the crown; but in the mean time, viz. 1324, by a council held at Vienna, all the lands of the Templers, leaft the fame fhould be put to prophane ufes, were given to the Knights hofpitalers, of the order of St. John Baptift, called St. John of Jerufalem; which knights had driven the turks out of the ifle of Rhodes, and gained divers other advantages over them; the premifes were therefore granted by king Edward III. to them, who poffeffed it fome time, and in the eighteenth year of that king's reign, were forced to repair the bridge of the faid temple.

As these knights had their chief house for England at Clerkenwell, near west Smithfield, they, in the reign of the said king Edward III. granted, for a certain rent of ten pounds by the year, the said temple, with the appurtenances thereunto adjoining, to the students of the common laws of England. In their possession the same has ever since remained, and is now divided into two houses for several students, by the name of the Inns of Court, viz. the Inner Temple and the Middle Temple, who keep two several halls; but they all resort to the said temple church.

In the round walk, the spot here represented, which is the west part without the choir, there remain monuments of noblemen there buried, to the number of eleven, eight of them are images of armed knights, five lying cross legged, as crusaders, or persons under a vow to visit the holy land, the other three not crossed; the rest are coped stones, all of grey marble. The first of the cross legged was William Marshall, the elder Earl of Pembroke, who died 1219; the second, William, his son, who died 1231; the third, Gilbert Marshall, his brother, also Earl of Pembroke, slain in a tournament at Hertford, near Ware, twenty miles from London, in the year 1241. After this, Robert Rose, otherwise called Furſan, who as Maitland has it, being made a templer in the year 1245, died and was buried there. These cross legged figures are commonly, though falsely, stiled knights templers, although scarce one of them ever belonged to that order, as the Rev. Doctor Nash has very sufficiently proved in his history of Worcester. " It is an opinion, says he, which universally prevails with regard to these cross legged monuments, that they were all erected to the memory of knights templers; now to me it is very evident, that not one of them belonged to that order, but as Mr. Habingdon, in describing those at Alvechurch, hath justly expressed it, to knights of the holy voyage; for the order of knights templers followed the rule of the canons regular of St. Austin, and as such were under a vow of celibacy. Now there is scarce one of these monuments which is certainly known for whom it was erected, but it is as certain that the person it represents was a married man. The knights templers always wore a white habit, with a red cross on the left shoulder; I believe not a single instance can be produced of either the mantle or cross being carved on any of these monuments, which surely would not have been omitted, as by it they were distinguished from all other orders, had these been really designed to represent knights templers. Lastly, this order was not confined to England only, but dispersed itself all over Europe, yet it will be very difficult to find one cross legged monument any where out of England; whereas no doubt they would have abounded in France, Italy, and elsewhere, had it been a fashion peculiar to that famous order. But though for these reasons I cannot allow the cross legged monuments to have been erected for knights templers, yet they have some relation to them; being memorials of those zealous devotees, who had either been in Palestine, personally engaged in what is called the Holy War, or had laid themselves under a vow to go thither, though perhaps they were prevented from it by death; some few indeed might possibly be erected to the memory of persons who had made pilgrimages thither, merely out of devotion; among the latter probably was the lady of the family of Mepham, of Mepham in Yorkshire, to whose memory a cross legged monument was placed in a chapel adjoining to the once collegiate church of Howden, in Yorkshire, and is at this day remaining, together with that of her husband, on the same tomb. As this religious madness lasted no longer than the reign of our Henry III. (the tenth and last crusade being published in the year 1268) and the whole order of knights templers was dissolved 7th of Edward II. Military expeditions to the holy land, as well as devout pilgrimages thither, had their period by the year 1312, consequently none of those cross legged monuments are of a later date than the reign of Edward II. or beginning of Edward III. nor of an earlier than that of king Stephen, when these expeditions first took place in this kingdom."

This view was drawn anno 1784.

White Tower, or Tower of London.

THE WHITE TOWER, OR TOWER OF LONDON.

THE following particulars respecting this fortress are in substance related by Maitland, in his History of London, from the authorities of Mat. Paris, Roger Windover, John Bever, Stow, and other ancient writers.

THIS tower was erected anno 1079, by William the Conqueror, as a keep to a fortress begun by him in the year 1067, to awe the citizens of London; the architect was Gundulph, bishop of Rochester. Fitz Stephens has falsely attributed this edifice to Julius Cæsar.

ANNO 1090 a violent storm of wind did great damage to this building, for the repairs of which, his works at Westminster and London Bridge, William Rufus exacted great sums of money from his people. Notwithstanding these repairs were not finished till the reign of Henry I. The tower was found to stand in need of further help in the year 1155, when Thomas Becket, archbishop of Canterbury, caused it to be again repaired.

IN 1190 Lord Chancellor Longschamp, bishop of Ely, encompassed the premises with a wall and ditch, for the doing which, he deprived the Priory of Holy Trinity, without Aldgate, and the Hospital of St. Catherine's of a mill and other parts of their property.

IN 1239, several bulwarks were added by Henry III. These were much damaged the next year by an earthquake, but the king caused them to be restored and augmented, with a stone gate, bulwark, &c. on the west side or entrance. This new work, which is recorded to have cost more than 12000 marks, fell down a few years after. The same king caused the garner within the tower to be repaired, and the leaden gutters of the great tower to be lengthened from the top, so that they should reach the ground for the conveyance of rain water, and to be made up on the south side above the said tower, deep alures of good and strong timber, and well leaded all over, by which people might see even to the foot of the said tower, and if needful, the better ascend and descend. He also caused the chapel of St. John the Evangelist in the said tower, as well as the old walls of the tower itself, to be whitened over, from whence probably this building obtained the name of the White Tower.

KING EDWARD I. in the 2d year of his reign, directed the finishing the work of the ditch, then new made about the bulwark, called the Lyon Tower, from lyons and other wild beasts kept there. Lyons were first lodged in the tower, by Henry I.

KING EDWARD IV. added to the fortifications here, and enclosed within a brick wall that parcel of ground which before was only encroached upon by a mud wall, taken out of Tower Hill, west from the lyons tower now called the bulwark. Anno 1484, masons, bricklayers, and other workmen were pressed to expedite the repairs directed to be made here by Richard III.

Anno 1512, the chapel of the White Tower was burned, and in 1532, Henry VIII. repaired the White Tower, and other parts of this fortress ; and in the next reign a Frenchman who lodged in the round bulwark, between the west gate and the postern or drawbridge, called the warders gate, blew up the said bulwark and himself therewith, without any further damage, which bulwark was immediately rebuilt.

IN the reign of Queen Elizabeth diverse encroachments were made here, by erecting tenements over the ditch, &c. these by order of the privy council were pulled down.

GREAT repairs were made here anno 1663, when the ditch was scoured, the wharfing new built with brick and stone, sluices made, letting in, and retaining the Thames water as occasion may require. The walls and windows of the White Tower then much decayed, were mended, two of the turets wholly taken down and new fanes set up, with the king's arms and imperial crowns over them, the old ones having been defaced by the parliamentary garrison ; since which time a variety of repairs have been done at different parts, and diverse new buildings erected, as occasion or conveniency required.

THIS fortress is situated on the east side of the city, part of its western extremity standing within the limits of the ancient city wall ; the area contained within its walls is estimated at twelve acres and five rods. Its circumference on the outside of the ditch three thousand one hundred and fifty-six feet. It is surrounded by a ditch in some places one hundred and twenty feet broad, supplied from the Thames, that washes its south boundaries, within which is a lofty wall.

IT is defended by eighteen towers, known by the following names : the White Tower, Bloody, Hall, St. Thomas's, Lanthorn, Cradle, Well, Salt, Broad Arrows, Castle, Martins, Bower, Flint, Dwelling, Beauchamp, the Bell, the Middle, and the Lyons Towers. There is a spacious wharf next the river.

ALL the portion of the tower which is environed within the site of the ancient city wall, or on the west part thereof, is within the city of London, ward of Tower, and Parish of Alhallows Barking ; the rest lying on the east side of the said wall, is within the county of Middlesex.

THIS view, which shews the north-west aspect, was drawn in 1784.

A Gateway, called King John's Castle, Oldford, Middlesex.

KING HENRY VIII.'s HOUSE, OLD FORD, MIDDLESEX.

THIS building, vulgarly known by the appellation of King John's Houfe, ftands in Old Ford, in the parifh of Stratford le Bowe. It was the gate of a royal manfion belonging to king Henry VIII. is of brick, and by its ftile feems at leaft as old as the reign of king Henry VII. Several foundations of the interior buildings are ftill vifible, particularly thofe of the chapel, which was ftanding within the memory of fome ancient perfons now (1787) refiding near the fpot; who report that it was adorned with fine paintings and curious painted glafs, and was called the Romifh Chapel. The extremity of thefe premifes is bounded by a ditch, which has ferved as a fhore to them and the adjacent buildings time immemorial. This was lately enlarged, in order to admit the coal barges from the river Lea, and to make a wharf; in doing which, a ftone wall was difcovered twenty-feven paces in length, having over it a layer of brick. This feems to have been the boundary and breadth of the whole premifes: their length is but little more; fo that the area of the whole was extremely fmall for a royal manfion. Many ancient glazed tiles have been digged up here, ornamented with fcroll-work painted in yellow, four of them completing one pattern. Thefe, it is likely, were part of the pavement of the chapel, many such tiles being applied to that use in different old buildings, such as the cathedrals at Winchester and Gloucester; Christ Church, Hants; Romsey, &c. &c. Several ancient coins have been also found here.

This estate is held on a lease from Christ's Hospital, London; originally granted to the late Mr. Edmond Smith, scarlet dyer, for 61 years; many of which are at present unexpired. Probably this mansion was granted to the hospital by its founder king Edward VI. The ruinous state of this building, makes it unlikely that it will stand through the ensuing winter.

This view, which shews the inside of the gate, was drawn A. D. 1786.

Savoy Church, London.

CHAPEL OF ST. JOHN THE BAPTIST, IN THE SAVOY, LONDON.

(PLATE I.)

This was the chapel to a manfion originally built in the year 1245 by Peter of Savoy and Richmond, uncle to Eleanor, wife of king Henry III. This queen afterwards purchafed it for her fon, Edmond earl of Lancafter, from the fraternity of Mountjoy, unto whom Peter of Savoy had given it. Henry duke of Lancafter, repaired, or rather rebuilt, the houfe, which Maitland fays had been pulled down; according to Stowe he laid out on it 52000 marks. This money he had gathered together at the town of Bridgerike.

In the year 1381, the rebels of Kent and Effex, headed by Wat Tyler, out of hatred to John of Gaunt, duke of Lancafter, burned this houfe to the ground, not fuffering any part of the plate, jewels, or rich furniture, to be faved. The plate they cut in fmall pieces, and threw into the Thames; the precious ftones they broke to powder in a mortar. A proclamation having been previoufly made by order of their leaders, threatening death to any one who fhould attempt to convert any article to his own ufe, one of the rebels was thrown into the fire by his companions, for endeavouring to fecrete a valuable piece of plate. Among other articles, the rebels found fome barrels of gun-powder, which they miftook for gold or filver; thefe they threw into the fire, whereby the hall was blown up, the adjacent buildings deftroyed, and themfelves all expofed to great danger; doubtlefs, many of them were killed or wounded. Befides this time, the Savoy has more than once experienced the fury of the flames.

This manfion thus defaced and in ruins, afterwards came into the king's hands, and was rebuilt from the ground for an hofpital of St. John the Baptift, by king Henry VII. about the year 1509. Wever fays the following infcription was over the great gate:

Hofpitium hoc inopi turba Savoia vocatum
Septimus Henricus fundavit ab imo Solo.

This hofpital confifted of a mafter and four brethren, who were to be in prieft's orders, and to officiate in their turns; they were alfo alternately to ftand at the gate of the Savoy, and if they faw any object of charity, they were obliged to take him in and feed him. If he proved to be a traveller, he was entertained for one night, and a letter of recommendation, with as much money, given him, as would defray his expences to the next hofpital. Stowe fays that king Henry purchafed for this hofpital, lands fufficient to enable them to relieve an hundred poor people. I fuppofe he means daily; it being eftimated that they might expend 529 l. 15 s. yearly.

On the 10th of June, in the 7th year of king Edward VI. this hofpital was fuppreffed, and the beds, bedding and other furniture, with lands of the yearly value of 700 marks, given by the king, for the furnithing his houfe at Bridewell, which he had given to the citizens of London, to be a workhoufe for the poor and idle perfons, and the hofpital of St. Thomas in Southwark lately fuppreffed.

The hofpital of the Savoy was again new founded, corporated, and endowed with lands, by queen Mary, the 3d of November, in the fourth year of her reign, when one Jackfon was appointed mafter. The ladies of the court and maids of honor, in compliment to the queen, furnifhed it with new beds, bedding and other furniture, in a very ample manner. It confifted of a mafter and four brethren, as before; a receiver of the rents, who was alfo the porter and locked the gates every night, and chofe a watchman. Maitland fays, on the acceffion of queen Elizabeth it was again fuppreffed.

The original rents amounted to 22000 l. per annum; which being deemed too large an endowment, an act of refumption was obtained in the 4th and 5th of Philip and Mary, fo that the lands reverted to the crown. But thofe who had taken leafes from the mafter of the Savoy, had their lands confirmed to them for ever, upon the payment of twenty years purchafe; a referve being made of 800 or 1000 l. per ann. in perpetuity for the mafter and four brethren; and over a houfe, inhabited A. D. 1732 by Mr. Collins, the king's diftiller, which was part of the great gate of the Savoy, was placed the effigies of St. John the Baptift, curioufly carved at full length in ftone.

This view was drawn A. D. 1786.

Savoy Church, London &c.

THE CHAPEL OF ST. JOHN THE BAPTIST, IN THE SAVOY, LONDON.

(PLATE II.)

The chapel in the Savoy, (which is very erroneously called St. Mary le Savoy) is properly the chapel of St. John the Baptist. It is all stone-work, and carries the aspect of antiquity. It was repaired with great cost in the year 1600, and the gallery at the south end, built in the year 1618. It was again repaired anno 1721, at the sole charge of his late majesty king George I. who also enclosed the burial-ground with a strong brick wall, and added a door to it, half of which consists of iron-work.

The inhabitants of St. Mary le Strand, after their church was pulled down to enlarge the garden belonging to Somerset-house, congregated here for many years; but when Dr. Killigrew was made master, he would not permit them to frequent the church till they had signed an instrument, whereby they renounced their having any right or property in or to the said chapel, or any part of the Savoy; and then he allowed them to make collections at the chapel door nine months in the year, for the support of their own poor. The Dr. soon broke the old constitution, and not only appointed two overseers, (one chosen by himself, and the other by the inhabitants of the precinct) but he also set up a vestry, (without authority) to consist of the master and fourteen inhabitants. By virtue of his patent, he had liberty to grant leases, for three lives, for ninety-one years; which he did by taking fines, and reserving only a small quit-rent, to the diminution of the annual income of the hospital.

Soon after the Dr.'s decease, viz. in the first year of the late queen Anne, com-missioners were appointed to visit the hospital, who were seven lords spiritual, and as many lords temporal. The commission was opened by sir Nathan. Wright, then lord-keeper of the great seal; and three of the brethren, or chaplains, were discharged because they had other benefices; and also the fourth, for being a teacher of a seperate congregation. The last mentioned chaplain was put in by Dr. Killigrew, though he knew that he was a dissenting preacher.

Some time after this, Dr. Prat, who was chaplain of the hospital, endeavoured to obtain an act of parliament to have it dissolved, and to be made parochial. The bill passed the house of commons, but meeting with great opposition from the chancellors of the two universities, from the bishops and other lords, it was thrown out of their house.

The chapel stands north and south, and is situated by the church-yard of the Savoy, which lies between the south side of the Strand and the Thames: it consists only of a nave, without any side aile. The ceiling, which is coveing, is orna-mented with a kind of regular pattern, formed of four-leaved roses, many of which have in their centers the crown of thorns, some have armorial bearings, and others animals supporting banners. Among them, the bull, the stag, the wolf, the greyhound and griffin, seemingly the supporters borne by several of our kings. These were all originally painted in their proper colours, but have since been defaced by white-washing.

Here are several mural monuments, one seemingly of the age of Edward IV. or Henry VII. divers others of the time of queen Elizabeth and James I. Several stones on the floor have the marks of brasses, and one or two inscriptions are still remaining.

Plate I. shews part of the east side of the chapel, with an arch of a window of the refectory or great hall of the ancient hospital. The remains of twelve large arched windows on the south side, are still visible; as also part of a fire-place. This building was lately used as a barrack, and burned down by accident. The west end, bounded by an arch, is seen in profile beyond the church.

Plate II. shews the front of this window, with two of its northern side.

THIS view was drawn A. D. 1787.

LLANHODENEI, LANTONY, OR LANTONIA PRIMA, MONMOUTHSHIRE.

This monastery stands in the northernmost corner of the county of Monmouth, amongst the Hatterell hills. Its situation is thus described by Giraldus Cambrensis: In the low vale of Ewias, which is about a bow shot over, and inclosed on all sides with high mountains, stands the church of St. John Baptist, covered with lead; and considering the solitariness of the place not unhandsomely built, with an arched roof of stone, in the same place where formerly stood a small chapel of St. David the Archbishop. recommended with no other ornaments than green moss and ivy, a place fit for the exercise of religion, and the most conveniently seated for canonical discipline of any monastery in the island of Britain: built first to the honour of that solitary life by two hermits, in this desart, remote from all the noise of the world, upon the river Hodeni, which glides through the midst of the vale, whence it was called Llan Hodeni. the word Llan signifying a church or religious place. But to speak more accurately, the true name of that place is Nent Hodeni, for the inhabitants call it at this day Llan-dhewi-yn nent Hodeni, i. e. St. David's church on the river Hodeni. The rains which mountainous places produce are here very frequent, the winds exceedingly fierce, and the winters almost continually cloudy; yet notwithstanding that gross air, it is so tempered that this place is very little subject to diseases: the monks sitting here in their cloisters, when they chance to look out for fresh air, have a pleasing prospect on all hands, of exceeding high mountains, with plentiful herds of wild deer feeding aloft at the furthermost limits of the horizon. The body of the sun surmounts these hills so as to be visible to them, only between the hours of one and three, nor even that but when the air is moft clear. And a little after, The form of this place drew hither Roger, Bifhop of Salifbury, Prime Minifter of ftate, who having for fome time admired the fituation and retired folitarinefs of it, and alfo the contented condition of the monks, ferving God with due reverence, and their moft agreeable and brotherly converfation ; and being returned to the king, and having fpent the beft part of the day in the praife of it, he at laft thus concluded his difcourfe: What fhall I fay more, all the treafure of your Majefty and the kingdom would not fuffice to build fuch a cloifter ; at which both the king and courtiers being aftonifhed, he at length explained that paradox, by telling them he meant the mountains wherewith it was on all hands inclofed.

The hiftory of this houfe is given by Tanner in the following words: Here, in a very folitary valley, not long after the year 1108, was fettled a priory of canons regular, of the order of St. Auftin, dedicated to St. John Baptift, who acknowledged Hugh Lacy for their founder. In the beginning here were above forty Religious, but by reafon of the hard ufage they met with from the rudenefs, poverty and barrennefs of the neighbouring country and people, the greateft part of them removed; firft to the Bifhop's palace, in Hereford, and after, viz. A. D. 1136, to a place near Gloucefter, which was alfo called, from this mother monaftery, Lantony (and fometimes, for diftinction's fake, Lantony the fecond), fo that only thirteen canons were left here, which number in procefs of time decreafed, and the houfe was almoft ruined. When King Edward IV. (anno 21.) gave leave for the annexing this priory to Lantony, near Gloucefter, here being to be maintained a prior dative, and four canons: but it is to be doubted whether this union ever took full effect; becaufe the eftate of Lantony the firft is valued diftinct in 26 Hen. VIII. at 87 l. 9 s. 5 d. per ann. M. S. Corp. Chrift. Col. Cant. 99 l. 19 s. od. ob. Dugd. 71 l. 3 s. 2 d. Speed. 112 l. 5 d. fumma inde M. S. Val. The fite was granted 38 Hen. VIII. to Nic. Arnold.

It is neceffary to obferve that, in the defcription here quoted from Giraldus, there is a fmall miftake refpecting the fun, the monks of this houfe having enjoyed a greater portion of its rays than he has affigned them. The author of the Tour through Wales, as well as a note in Gibfon's Camden, bear teftimony to this. The former fays, That luminary fhone upon the ruins at the time he faw it, which was eleven o'clock.

The Abbey-church is in the form of a crofs, and was, according to Speed, built about the year 1137, and the prefent ruins feem of a later period, having a mixture of circular and pointed arches ; thofe below being pointed, and thofe above circular. The whole feems to have been built at the fame time, and from one plan.

The whole nave is ftill remaining from eaft to weft, the roof excepted. It meafures, according to the author before cited, 212 feet in length, 27 feet 4 inches in breadth. The aifles are no more than 8 feet 8 inches broad. The diagonal ftone vault, over the body of the church, fprung from fmall cluftered flying pillars; thefe are ftill feen projecting from the walls between the Gothic arches of the nave.

Two fides of the high tower, are ftill extant, which rife from nearly the centre of the church.

The whole ftructure is faced with a durable and well worked ftone.

This View was drawn Anno 1777.

A View of the Abbey Church at Llantony
from within the West Door.

MONNOW GATE AND BRIDGE, MONMOUTH.

THIS plate prefents the fouth afpect of Monnow Gate and Bridge, fo called from the river over which it is conftructed. Both are mentioned in Leland's Itinerary, and indeed have undoubted marks of antiquity, but neither hiftory nor tradition afford any lights refpecting the date of their erection. As a picturefque object they have long been noticed by the connoiffeurs.

THIS view was drawn anno 1775.

Ragland Castle, Monmouth &c.
as well as of a ... lodgings.

RAGLAND CASTLE, MONMOUTHSHIRE.

THIS caftle is of no great antiquity, its foundations are faid to have been laid about the time of Henry VII. fince which additions have been made to it at different periods. Leland thus defcribes it, " Ragland vn middle Veneeland ys a fair and pleafant caftel viii myles " from Chapftow and vii from Bergevenny. The towne by ys bare ther ly to goodly parkes " adjacent to the caftel." And in another place " Morgan tolde me that one of the lafte " Lord Herbertes buildid al the befte logges of the caftel of Ragland." Camden calls it a fair houfe of the Earl of Worceefter's, built caftle like. In the troubles under Charles I. this houfe was a garrifon for the King, being fortified with many outworks by the Earl of Wor- ceefter, and was the laft garrifon held by the royalifts. The circumftances of its fiege are in fubftance thus related in Rufhworth's Hiftorical Collections.

RAGLAND Caftle was invefted, or, as it is termed, ftreightened firft by Sir Trevor Williams and Major General Langhorn, and afterwards by Colonel Morgan, ordered from Worceefter to command in chief, the force then only fifteen hundred men, and the garrifon confifted of eight hundred; but after the reduction of Oxford, Morgan was reinforced with two thoufand men, when he fent a fummons; before this reinforcement, the garrifon in a fally, had killed a Cornet of Morgan's regiment and taken his colours. This fummons required the Marquis to yield up the caftle, with all the ammunition and provifion, as the fole condition on which he might expect mercy; that this was the laft place held out in the whole kingdom, and Sir Thomas Fairfax had fpared his forces for its reduction, having completed his other work: he likewife enclofed a copy of a letter from the King, directing the furrender of all his garrifons, in order to fhew that he could have no hopes of relief. This letter was dated, June 28, 1646.

THE Marquis in anfwer, begged leave to doubt the authenticity of the letter, and Ragland not being mentioned, refufed to furrender, faying, he made choice, if it fo pleafed God, rather to dye nobly, than to live with infamy. Colonel Morgan then offered to permit him to fend an officer to Oxford to thofe Lords to whom his Majefty's letters were directed, but the Mar- quis, without taking notice of the offer, perfifted in the refufal. General Fairfax fhortly after arrived in perfon from Bath to haften the fiege, when he repeated the fummons, in anfwer to which the Marquis requefted leave to afk his Majefty's pleafure refpecting the garrifon, but as to the caftle, it being his own and only houfe, he prefumed the King would command nothing, nor could he perceive how either by law or confcience he could be forced out of it.

This request Fairfax by letter refused, saying it had not been allowed to the most considerable garrisons, farther than sending an account to his Majesty of the thing done upon the surrender, which he freely granted his Lordship, and as to the distinction of its being his house, had it not been converted into a garrison he should not have been troubled ; having sent this answer he considered his conscience discharged respecting the consequences of a farther refusal. The Earl then relinquished his request of sending to the King, but said, that having laid out twenty thousand pounds in consequence of his Majesty's promises, if he offended the King that would be lost without any benefit to the Parliament, but that if he might quietly receive his means of subsistance and live in security, he would peaceably quit the garrison, and that if the General knew how intimate he was with his grandfather in the time of Henry, Earl of Huntingdon, he would not refuse his request.

Diverse other letters passed between them, in which the Earl requested a cessation of arms, in order to treat, which Fairfax offered to grant, on August 14th, for the morrow, from nine in the morning till two in the afternoon, but the Earl sent him his proposals, which were deemed inadmissable by the General, who in return sent him word he might still have the conditions first offered, provided he returned his resolution by six in the evening.

In the mean time the approaches were carried on, being not above sixty yards distant, and two bomb batteries erected at different places, one of four, and the other of two twelve inch mortars. The General ordered another approach, in which the engineer, Captain Hooper, had made a considerable progress : when on 15th August, the Earl agreed to treat on the General's propositions, and by Monday 17th, the treaty was concluded as follows : The castle and garrison, with the ordinance, arms, ammunition, and provisions of war, to be delivered to Sir Thomas Fairfax without spoil, on Wednesday the 19th, by ten in the forenoon, the garrison to march out with colours flying, trumpets sounding, drums beating, matches lighted at both ends, and bullets in their mouths ; every soldier with twelve rounds of powder, with match and bullets in proportion, and bag and baggage, thence to march to any place within ten miles which the Governor should nominate, where the arms were to be delivered up and the men disbanded, under an engagement not to serve hereafter against the Parliament ; this was accordingly put in execution at the day assigned : in the castle were delivered up twenty pieces of ordnance, only three barrels of powder, there being a mill with which they could make three barrels per day. There was great store of corn and malt, wine and beer ; the few horses they had were almost starved for want of hay, so that they had like to have eaten one another, and were therefore tied with chains. There were also, great store of goods and rich furniture, which General Fairfax committed to the custody of Mr. Herbert, commissioner of the army, Mr. Roger Williams, and Major Taliday. There marched out of the castle, the Marquis of Worcester, who was then above four-score years of age, the Lord Charley, the Marquis's son, the Countess of Glamorgan, the Lady Jones, Sir Phillip Jones, Dr. Bailey, Commissary Gwilliam, four Colonels, eighty-two Captains, sixteen Lieutenants, six Cornets, four Ensigns, four Quarter Masters, fifty-two Esquires and gentlemen.

The following account of the present state of this castle is given by Mr. Gilpin, in his ingenious description of the picturesque beauties of the Wye.

Ragland Castle seems (as we saw it from the height) in a rich vale, but as we descended it took an elevated station, it is a large and very noble ruin, though more perfect than ruins of this kind commonly are, it contains two areas within the ditch, into each of which you enter by a very large and deep gateway. The buildings, which circumscribe the first area, consist of the kitchen and offices : it is amusing to hear the stories of ancient hospitality, " Here are the remains of an oven," said our conductor, " which was large enough to bake " a whole ox, and a fire range wide enough to roast him."

The grand hall, or banquetting room, a large and lofty apartment, forms the screen between the two areas, and is perfect except the roof. The music gallery may be distinctly traced, and the butteries which divide the hall from a parlour : near the hall is shewn a narrow chapel.

On viewing the comparative size of the halls and chapels in old castles, one can hardly at first avoid observing that the founders of these ancient structures supposed a much greater number of people would meet together to feast than to pray. And yet we may perhaps account for the thing, without calling in question the piety of our ancestors. The hall was meant to regale a whole county, while the chapel was intended only for the private use of the inhabitants of the castle. The whole area of the first inclosure is vaulted, and contains cellars, dungeons, and other subterraneous apartments. The buildings of the second area are confined merely to chambers.

Near the castle stands the citadel, a large octagonal tower, two or three sides of which are still remaining. This tower is incircled by a separate moat, and was formerly joined to the castle by a draw-bridge.

This view was drawn, anno 1775.

The Roman Tower at Caerleon, Monmouthshire.
Published 1st August 1789, by I. Boydell.

ROMAN TOWER AT CAERLEON, MONMOUTHSHIRE.

THE building whose ruins are here delineated stands at Caerleon in Monmouthshire, near the bridge laid over the river Usk; it is generally supposed of Roman construction, there having been a Roman station at this place, and the remains of an Amphitheatre; Baths, and other Roman works, being still discoverable, about and within the enceinte of its walls, which are said to have been near three miles in compass.

It seems difficult to assign the use for which this tower could have been built, its size for which the figures may serve as a scale, shew it could scarcely have been intended for defence, as from its smallness it could contain but very few men; perhaps it might be intended for a stair-case, or as the towers in Burgh castle near Yarmouth, the Gariononum of the Romans, for a buttress to prop and strengthen the adjacent wall.

This view was drawn anno 1778.

Uske Castle, Monmouthshire.

USK CASTLE, MONMOUTHSHIRE.

I HAVE not been able to gain the least information respecting the time when this castle was built, or who was the builder; which is the more extraordinary, as from the extent of its ruins, it seems to have been a building of some consequence. It is pleasantly seated on the river Usk, near its concourse with the Berthin. The present owner is the lord Mountstuart.

THIS view, which shews a square tower, part of the defence of the castle, was drawn A. D. 1785.

BILLOCKBY CHURCH, NORFOLK.
ad Delity a...

BILLOCKBY CHURCH, NORFOLK.

THIS church ftands near the eaftern extremity of the county of Norfolk, on the road leading from Yarmouth to Norwich. According to Blomfield it is mentioned in the Domefday Survey, when it was endowed with feven acres of land, then valued at but 7d. per annum.

IN the 10th of Henry III. Ralph de Bray paffed the advowfon of this church by fine to Nicholas de Holedis.

REGINALD de ECCLES who was poffeffed of confiderable property here, by his will dated 1380 and proved 1381, directed that his body fhould be buried on the north fide of the chancel of this church.

JOHN de ECCLES his fon, by his laft will and teftament, dated 1383 and proved 1384, bequeathed the reverfion of this manor to be fold, and all the produce exceeding one hundred pounds to be expended in the repairs of this church and chancel, mending the caufeways of Weybridge and Baftwick, and putting out poor girls as apprentices. It feems likely from the ftile of this building, that a thorough repair almoft equal to a re-edification took place at this time, as fcarce any part of it appears of the age afcribed to the original building.

In the 7th of Henry VII. the advowfon belonged to Thomas Snytterton and Robert Pylalie, who conveyed it to Thomas Godfalve, he in the 32d of the fame reign granted it to Henry Hobart.

ANNO 1552 Robert Mahew was prefented to this church, and Thomas Mahew in 1631. In 1740 Sir George England.

THE Church is dedicated to all Saints, is a rectory, the ancient valor is 6 marks and Peter-pence 5d. ob. The prefent valor is 2l. 18s. 9d. and is difcharged. Here, fays Blomfield, were the lights of St. Mary and St. Nicholas, probably he means tapers kept burning to the honor of thofe Holy Perfonages. In the chancel window were the arms of Harvey impaling Dengayn and Jenny.

THIS edifice exhibits a more picturefque appearance than can be conveyed by an engraving, the mixture of free-ftone, flint, and brick in its walls; the ancient thatch with which the chancel is moftly covered, enriched with grafs, mofs, and ftained of different hues, contrafted with new ftraw lately laid on, together afford a variety of tints, which cannot be expreffed by black and white.

The nave and tower of this church are in ruins, the chancel is patched up and ftill ufed for divine fervice.

This view was drawn anno 1776.

St. MARY's PRIORY, THETFORD, NORFOLK.

PLATE I.

OF this Monastery the following account is given by Tanner in the *Notitia Monastica :*

" IN this then famous Town was a society of religious persons in the church
" of St. Mary, as early as the reign of King Edward the Confessor, if not be-
" fore. Hither Arfastus, or Herfastus, bishop of the East Angles, removed
" his episcopal seat from North Elmham, A. D. 1075. But it continued here
" only nineteen or twenty years, and then was translated to Norwich. After
" which, that great nobleman, Roger Bigod, or Bigot, by the advice of bishop
" Herbert, and others, built a monastery here, about A. D. 1104; and shortly
" after brought Cluniac monks from Lewes in Suffex, and placed them in it,
" making it subordinate to the abby of Cluny, in France. But this House and
" Place being found inconvenient, the same generous nobleman began on the
" other side of the water, a little without the town, a most stately monastery
" and church, to the honor also of the blessed Virgin Mary ; but dying shortly
" after, Prior Stephen carried on the Work, and met with so much encou-

" ragement that he finished it in about seven years, and removed his convent
" into it on the feast of St. Martin, A. D. 1114. This priory was made de-
" nison 50 Edw. III. and 26 Henry VIII. was found to be endowed with
" three hundred and twelve pounds, fourteen shillings, and four pence, ob. 9
" per ann. as Dugdale; and four hundred and eighteen pounds, six shillings
" and three pence, as Speed; and was granted in exchange, 32 Henry VIII,
" to its patron, Thomas duke of Norfolk, who once intended to refound
" herein a college of secular priests."

THIS monastery was the burial-place of the Bigods, and after them, of the Mowbreys, created dukes of Norfolk, as also of the Howards, their successors.

HERE were seventeen monks. The names of the priors are thus recorded by Browne Willis, in his History of Abbies, taken, as he says, from Dr. Tanner's Collections.

STEPHEN occurs prior anno 1130. In the Monasticon, after him, I meet with

CONSTANTINE: and then

MARTIN, anno 1189, and 1197.

RICHARD was prior anno 1216, and 1236; as was

STEPHEN, anno 1257, 41 H. III. and

WILLIAM, anno 1261, 55 H. III. The next I find is

VINCENT, who occurs anno 1286, and 1297. His successor, I guess, was

THO. LE BIGOD, confirmed prior, 31 Dec. 1304, after him I met with

JAMES, anno 1335, on whose deposition on account of his age, anno 1355,

JEFFRY DE ROCHERIO was placed in his stead. He presided anno 1369, as did

JOHN DE FORDHAM, anno 1372, who was, as I suppose, the same person that was made anno 1388, bishop of Ely. His successor was one

JOHN, whose surname I do not meet with. He occurs anno 1390, and also 1395, as does one

JOHN IXWORTH, in 1428. Whether he be the same with the last I cannot determine. The next in my catalogue is

NICHOLS anno 1431. On whose death or cession the priory became vacant, anno 1438. After him I met with one

JOHN, anno 1441. Query if he be the same with

JOHN VEYSEY, who governer'd anno 1461, and 1479. His successor seems to have been

ROBERT, who occurs anno 1485 and 1497, as does one

ROGER, anno 1503, and

WILLIAM, anno 1519, and again at the dissolution, anno 1540, at which time he, with thirteen canons or monks, surrendered this house.

This View was drawn anno 1777.

THE GATE OF ST. MARY'S ABBEY THETFORD, NORFOLK.

This Gate stands on the north-east side of the Abbey. It is built mostly with pebble and flint, coigned with square stones and had over it two stories of apartments; adjoining to it are some rooms and stables, used as such by the monks. From the stile of the architecture this gate does not seem older than the reign of Richard the Third or Henry the Seventh.

The view here given shews its inner side, and was drawn anno 1777.

THE PRIORY OF THE OLD HOUSE, THETFORD, NORFOLK.

A COUNCIL held by Lanfranc, Archbishop of Canterbury, having determined that all Bishop's sees which were settled in villages, should be removed to the most eminent cities in their dioceses; in consequence of this regulation the see of Norfolk was removed to Thetford, anno 1075, as being a more populous and wealthy place than Elmham, where it had before been established.

THE mother church of this place (says Blomfield) was dedicated to St. Mary, and stood where the free-school and master of the hospitals house now stands, this, in all probability belonged to the Bishop of that province (who it is thought had a house near it) till Stigand retained it in his hands with other revenues of the Bishopric after he had left the see; but on his disgrace, the King gave it with the four churches appendant and all that belonged to them, to Bishop Arfast and his heirs, in fee and inheritance. Arfast here placed his episcopal chair, and afterwards gave the inheritance of it to Richard his eldest son, and the four other churches to his other sons and their heirs.

THIS Arfast assisted by Roger Bigod rebuilt the church, dedicating it to St. Mary, the Holy Trinity and all Saints, and joined his palace or mansion-house to the north side of it towards the west end, of which there is so much now standing, which serves for the wall to a garden facing the Canons, that we can plainly distinguish its breadth. It consisted of a nave, two Isles, a north and south transept (the arch of which now divides the school and master's appartments) and a chancel or choir, the east end of which reached the street within about twelve yards, as its foundation discovers, so that it was a noble church fit for the cathedral of such a see.

The Bishops see being translated to Norwich, Robert Bigod, continues Blomfield, purchased the cathedral or church of St. Mary, of Richard son of Bishop Arfast, and by the advice and consent of Henry I, and at the request of Bishop Herbert, placed therein Cluniac Monks, having erected a timber building for their reception.

He soon after begun a cloister of stone, the area of which is now visible between the church and river, the walls of the refectory, which were on the north side of the court, not far from it, are now in a great measure standing. The cloister was near three years building, during which time this situation being found too small and inconvenient, their founder was prevailed upon to remove them to the Norfolk side of the river; he accordingly built the monastery now called the Abbey, and in the year 1107, or according to others 1114, the whole convent removed thither except two or three monks, who for a while kept it as a cell to their new house, but afterwards totally forsook it, and it was exchanged by them for lands more convenient to their new situation, and so became joined to the dominion or lordship. The buildings continued desolate and in ruins till the time of King Edward III, when Sir Edward Gonvile, parson of Terrington in Norfolk, steward to Henry Earl of Lancaster, persuaded that nobleman to repair the church and buildings, and to introduce there friars, preachers of the order of St. Dominic. This being accomplished about the year 1327, it became a priory of friars preachers, and the priors were always nominated by the Lords of the dominion of Thetford, to which the Earl annexed the patronage, and confirmed by the superior of their order.

In 1347, the Earl of Lancaster enlarged their premises with the site of the Domus Dei, an hospital which stood between their cloister and the High-street, on which they cleared away all the buildings except the hospital-house, wherein they kept a brother or two, who daily begged what he could of the passengers for the benefit of the house, this sometimes has occasioned the priory to be confounded with the Domus Dei.

This priory was surrendered to King Henry VIII. the prior and five bretheren only signing the instrument: Blomfield supposes there might have been a great number in the cloister who would not join in it; Willis says, the church of the Dominicans at Thetford was thirty-six paces long. The site was granted to Sir Richard Fulmerston, by the name of the Site of the Friars Preachers, formerly called the Hospital-House of God in Thetford, who was to hold it in capite of the Queen, by the service of the 20th part of a fee, and 5d. ob. per ann. rent. He left it to his heiress, and it descended to Sir Edward Clere, who sold it with the canons farm, to which it now belongs, to Robert Causfield and others, in trust for the Earl of Arundel, and thus came to the noble family of the Howards, to whom it now belongs.

In this view is also shewn the back of the school and hospital, built in pursuance of the will of Sir Richard Fulmerston, dated anno 1566, on the ruins of the old cathedral; there had been a school in this town very early, as is evident from the many collations to it by the Bishop in whose donation it was, one as early as 1328, but from 1496 no more occur, so that it seems probable the school ceased till Sir Richard Fulmerstons time, who erected one and paid the master during his life, and made the above provision by his will.——The hospital part is for the habitation of four poor persons, two men and two women. This house is said to have been the birth-place and residence of that well known antiquary, Mr. Thomas Martin.

This view was drawn anno 1777.

OUR LADY's MOUNT LYNN, NORFOLK.

THIS very fingular edifice ftands upon a circular mount on the eaftern fide of the town of Lynn in Norfolk, now making part of the mound of the modern fortifications thrown up round that place; it is included within a Baftion.

THE lower octagonal part is built with brick faced with ftone, the upper part, in the form of a crofs is of polifhed ftone, the top part of brick. It confifts of three ftories of appartments, the loweft is arched and has within it a ciftern which feems not to have been an original part of the building, but to have been added fince, for the purpofe, perhaps of a refervoir for water during the time when the town was befieged in the civil wars; the fecond ftory is likewife arched, a flight of ftone ftairs, now in ruins, ran round thefe appartments towards the internal circumference of the octagonal part, and led up to the upper ftone building which certainly was a chapel : common information fays, the uppermoft multangular brick part has been chimneys, but as no leading flues to the chimneys are to be feen, it is rather probable it was the fhaft of a crofs elevated above the whole. Thus much as to the prefent ftate of this building, as to its antiquity the reader will be pleafed to receive his information on that point from Parkens's continuation of Blomfield's Hiftory of Norfolk, where it is thus confufedly defcribed :

" Our Lady on the Mount or Wall and Gild.

" This chapel was defaced before the 3d of Elizabeth, as appears from an " inquisition then taken.

" In Doctor Browns travels, fol. edit. p. 43, is a cut of a Greek monastery, " very much in the form of this chapel, of four stories in height, one less than " the other, the three lowest square, the uppermost story an octagon, like a " steeple.

" These are the brethren and sisters of the Guild, Tigulat founded to the " honour and purification of the blessed Virgin Mary anno 3d Edward III.

" Thomas de Langham and Christian his wife.

" Charles de Secheford and Alice his wife.

" Robert de Derby and Margery his wife, William son of the said Ro- " bert, &c.

" Robert seems to be alderman of the Guild.

" These are the four morwespeche of the said Guild. The first morwespeche " is on the Sunday (le Demeynge prochein) after the Purification of the Blessed " Virgin ; the second on the day of the Annunciation of our Lady, the third " on the day of the Assumption of our Lady, the fourth on the day of the " Conception of our Lady.

" It is ordained that if any of the brethren be summoned on any of the " four morwespeches, and are in the said town and make default, they shall " pay one penny to the honour of our Lady.

" There is a chimney now standing in it, erected during the plague, where it " was made a post-house.

" In 1509 It was in use, when in the compotus of the prior of St. Margaret " we find."

De pixidib. omnium sanctor. in eccles, St. Margaret et Capellis St. Nicholai et St. Jacobi una cum Capella Beatæ Mariæ ad Pontem. 6s. 4d.

De Capella beatæ Mariæ de Monte. 16s. 10d. which shews how great the Madona here was held.

" This building is likewise mentioned by Macharel in his history of Lynn, " who says, at a little distance from the town stands another ruinous fabrick, " called the Lady's Mount, in which (no doubt) by some remains of architecture, " it appears there has been a chapel dedicated to the blessed Virgin. This reli- " gious place, say the ancient inhabitants, was a receptacle for the pilgrims, who " took this in the way to say their orisons at as they travelled along towards that " sometime famous and celebrated priory or convent of our Lady of Walsing- " ham, a village so much renowned all over England for pilgrimage to the Virgin " Mary, that he who had not in that age visited and presented it with offerings " was accounted irreligious."

This view was drawn anno 1776.

Holdenby House, Northamptonshire.

HOLDENBY HOUSE, NORTHAMPTONSHIRE.

HOLDENBY HOUSE stands on a pleasant eminence, about six miles South-west of Northampton; it was built by Sir Christopher Hatton, Privy Counsellor to Queen Elizabeth, Lord High Chancellor of England, and Knight of the Garter. He is said to have called it Holdenby House in honour of his great grandmother, heiress of the ancient family of the Holdenbys. The gate here represented, was built in the year 1583, as is evident from that date carved over the arch. It is most likely that the rest of the buildings were erected about the same time. The stile is neither that called Gothic nor Grecian, but a mixture of both, a manner of building much in fashion about the latter end of the reign of Queen Elizabeth, and that of her successor King James. Sir Christopher Hatton dying unmarried, left this house to Sir William Newport, Knight, his sister's son, who, in default of male issue, gave it to Sir Christopher Hatton, his godson, and nearest kinsman: afterwards it became a palace to King Charles I. and when he was delivered to the Parliament, he was kept here three months, and hence was seized and carried to the army by Cornet Joyce. It afterwards belonged to the victorious Duke of Marlborough, and was part of the jointure of the Marchioness of Blandford, relict of his grandson. At present it is let to a farmer who resides here, and has pulled down great part of the buildings, and converted the rest to barns and stables. The entrance into the yard on the North side, was through a gate, similar to that here delineated; it was standing in 1761, when this view was taken: the house stood a small distance to the West; its roof and ornamented chimnies are seen in the drawing, over the wall.

Alnemouth Church Northumberland.
Published According to J. Harper

ALNEMOUTH CHURCH, NORTHUMBERLAND.

ALNEMOUTH Church ſtands within the pariſh of Workworth, about two miles and a half diſtant from that town. It is ſituated on a mount or hill near the ſouth bank of the river Alne, which divides it from the Village of Alnemouth, whence it derives its name. The ſea which waſhes the eaſt ſide of this hill has frequently, by encroaching on the ſoil, thrown up bones of an enormous ſize, theſe being found ſo near a church-yard, has made the credulous vulgar ſuppoſe they were the bones of Giants, ſlain in an invaſion and buried here. When moſt probably they were only the bones of horſes killed near the ſpot in ſome of the many ſkirmiſhes and battles that ſo long and ſo often diſturbed this coaſt.

NEITHER the Founder of this church nor the time of its erection are known. As parochial churches were moſtly built either by the Lord of the Manor or private contributions of pious perſons, their origin is in general difficult to aſcertain, ſcarce any records or memorandums of them being preſerved in any publick muni-ments, except that ſometimes the date of their conſecration is entered in the Biſhop's Regiſter.

ALNEMOUTH CHURCH, NORTHUMBERLAND.

THE same obfcurity occurs refpecting this church as to the time of its being thus ruined; which perhaps was not effected by any violent means, but fimply by the gradual fappings of time and want of proper repairs. Divine fervice has not been performed in it for many years, owing to its ruinous ftate, the church-yard is however ftill ufed for burials. The inhabitants of the Village go to the neighbouring church of Lifbury.

THE ftile of this building pronounces it of great antiquity, and from its ruins it may be feen it was in the form of a crofs.

This view was drawn anno 1775.

BLINKENSOP CASTLE NORTHUMBERLAND.

BLENKENSOP CASTLE, NORTHUMBERLAND.

THIS was one of the castles or towers, built for the defence of the borders; it stands at the western extremity of the county near Cumberland, and on the southermost bank of a rivulet called Tippal, a small distance from the Roman Wall.

BLENKENSOP was anciently part of the barony of Nicholas de Bolteby, and according to a court roll for Northumberland, transcribed by Leland in his Collectanea, was held by Radulphus de Blenkensop; but what time is not mentioned. Camden, in the following passage in his Britannia, both gives some information as to that point, and also shews that this castle was not the place of residence of the Blenkensops, as has by some been supposed; his words are,

" THEN saw we Blenkensop, which gave name to a generous family, as also " their habitation in a right pleasant country southward, which was the baronie " of Sir Nicholas of Bolteby, a Baron of renowne in the time of Edward I."

IN all likelihood the castle was entire and garrisoned in the 6th of Edward VI. when, according to Bishop Littleton's Border History, the following regulations for guarding this district were made, as is it not probable a fortress or castle would be suffered to fall to decay on a post where so strict a watch was thought necessary.

" The order of the watches upon the middle marches made by the Lord Wharton, " Lord Deputy General of all the three marches, under my Lord of Northum- " berland's Grace, Lord Warden General of all the said Marches, in the month of " October, in the sixth year of the reign of our Sovereign Lord King Edward VI." among which were these articles above alluded to.

FROM Blenkensop Castle to Therlway Castle to be watched nightly with two men of the inhabitants, dwelling between the said two castles.

FROM Blenkensop Castle to the Redpethe, to be watched nightly with two men of the inhabitants, dwelling within the same.

THE day watch of the lordfhip of Blenkynfop to be kept with one man every day at Dongham-gate with the inhabitants of the faid lordfhip. Setters and fearchers of the fame watch, John Noble and Arche Story; overfeers of the fame, Albany Fetherftonhalfs and Harry Walles.

MR. Wallis in his Hiftory of Northumberland gives the following account and defcription of this caftle, in which among others he fays, this caftle was the feat of the Blenkenfopps.

" BLENKENSOPP CASTLE, the feat of the antient family of the Blenkenfopps, " of Ralph de Blenkenfopp, 1 K. Edward I. of Thomas de Blenkenfopp, 39th 42. " K. Edward III. and of William Blenkenfopp, 10th Q. Elizabeth; who held " it of the honour of Langley paying annually for all fervices 6s. 8d. one half at " Martinmas and the other at Whitfontide. In the fouth-weft end of Haltwefel " Church is the ftone effigie of one of the family, recumbent, in armour, his " legs acrofs and hands elevated; the habit; the habit and attitude of a Knight " Templer, or fuch as made the Crufade; on which, and for the ranfom of our " Cœur de Lion, K. Richard I. fo much money was fwept out of the kingdom, " that not one genuine coin of his is faid to be met with in the cabinets of the " curious; his ranfom alone cofting one hundred thoufand pounds in filver, equal " to three hundred thoufand pounds of our prefent money: Gawen Blenkenfopp, " D. D. is on record for being a benefactor to that renouned feminary of learn- " ing, Pembroke Hall, in Cambridge, of which he was fellow.

" THE Caftle of Blenkenfopp is about a mile to the fouth-eaft of Thirlwall " Caftle, on the fouther banks of the Tippal; upon an eminence, and overlooked " by another; the weft and north-weft fide of it protected by a very high cefpi- " titious wall, and a deep fofs; a vault going through it north and fouth, thirty- " three feet in length, and in breadth eighteen feet and a half; two lefler ones " on the north fide. The facing of the weftern wall has been down beyond " the memory of any perfon now living in the neighbourhood. It has been a " very ftrong building; it is now in the poffeffion of John Blenkenfopp Coulfon, " of Jeffmont, Efq." Mr. Hutchenfon who vifited this caftle fince Mr. Wallis, differs with him in fome particulars, and mentions others not taken notice of by him; as his account of it is fhort, the whole is here tranfcribed.

" BLENKENSOP Caftle is fituate on the fouthern banks of the brook Tippal, " by the remains it appears this caftle has confifted of a fquare tower, built on " an artificial mount furrounded by an outward wall, at the diftance only of " four paces, of equal height with interior building, defended towards the north " by a very deep ditch and outward mound. The out wall towards the weft " has been removed of late years and lays the tower open on that fide; three " vaults fupport the building, one of which is eighteen feet wide. This caftle " is the property of J. Blenkenfop Coulfon, Efq; has been in the family of the " Blenkenfops for many centuries, and held of the manor of Langley."

This view was drawn anno 1774.

PAROCHIAL CHURCH OF BOTHALL, IN NORTHUMBERLAND.

THE Parochial Church of Bothall, in Northumberland, stands a small distance east of the castle, in a most pleasant and retired situation. It is a very neat building, though of no very great antiquity, but seems a cathedral in miniature. The ancient monument of the Lord Ogle and his lady, with the geneological table of that family, shewn in this church, have been mentioned in the second plate of the castle.

THE view from which this plate was engraved was drawn anno 1773.

S.t Cuthbert Hermitage.

St. CUTHBERT's ORATORY ON COCQUET ISLAND, NORTHUMBERLAND.

This View shews the remains of the Hermitage or Oratory, in which St. Cuthbert is said to have resided before he was made bishop of Lindisfarne, and in which he ended his days, after retiring from that office.

It stands in one of the Farn islands, situated in the German ocean, about a mile and a half from the shore, called also Coquet and House Island, the first from its vicinity to the mouth of the river Coquet, and the latter from the buildings here represented. This island contains about six acres of rich pasture land, and is therefore often rented for feeding sheep, as well as for the convenience of gathering sea-weed. It has but one spring, the water of which is brackish; it formerly belonged to Mr. Greaves, who sold it to the present proprietor his Grace the Duke of Northumberland.

The building with the church-like windows is said to be the Oratory, probably much altered, if not rebuilt since the death of St. Cuthbert, especially as tradition says, it was converted into a Monastery for eleven monks; indeed the traces of ruined walks shew there were diverse erections adjoining to or near it; the other building here shewn, might be some office belonging to the Monastery.

The Oratory is now fitted up for a dwelling-house, and has been occasionally inhabited by persons tending sheep pastured here, or employed to collect sea-weed; the other building is used for a light-house, the irons seen on its top, being contrivances for holding the fire.

The stone coffin shewn in the drawing, is said to be that in which St. Cuthbert was originally buried, it now lies within the walls of the light-house, nearly in that part opposite the figures.

This view was drawn anno 1778.

HISTORY PRESERVING THE MONUMENTS OF ANTIQUITY.

The side View of Lindisfarne Holy Island Monastery Northumberland

of hufbandry, made many breaches and paffages therein, by which they could eafily pafs to and fro. From thefe openings, which in the Englifh language are pronounced Thirlit-wall, it took its prefent name, fignifying in Latin the pierced wall. Mr. Wallis fays the place where the Scots made this breach, ftill retains the name of the Gap. Probably this caftle with the neighbouring fortifications of turf, were made to prevent a like infult.

THIRLWALL caftle, was anno 1333, 7 Edward III. the property of John de Thirlwall. And in the 10th of Elizabeth belonged to Robert de Thirlwall. The laft proprietor of that family was Elenora, married anno 1738, to Mathew Swinburne, Efq; by whom the caftle and its demefnes were fold to the Earl of Carlifle.

THIS view which was drawn anno 1774, fhews the fouth afpect of the caftle.

N.E. View of Tynemouth Priory, Northumberland.

THE

Hermit of Warkworth,

A NORTHUMBERLAND BALLAD.

IN THREE FITS OR CANTOS.

A NEW EDITION WITH ADDITIONS.

LONDON,

PRINTED FOR T. EVANS IN THE STRAND.

M. DCC. LXXXII.

This Poem is Written by

Dr: Percy —

who Published the

Reliques of Ancient Poetry

The Views of this Hermitage
are in the Prior part of Grose's
Antiquities............ Vol: 3. P.ª 71.
& in the Antiquities of Great Brittain

also in Buck's Views & this
is only the Castle —
of
Warkworth —

TO HER GRACE

ELIZABETH

DUCHESS AND

COUNTESS OF NORTHUMBERLAND,

IN HER OWN RIGHT

BARONESS PERCY,

&c. &c. &c.

DOWN in a northern vale wild flowrets grew,
   And lent new sweetness to the summer gale;
The Muse there found them all remote from view,
Obscur'd with weeds, and scatter'd o'er the dale.

   O Lady, may so slight a gift prevail,
And at your gracious hands acceptance find?
Say, may an ancient legendary tale
Amuse, delight, or move the polish'd mind?

   Surely the cares and woes of human kind,
Tho' simply told, will gain each gentle ear:
But all for you the Muse her lay design'd,
And bade your noble Ancestors appear:

   She seeks no other praise, if you commend,
Her great protectress, patroness, and friend.

M. DCC. LXX.

ADVERTISEMENT.

WARKWORTH CASTLE in Northumberland stands very boldly on a neck of land near the sea-shore, almost surrounded by the river Coquet, (called by our old Latin Historians, COQUEDA) which runs with a clear rapid stream, but when swoln with rains becomes violent and dangerous.

About a mile from the Castle, in a deep romantic valley, are the remains of a HERMITAGE; of which the Chapel is still intire. This is hollowed with great elegance in a cliff near the river; as are also two adjoining apartments, which probably served for the Sacristy and Vestry, or were appropriated to some other sacred uses: for the former of these, which runs parallel with the Chapel, appears to have had an Altar in it, at which Mass was occasionally celebrated, as well as in the Chapel itself.

Each of these apartments is extremely small; for that which was the principal Chapel does not in length exceed eighteen feet; nor is more than seven feet and a half in breadth and height: it is however very beautifully designed and executed in the solid rock; and has all the decorations of a compleat Gothic Church or Cathedral in miniature.

But what principally distinguishes the Chapel, is a small Tomb or Monument, on the south side of the altar: on the top of which, lies a Female Figure extended in the manner that effigies are usually exhibited praying on ancient tombs. This figure, which is very delicately designed, some have ignorantly called an image of the Virgin Mary; though it has not the least resemblance to the manner in which she is represented in the Romish Churches; who is usually erect, as the object of adoration, and never in a prostrate or recumbent posture. Indeed the real image of the Blessed Virgin probably stood in a small nich, still visible behind the altar: whereas the figure of a Bull's Head, which is rudely carved at this Lady's feet, the usual place for the Crest in old monuments, plainly proves her to have been a very different personage.

About

ADVERTISEMENT.

About this tomb are feveral other Figures; which, as well as the principal one above-mentioned, are cut in the natural rock, in the fame manner as the little Chapel itfelf, with all its Ornaments, and the two adjoining Apartments. What flight traditions are feattered through the country concerning the origin and foundation of this Hermitage, Tomb, &c are delivered to the Reader in the following rhimes.

It is univerfally believed, that the Founder was one of the BERTRAM family, which had once confiderable poffeffions in Northumberland, and were anciently Lords of Bothal Caftle, fituate about ten miles from Warkworth. He has been thought to be the fame BERTRAM that endowed BRINKBURN Priory, and built BRINKSHAUGH Chapel: which both ftand in the fame winding valley, higher up the river.

But BRINKBURN Priory was founded in the reign of K. Henry I.* whereas the form of the Gothic Windows in this Chapel, efpecially of thofe near the altar, are found rather to refemble the ftyle of architecture that prevailed about the reign of K. Edward III. And indeed that the fculpture in this Chapel cannot be much older, appears from the Creft which is placed at the Lady's feet on the tomb; for Camden † informs us, that armorial Crefts did not become hereditary till about the reign of K. Edward II.

Thefe appearances ftill extant, ftrongly confirm the account given in the following poem, and plainly prove that the HERMIT of WARKWORTH was not the fame perfon that founded BRINKBURN Priory in the twelfth century, but rather one of the BERTRAM family, who lived at a later period.

* Tanner's Notitia Monaft. † See his Remains.

⁎⁎⁎ FIT was the word used by the old Minstrels to signify a PART or DIVISION of their Historical Songs, and was peculiarly appropriated to this kind of compositions. See Reliques of Ancient Eng. Poetry, Vol. II. p. 166 and 397. 2d Ed.

...ib. 166 & 400. 3d Ed.

HERMIT of WARKWORTH.

A

NORTHUMBERLAND BALLAD.

FIT the FIRST.

DARK was the night, and wild the ſtorm,
  And loud the torrent's roar;
And loud the ſea was heard to daſh
  Againſt the diſtant ſhore.

Muſing on man's weak hapleſs ſtate,
  The lonely Hermit lay;
When, lo! he heard a female voice
  Lament in ſore diſmay.

With hofpitable hafte he rofe,
   And wak'd his fleeping fire;
And fnatching up a lighted brand,
   Forth hied the reverend fire.

All fad beneath a neighbouring tree
   A beauteous maid he found,
Who beat her breaft, and with her tears
   Bedew'd the mofly ground.

O! weep not, lady, weep not fo;
   Nor let vain fears alarm;
My little cell fhall fhelter thee,
   And keep thee fafe from harm.

It is not for myfelf I weep,
   Nor for myfelf I fear;
But for my dear and only friend,
   Who lately left me here:

And while fome fheltering bower he fought
   Within this lonely wood,
Ah! fore I fear his wandering feet
   Have flipt in yonder flood.

                                             O!

O! truſt in heaven, the Hermit ſaid,
  And to my cell repair;
Doubt not but I ſhall find thy friend,
  And caſe thee of thy care.

Then climbing up his rocky ſtairs,
  He ſcales the cliff ſo high;
And calls aloud, and waves his light
  To guide the ſtranger's eye.

Among the thickets long he winds
  With careful ſteps and ſlow:
At length a voice return'd his call,
  Quick anſwering from below:

O! tell me, father, tell me true,
  If you have chanc'd to ſee
A gentle maid, I lately left
  Beneath ſome neighbouring tree:

But either I have loſt the place,
  Or ſhe hath gone aſtray:
And much I fear this fatal ſtream
  Hath ſnatch'd her hence away.

Peric.

Praife heaven, my fon, the Hermit faid ;
    The lady's fafe and well :
And foon he join'd the wandering youth,
    And brought him to his cell.

Then well was feen, thefe gentle friends
    They lov'd each other dear :
The youth he prefs'd her to his heart ;
    The maid let fall a tear.

Ah ! feldom had their hoft, I ween,
    Beheld fo fweet a pair :
The youth was tall, with manly bloom ;
    She flender, foft, and fair.

The youth was clad in foreft green,
    With bugle-horn fo bright :
She in a filken robe and fcarf
    Snatch'd up in hafty flight.

Sit down, my children, fays the Sage ;
    Sweet reft your limbs require :
Then heaps frefh fewel on the hearth,
    And mends his little fire.

                      Partake,

Partake, he faid, my fimple ftore,
    Dried fruits, and milk, and curds;
And fpreading all upon the board,
    Invites with kindly words.

Thanks, father, for thy bounteous fare;
    The youthful couple fay:
Then freely ate, and made good chear,
    And talk'd their cares away.

Now fay, my children, (for perchance
    My councel may avail)
What ftrange adventure brought you here
    Within this lonely dale?

Firft tell me, father, faid the youth,
    (Nor blame mine eager tongue)
What town is here? What lands are thefe?
    And to what lord belong?

Alas! my fon, the Hermit faid,
    Why do I live to fay,
The rightful lord of thefe domains
    Is banifh'd far away?

                    C   Ten

Ten winters now have shed their snows
  On this my lowly hall,
Since valiant HOTSPUR (so the North
  Our youthful lord did call)

Against Fourth HENRY BOLINGBROKE
  Led up his northern powers,
And stoutly fighting lost his life
  Near proud Salopia's towers.

One son he left, a lovely boy,
  His country's hope and heir ;
And, oh! to save him from his foes
  It was his grandsire's care.

In Scotland safe he plac'd the child
  Beyond the reach of strife,
Nor long before the brave old Earl
  At Bramham lost his life.

And now the PERCY name, so long
  Our northern pride and boast,
Lies hid, alas ! beneath a cloud ;
  Their honors rest and lost.

                              No

No chieftain of that noble houfe
   Now leads our youth to arms;
The bordering Scots difpoil our fields,
   And ravage all our farms.

Their halls and caftles, once fo fair,
   Now moulder in decay;
Proud ftrangers now ufurp their lands,
   And bear their wealth away.

Nor far from hence, where yon full ftream
   Runs winding down the lea,
Fair WARKWORTH lifts her lofty towers,
   And overlooks the fea.

Thofe towers, alas! now ftand forlorn,
   With noifome weeds o'erfpread,
Where feafted lords, and courtly dames,
   And where the poor were fed.

Meantime far off, mid Scottifh hills,
   The PERCY lives unknown:
On ftrangers' bounty he depends,
   And may not claim his own.

                        O might

O might I with thefe aged eyes
   But live to fee him here,
Then fhould my foul depart in blifs!
   He faid, and dropt a tear.

And is the PERCY ftill fo lov'd
   Of all his friends and thee?
Then blefs me, father, faid the youth,
   For I thy gueft am HE.

Silent he gaz'd, then turn'd afide
   To wipe the tears he fhed;
And lifting up his hands and eyes,
   Pour'd bleffings on his head.

Welcome, our dear and much-lov'd lord,
   Thy country's hope and care:
But who may this young lady be,
   That is fo wonderous fair?

Now, father, liften to my tale,
   And thou fhalt know the truth:
And let thy fage advice direct
   My unexperienc'd youth.

In

In Scotland I've been nobly bred
  Beneath the Regent's* hand,
In feats of arms, and every lore,
  To fit me for command.

With fond impatience long I burn'd
  My native land to fee :
At length I won my guardian friend,
  To yield that boon to me.

Then up and down in hunter's garb
  I wandered as in chace,
Till in the noble NEVILLE's† house
  I gain'd a hunter's place.

Sometime with him I liv'd unknown,
  Till I'd the hap so rare,
To please this young and gentle dame,
  That baron's daughter fair.

D

Now,

---

* ROBERT STUART, duke of Albany. See the continuator of FORDUN's Scoti-Chronicon, cap. 18, cap. 23, &c.

† RALPH NEVILLE, first Earl of Westmorland, who chiefly resided at his two Castles of BRANCEPETH, and RABY, both in the bishoprick of Durham.

Now, Percy, faid the blufhing maid,
 The truth I muft reveal;
Souls great and generous, like to thine,
 Their noble deeds conceal.

It happened on a fummer's day,
 Led by the fragrant breeze,
I wandered forth to take the air
 Among the green-wood trees.

Sudden a band of rugged Scots,
 That near in ambufh lay,
Mofs-troopers from the border-fide,
 There feiz'd me for their prey.

My fhrieks had all been fpent in vain,
 But heaven, that faw my grief,
Brought this brave youth within my call,
 Who flew to my relief.

With nothing but his hunting fpear,
 And dagger in his hand,
He fprung like light'ning on my foes,
 And caus'd them foon to ftand.

He

He fought, till more affiftance came;
   The Scots were overthrown;
Thus freed me, captive, from their bands,
   To make me more his own.

O happy day! the youth replied:
   Bleft were the wounds I bare!
From that fond hour fhe deign'd to fmile,
   And liften to my prayer.

And when fhe knew my name and birth,
   She vowed to be my bride;
But oh! we fear'd, (alas, the while!)
   Her princely mother's pride.

Sifter of haughty BOLINGBROKE, *
   Our houfe's ancient foe,
To me I thought a banifh'd wight
   Could ne'er fuch favour fhow.

Defpairing then to gain confent;
   At length to fly with me
I won this lovely timorous maid;
   To Scotland bound are we.

                       This

* JOAN, countefs of Weftmoreland, mother of the young lady, was daughter of JOHN of GAUNT, and half-fifter of king HENRY IV.

This evening, as the night drew on,
  Fearing we were pursu'd,
We turn'd adown the right-hand path,
  And gain'd this lonely wood:

Then lighting from our weary steeds
  To shun the pelting shower,
We met thy kind conducting hand,
  And reach'd this friendly bower.

Now rest ye both, the Hermit said;
  Awhile your cares forego:
Nor, lady, scorn my humble bed;
  —— We'll pass the night below. *

* Adjoining to the cliff, which contains the Chapel of the Hermitage, are the remains of a small building, in which the Hermit dwelt. This consisted of one lower Apartment, with a little Bed-chamber over it, and is now in ruins: whereas the Chapel, cut in the solid rock, is still very intire and perfect.

THE END OF THE FIRST PART

THE

HERMIT of WARKWORTH.

A

NORTHUMBERLAND BALLAD.

FIT THE SECOND.

LOVELY smil'd the blushing morn,
　　And every storm was fled:
But lovelier far, with sweeter smile,
　　Fair ELEANOR left her bed.

She found her HENRY all alone,
　　And cheer'd him with her sight;
The youth consulting with his friend
　　Had watch'd the livelong night.

What sweet surprize o'erpower'd her breast!
　　Her cheek what blushes dyed!
When fondly he besought her there
　　To yield to be his bride.

E　　　　　　　Within

Within this lonely hermitage
　　There is a chapel meet:
Then grant, dear maid, my fond requeſt,
　　And make my blifs compleat.

O HENRY! when thou deign'ſt to fue,
　　Can I thy fuit withſtand?
When thou, lov'd youth, haſt won my heart,
　　Can I refufe my hand?

For thee I left a father's fmiles,
　　And mother's tender care;
And whether weal or woe betide,
　　Thy lot I mean to ſhare.

And wilt thou then, O generous maid!
　　Such matchlefs favour ſhow,
To ſhare with me a banifh'd wight
　　My peril, pain, or woe?

Now heaven, I truſt, hath joys in ſtore
　　To crown thy conſtant breaſt;
For, know, fond hope aſſures my heart
　　That we ſhall foon be bleſt.

　　　　　　　　　　　　　　　　Not

Not far from hence ftands COQUET Ifle,*
  Surrounded by the fea;
There dwells a holy friar, well-known
  To all thy friends and thee:

'Tis father Bernard, fo rever'd
  For every worthy deed;
To RABY caftle he fhall go,
  And for us kindly plead.

To fetch this good and holy man
  Our reverend hoft is gone;
And foon, I truft, his pious hands
  Will join us both in one.

Thus they in fweet and tender talk
  The lingering hours beguile:
At length they fee the hoary fage
  Come from the neighbouring ifle.

With pious joy and wonder mix'd
  He greets the noble pair,
And glad confents to join their hands
  With many a fervent prayer.

                                      Then

---

* In the little Ifland of COQUET, near Warkworth, are ftill feen the ruins
of a Cell, which belonged to the Benedictine monks of Tinemouth-Abbey.

Then ſtraight to R a b y's diſtant walls
 He kindly wends his way ;
Mean-time in love and dalliance ſweet
 They ſpend the livelong day.

And now attended by their hoſt,
 The Hermitage they view'd,
Deep-hewn within a craggy cliff,
 And over-hung with wood.

And near a flight of ſhapely Steps,
 All cut with niceſt ſkill,
And piercing thro' a ſtony Arch,
 Ran winding up the hill.

There deck'd with many a flower and herb
 His little Garden ſtands ;
With fruitful trees in ſhady rows,
 All planted by his hands.

Then, ſcoop'd within the ſolid rock,
 Three ſacred Vaults he ſhows ;
The chief a Chapel, neatly arch'd,
 On branching Columns roſe.

Each

Each proper ornament was there,
   That fhould a chapel grace;
The Latice for confeffion fram'd,
   And Holy-water Vafe.

O'er either door a facred Text
   Invites to godly fear;
And in a little Scutcheon hung
   The crofs, and crown, and fpear.

Up to the Altar's ample breadth
   Two eafy fteps afcend;
And near a glimmering folemn light
   Two well-wrought Windows lend.

Befide the altar rofe a Tomb
   All in the living ftone;
On which a young and beauteous Maid
   In goodly fculpture fhone.

A kneeling Angel fairly carv'd
   Lean'd hovering o'er her breaft;
A weeping warrior at her feet;
   And near to thefe her Creft.*

F

The

* This is a Bull's Head, the creft of the WIDDRINGTON family. All the Figures,
&c. here defcribed are ftill vifible, only fomewhat effaced with length of time.

The cliff, the vault, but chief the tomb,
 Attract the wondering pair:
Eager they afk, What haplefs dame
 Lies fculptur'd here fo fair?

The Hermit figh'd, the Hermit wept,
 For forrow fcarce could fpeak:
At length he wip'd the trickling tears
 That all bedew'd his cheek:

Alas! my children, human life
 Is but a vale of woe;
And very mournful is the tale,
 Which ye fo fain would know.

THE HERMIT's TALE.

Young lord, thy grandfire had a friend
 In days of youthful fame;
Yon diftant hills were his domains;
 Sir BERTRAM was his name.

Where'er the noble PERCY fought
 His friend was at his fide;
And many a fkirmifh with the Scots
 Their early valour try'd.

Young

Young Bertram lov'd a beauteous maid,
   As fair as fair might be ;
The dew-drop on the lily's cheek
   Was not fo fair as fhe.

Fair WIDDRINGTON the maiden's name,
   Yon tow'rs her dwelling place ;*
Her fire an old Northumbrian chief
   Devoted to thy race.

Many a lord, and many a knight,
   To this fair damfel came ;
But Bertram was her only choice ;
   For him fhe felt a flame.

Lord PERCY pleaded for his friend,
   Her father foon confents ;
None but the beauteous maid herfelf
   His wifhes now prevents.

But fhe with ftudied fond delays
   Defers the blifsful hour ;
And loves to try his conftancy,
   And prove her maiden power.

                       That

* WIDDRINGTON caftle is about five miles fouth of Warkworth.

That heart, she said, is lightly priz'd,
　　Which is too lightly won ;
And long shall rue that easy maid,
　　Who yields her love too soon.

Lord PERCY made a solemn feast
　　In Alnwick's princely hall ;
And there came lords, and there came knights,
　　His chiefs and barons all.

With wassel, mirth, and revelry
　　The castle rung around :
Lord PERCY call'd for song and harp,
　　And pipes of martial sound.

The minstrels of thy noble house,
　　All clad in robes of blue,
With silver crescents on their arms,
　　Attend in order due.

The great atchievements of thy race
　　They sung : their high command :
" How valiant MAINFRED o'er the seas
　" First led his northern band. *

　　　　　　　　　　　　　　　" Brave

* See Dugdale's Baronage, page 269, &c.

" Brave GALFRED next to Normandy
  " With venturous Rollo came ;
" And from his Norman caſtles won,
  " Aſſum'd the PERCY name.*

" They ſung, how in the Conqueror's fleet
  " Lord WILLIAM ſhipp'd his powers,
" And gain'd a fair young Saxon bride,
  " With all her lands and towers.†

" Then journeying to the Holy Land,
  " There bravely fought and dy'd :
" But firſt the ſilver Creſcent wan,
  " Some Paynim Soldan's pride.

G   " They

* In Lower Normandy are three Places of the name of PERCY : whence the
Family took the ſurname DE PERCY.

† WILLIAM DE PERCY, (fifth in Deſcent from GALFRED, or
GEFFREY DE PERCY, ſon of MAINFRED,) aſſiſted in the conqueſt of
England, and had given him the large poſſeſſions in Yorkſhire, of EMMA DE
PORTE, (ſo the Norman writers name her,) whoſe father, a great Saxon lord,
had been ſlain fighting along with Harold. This young lady, WILLIAM, from
a principle of honour and generoſity, married : for having had all her lands beſtowed upon him by the Conqueror, " he (to uſe the words of the old Whitby
" Chronicle) wedded her that was very hine to them, in diſcharging of his
" conſcience." See Harl. MSS. 692. (26.) — He died at Mountjoy, near Jeru-
ſalem, in the firſt Cruſade.

" They fung how AGNES, beauteous heir,
    " The queen's own brother wed,
" Lord JOSCELINE, fprung from Charlemagne,
    " In princely Brabant bred.*

" How he the PERCY name reviv'd,
    " And how his noble line
" Still foremoft in their country's caufe,
    " With godlike ardour fhine."

With loud acclaims the liftening crowd
    Applaud the mafters' fong,
And deeds of arms and war became
    The theme of every tongue.

Now high heroic acts they tell,
    Their perils paft recall:
When, lo! a damfel, young and fair,
    Stepp'd forward thro' the hall.

                                    She

*AGNES DE PERCY, fole heirefs of her houfe, married JOSCELINE DE LOVAIN, youngeft fon of Godfrey Barbatus, duke of Brabant, and brother of queen Adeliza, fecond wife of king Henry I. He took the name of PERCY, and was anceftor of the earls of Northumberland. His fon, lord RICHARD DE PERCY, was one of the twenty-fix barons, chofen to fee the Magna Charta duly obferved.

She Bertram courteously addrefs'd;
  And kneeling on her knee;
Sir knight, the lady of thy love
  Hath fent this gift to thee.

Then forth fhe drew a glittering helme,
  Well-plated many a fold,
The cafque was wrought of tempered fteel,
  The creft of burnifh'd gold.

Sir knight, thy lady fends thee this,
  And yields to be thy bride,
When thou haft prov'd this maiden gift
  Where fharpeft blows are try'd.

Young Bertram took the fhining helme,
  And thrice he kifs'd the fame:
Truft me, I'll prove this precious cafque
  With deeds of nobleft fame.

Lord PERCY, and his barons bold,
  Then fix upon a day
To fcour the marches, late oppreft,
  And Scottifh wrongs repay.

The

The knights affembled on the hills
  A thoufand horfe and more:
Brave Widdrington, tho' funk in years,
  The P ɛ ʀ c ʏ-ftandard bore.

Tweed's limpid current foon they pafs,
  And range the borders round:
Down the green flopes of Tiviotdale
  Their bugle-horns refound.

As when a lion in his den
  Hath hear'd the hunters' cries,
And rufhes forth to meet his foes,
  So did the D o ᴜ ɢ ʟ ᴀ s rife.

Attendant on their chief's command
  A thoufand warriors wait:
And now the fatal hour drew on
  Of cruel keen debate.

A chofen troop of Scottifh youths
  Advance before the reft;
Lord P ɛ ʀ c ʏ mark'd their gallant mien,
  And thus his friend addrefs'd.

                        Now,

Now, Bertram, prove thy Lady's helme,
    Attack yon forward band;
Dead or alive I'll refcue thee,
    Or perifh by their hand.

Young Bertram bow'd, with glad affent;
    And fpurr'd his eager fteed,
And calling on his Lady's name,
    Rufh'd forth with whirlwind fpeed.

As when a grove of fapling oaks
    The livid lightning rends ;
So fiercely 'mid the oppofing ranks
    Sir Bertram's fword defcends.

This way and that he drives the fteel,
    And keenly pierces thro' ;
And many a tall and comely knight
    With furious force he flew.

Now clofing faft on every fide
    They hem Sir Bertram round;
But dauntlefs he repels their rage,
    And deals forth many a wound.

H
                                                  The

The vigour of his single arm
   Had well-nigh won the field ;
When ponderous fell a Scottish ax,
   And clove his lifted shield.

Another blow his temple took,
   And reft his helme in twain ;
That beauteous helme, his Lady's gift !
   —— His blood bedew'd the plain.

Lord PERCY saw his champion fall
   Amid the unequal fight ;
And now, my noble friends, he said,
   Let's save this gallant knight.

Then rushing in with stretch'd-out shield
   He o'er the warrior hung ;
As some fierce eagle spreads her wing
   To guard her callow young.

Three times they strove to seize their prey,
   Three times they quick retire :
What force could stand his furious strokes,
   Or meet his martial fire ?

                                  Now

Now gathering round on every part,
　The battle rag'd amain;
And many a lady wept her lord
　That hour untimely flain.

Percy and Douglas, great in arms,
　There all their courage fhow'd;
And all the field was ftrew'd with dead,
　And all with crimfon flow'd.

At length the glory of the day
　The Scots reluctant yield,
And, after wonderous valour fhown,
　They flowly quit the field.

All pale extended on their fhields,
　And weltering in his gore,
Lord Percy's knights their bleeding friend
　To Wark's fair caftle bore.

Well haft thou earn'd my daughter's love,
　Her father kindly fed;
And fhe herfelf fhall drefs thy wounds,
　And tend thee in thy bed.

　　　　　　　　　　　A meffage

A meſſage went, no daughter came;
  Fair IsABEL ne'er appears:
Beſhrew me, ſaid the aged chief,
  Young maidens have their fears.

Cheer up, my ſon, thou ſhalt her ſee
  So ſoon as thou canſt ride;
And ſhe ſhall nurſe thee in her bower,
  And ſhe ſhall be thy bride.

Sir Bertram at her name reviv'd,
  He bleſs'd the ſoothing ſound;
Fond hope ſupplied the Nurſe's care,
  And heal'd his ghaſtly wound.

⁎⁎⁎ WARK caſtle, a fortreſs belonging to the Engliſh, and of great note in ancient times, ſtood on the ſouthern bank of the river TWEED, a little to the eaſt of TIVIOTDALE, and not far from Kelſo. It is now entirely deſtroyed.

THE END OF THE SECOND PART.

THE

HERMIT of WARKWORTH.

A

NORTHUMBERLAND BALLAD.

FIT THE THIRD.

O NE early morn, while dewy drops
　　Hung trembling on the tree,
　Sir Bertram from his fick-bed rofe,
　　His bride he would go fee.

A brother he had in prime of youth,
　Of courage firm and keen,
And he would tend him on the way
　Becaufe his wounds were green.

All day o'er mofs and moor they rode,
　By many a lonely tower;
And 'twas the dew-fall of the night
　Ere they drew near her bower

　　　　　　　　I　　　　　　　　Moft

Moſt drear and dark the caſtle ſeem'd,
  That wont to ſhine ſo bright;
And long and loud Sir Bertram call'd
  Ere he beheld a light.

At length her aged Nurſe aroſe,
  With voice ſo ſhrill and clear:
What wight is this, that calls ſo loud,
  And knocks ſo boldly here?

'Tis Bertram calls, thy Lady's love,
  Come from his bed of care:
All day I've ridden o'er moor and moſs
  To ſee thy Lady fair.

Now out, alas! (ſhe loudly ſhriek'd)
  Alas! how may this be?
For ſix long days are gone and paſt
  Since ſhe ſet out to thee.

Sad terror ſeiz'd Sir Bertram's heart,
  And ready was he to fall;
When now the draw-bridge was let down,
  And gates were open'd all.

                                   Six

Six days, young knight, are paſt and gone,
   Since ſhe ſet out to thee;
And ſure if no ſad harm had hap'd
   Long ſince thou wouldſt her ſee.

For when ſhe heard thy grievous chance
   She tore her hair, and cried,
Alas! I've ſlain the comlieſt knight,
   All thro' my folly and pride!

And now to atone for my ſad fault,
   And his dear health regain,
I'll go myſelf, and nurſe my love,
   And ſoothe his bed of pain.

Then mounted ſhe her milk-white ſteed
   One morn at break of day;
And two tall yeomen went with her
   To guard her on the way.

Sad terror ſmote Sir Bertram's heart,
   And grief o'erwhelm'd his mind:
Truſt me, ſaid he, I ne'er will reſt
   'Till I thy Lady find.

                          That

That night he spent in sorrow and care;
  And with sad boding heart,
Or ever the dawning of the day
  His brother and he depart.

Now, brother, we'll our ways divide,
  O'er Scottish hills to range:
Do thou go north, and I'll go west;
  And all our dress we'll change.

Some Scottish carle hath seiz'd my love,
  And borne her to his den;
And ne'er will I tread English ground
  'Till she is restor'd agen.

The brothers strait their paths divide,
  O'er Scottish hills to range;
And hide themselves in queint disguise,
  And oft their dress they change.

Sir Bertram clad in gown of gray,
  Most like a Palmer poor,
To halls and castles wanders round,
  And begs from door to door.

                     Sometimes

Sometimes a Minftrel's garb he wears,
　With pipes fo fweet and fhrill ;
And wends to every tower and town,
　O'er every dale and hill.

One day as he fate under a thorn,
　All funk in deep defpair,
An aged Pilgrim pafs'd him by,
　Who mark'd his face of care.

All Minftrels yet that ever I faw,
　Are full of game and glee :
But thou art fad and woe-begone !
　I marvel whence it be !

Father, I ferve an aged Lord,
　Whofe grief afflicts my mind ;
His only child is ftol'n away,
　And fain I would her find.

Cheer up, my fon ; perchance, (he faid)
　Some tidings I may bear :
For oft when human hopes have fail'd,
　Then heavenly comfort's near

K

Behind

Behind yon hills, so steep and high,
  Down in a lowly glen,
There stands a castle fair and strong,
  Far from th' abode of men.

As late I chanc'd to crave an alms
  About this evening hour,
Me-thought I heard a Lady's voice
  Lamenting in the tower.

And when I ask'd, what harm had happ'd,
  What Lady sick there lay?
They rudely drove me from the gate,
  And bade me wend away.

These tidings caught Sir Bertram's ear,
  He thank'd him for his tale;
And soon he hasted o'er the hills,
  And soon he reach'd the vale.

Then drawing near those lonely towers,
  Which stood in dale so low,
And sitting down beside the gate,
  His pipes he 'gan to blow.

                                          Sir

Sir Porter, is thy lord at home
   To hear a Minstrel's song?
Or may I crave a lodging here,
   Without offence or wrong?

My Lord, he said, is not at home,
   To hear a Minstrel's song:
And should I lend thee lodging here,
   My life would not be long.

He play'd again so soft a strain,
   Such power sweet sounds impart,
He won the churlish Porter's ear,
   And mov'd his stubborn heart.

Minstrel, he said, thou play'st so sweet,
   Fair entrance thou should'st win;
But, alas! I'm sworn upon the rood
   To let no stranger in.

Yet, Minstrel, in yon rising cliff
   Thou'lt find a sheltering cave;
And here thou shalt my supper share,
   And there thy lodging have.

                                 All

All day he fits befide the gate,
  And pipes both loud and clear:
All night he watches round the walls,
  In hopes his love to hear.

The firft night, as he filent watch'd,
  All at the midnight hour,
He plainly heard his Lady's voice
  Lamenting in the tower.

The fecond night the moon fhone clear,
  And gilt the fpangled dew;
He faw his Lady thro' the grate,
  But 'twas a tranfient view.

The third night wearied out he flept
  'Till near the morning tide;
When, ftarting up, he feiz'd his fword,
  And to the caftle hy'd.

When, lo! he faw a ladder of ropes
  Depending from the wall;
And o'er the mote was newly laid
  A poplar ftrong and tall.

                                    And

And foon he faw his love defcend,
   Wrapt in a Tartan plaid;
Affifted by a fturdy youth
   In highland garb y-clad.

Amaz'd, confounded at the fight,
   He lay unfeen and ftill;
And foon he faw them crofs the ftream,
   And mount the neighbouring hill.

Unheard, unknown of all within,
   The youthful couple fly.
But what can 'fcape the lover's ken?
   Or fhun his piercing eye?

With filent ftep he follows clofe
   Behind the flying pair,
And faw her hang upon his arm
   With fond familiar air.

Thanks, gentle youth, fhe often faid;
   My thanks thou well haft won:
For me what wiles haft thou contriv'd?
   For me what dangers run?

L   And

And ever fhall my grateful heart
  Thy fervices repay : —
Sir Bertram would no further hear,
  But cried, Vile traitor, ftay!

Vile traitor, yield that Lady up!
  And quick his fword he drew :
The ftranger turn'd in fudden rage,
  And at Sir Bertram flew.

With mortal hate their vigorous arms
  Gave many a vengeful blow :
But Bertram's ftronger hand prevail'd,
  And laid the ftranger low.

Die, traitor, die ! — A deadly thruft
  Attends each furious word.
Ah! then fair Ifabel knew his voice,
  And rufh'd beneath his fword.

O ftop, fhe cried, O ftop thy arm !
  Thou doft thy brother flay ! —
And here the Hermit paus'd, and wept : :
  His tongue no more could fay.

                                        At

At length he cried, Ye lovely pair,
  How ſhall I tell the reſt? —
'Ere I could ſtop my piercing ſword,
  It fell, and ſtabb'd her breaſt.

Wert thou thyſelf that hapleſs youth?
  Ah! cruel fate! they ſaid.
The Hermit wept, and ſo did they:
  They ſigh'd; he hung his head.

O blind and jealous rage, he cried,
  What evils from thee flow!
The Hermit paus'd; they ſilent mourn'd:
  He wept, and they were woe.

Ah! when I hear'd my brother's name,
  And ſaw my Lady bleed,
I rav'd, I wept, I curſt my arm,
  That wrought the fatal deed.

In vain I claſp'd her to my breaſt,
  And clos'd the ghaſtly wound;
In vain I preſs'd his bleeding corpſe,
  And rais'd it from the ground.

                        My

My brother, alas! fpake never more;
 His precious life was flown.
She kindly ftrove to foothe my pain,
 Regardlefs of her own.

Bertram, fhe faid, be comforted,
 And live to think on me:
May we in heaven that union prove,
 Which here was not to be!

Bertram, fhe faid, I ftill was true;
 Thou only hadft my heart:
May we hereafter meet in blifs!
 We now, alas! muft part.

For thee I left my father's hall,
 And flew to thy relief;
When, lo! near Chiviot's fatal hills
 I met a Scottifh chief.

Lord Malcolm's fon, whofe proffer'd love
 I had refus'd with fcorn;
He flew my guards, and feiz'd on me,
 Upon that fatal morn:

        And

And in thefe dreary hated walls
  He kept me clofe confin'd ;
And fondly fued, and warmly prefs'd
  To win me to his mind.

Each rifing morn increas'd my pain,
  Each night increas'd my fear ;
When wandering in this northern garb,
  Thy brother found me here.

He quickly formed this brave defign
  To fet me, captive, free ;
And on the moor his horfes wait,
  Ty'd to a neighbouring tree.

Then hafte, my love, efcape away,
  And for thyfelf provide ;
And fometimes fondly think on her,
  Who fhould have been thy bride.

Thus pouring comfort on my foul,
  Even with her lateft breath,
She gave one parting fond embrace,
  And clos'd her eyes in death.

M

In

In wild amaze, in fpeechlefs woe,
  Devoid of fenfe I lay:
Then fudden all in frantic mood
  I meant myfelf to flay:

And rifing up in furious hafte
  I feiz'd the bloody brand: *
A fturdy arm here interpos'd,
  And wrench'd it from my hand.

A crowd, that from the caftle came,
  Had mifs'd their lovely ward;
And feizing me to prifon bare,
  And deep in dungeon barr'd.

It chanc'd that on that very morn
  Their chief was prifoner ta'en:
Lord PERCY had us foon exchang'd,
  And ftrove to foothe my pain.

And foon thofe honour'd dear remains
  To England were convey'd;
And there within their filent tombs,
  With holy rites were laid.

                                                    For

* i. e. Sword.

For me, I loath'd my wretched life,
  And long to end it thought;
'Till time, and books, and holy men,
  Had better counsels taught.

They rais'd my heart to that pure source,
  Whence heavenly comfort flows :
They taught me to despise the world,
  And calmly bear its woes.

No more the slave of human pride,
  Vain hope, and sordid care;
I meekly vow'd to spend my life
  In penitence and prayer.

The bold Sir BERTRAM now no more,
  Impetuous, haughty, wild;
But poor and humble BENEDICT,
  Now lowly, patient, mild :

My lands I gave to feed the poor,
  And sacred altars raise ;
And here a lonely Anchorete
  I came to end my days.

This

This sweet sequester'd vale I chose,
   These rocks, and hanging grove;
For oft beside that murmuring stream
   My love was wont to rove.

My noble Friend approv'd my choice;
   This blest retreat he gave;
And here I carv'd her beauteous form,
   And scoop'd this holy cave.

Full fifty winters, all forlorn,
   My life I've linger'd here;
And daily o'er this sculptur'd saint,
   I drop the pensive tear.

And thou, dear brother of my heart,
   So faithful and so true,
The sad remembrance of thy fate
   Still makes my bosom rue!

Yet not unpitied pass'd my life,
   Forsaken, or forgot,
The PERCY and his noble Sons
   Would grace my lowly cot.

Oft

Oft the great Earl from toils of ſtate,
  And cumb'rous pomp of power,
Would gladly ſeek my little cell,
  To ſpend the tranquil hour.

But length of life is length of woe,
  I liv'd to mourn his fall:
I liv'd to mourn his godlike Sons,
  And friends and followers all.

But thou the honours of thy race,
  Lov'd youth, ſhalt now reſtore;
And raiſe again the PERCY name
  More glorious than before.

He ceas'd, and on the lovely pair
  His choiceſt bleſſings laid:
While they with thanks and pitying tears
  His mournful tale repaid.

And now what preſent courſe to take,
  They aſk the good old ſire;
And guided by his ſage advice,
  To Scotland they retire.

N

Mean-time their suit such favour found
 At RABY's stately hall,
Earl Neville, and his princely Spouse,
 Now gladly pardon all.

She suppliant at her Nephew's * throne,
 The royal grace implor'd:
To all the honours of his race
 The PERCY was restor'd.

The youthful Earl still more and more
 Admir'd his beauteous dame:
NINE noble SONS to him she bore,
 All worthy of their name.

* King Henry V. Anno 1414.

THE   END   OF   THE   BALLAD.

*** The account given in the foregoing ballad of young
PERCY, the son of HOTSPUR, is confirmed by the following Extract
from an old Chronicle formerly belonging to Whitby Abbey.

       " HENRY

" HENRY PERCY, the fon of Sir HENRY PERCY, that was
" flayne at Shrewefbury, and of ELIZABETH, the daughter of
" the Erle of Marche, after the death of his Father and Graunt-
" fyre, was exiled into Scotland * in the time of king Henry
" the Fourth: but in the time of king Henry the Fifth, by the
" labour of JOHANNE the countes of Weftmerland, (whofe
" Daughter ALLANOR he HAD WEDDED IN COMING INTO
" ENGLAND,) he recovered the King's grace, and the countye
" of Northumberland, fo was the SECOND ERLE of Northum-
" berland.

" And of this Alianor his wife, he begate IX Sonnes, and
" III Daughters, whofe names be JOHANNE, that is buried at
" Whytbye: THOMAS, lord Egremont: KATHARYNE GRAY of
" Rythyn: Sir RAFFE PERCY: WILLIAM PERCY, a Byfhopp:
" RICHARD PERCY · JOHN, that dyed WITHOUT ISSUE: [another
" JOHN, called by Vincent † ' Johannes Percy fenior de Wark-
" worth':] GEORGE PERCY, Clerk: HENRY that dyed WITHOUT
" ISSUE: ANNE ——" [befides the eldeft fon and fucceffor
" here omitted, becaufe he comes in below, viz.]

" HENRY PERCY, the THIRD Erle of NORTHUMBERLAND."

Vid. Harl. MSS. No. 692. (26.) in the Britifh Mufeum.

* i. e. remained an Exile in Scotland during the Reign of king Henry IV.
In Scotia exulavit tempore Henrici Regis quarti. Lat. MS. penes Duc. North.

† See his Great Baronag. No. 20, in the Heralds office.

POST.

POSTSCRIPT.

IT will perhaps gratify the curious Reader to be informed, that from a word or two formerly legible over one of the Chapel Doors, it is believed that the Text there inscribed was that Latin verse of the Psalmist,* which is in our Translation,

MY TEARS HAVE BEEN MY MEAT DAY AND NIGHT.

It is also certain, that the memory of the first Hermit was held in such regard and veneration by the PERCY Family, that they afterwards maintained a Chantry Priest, to reside in the Hermitage, and celebrate Mass in the Chapel: whose allowance, uncommonly liberal and munificent, was continued down to the Dissolution of the Monasteries; and then the whole Salary, together with the Hermitage and all its dependencies, reverted back to the Family, having never been endowed in mortmain. On this account we have no Record, which fixes the date of the Founda-tion, or gives any particular account of the first Hermit; but the following Instrument will shew the liberal Exhibition offered to his Successors. It is the Patent granted to the last Hermit in 1532, and is copied from an ancient MS. book of Grants, &c. of the VIth Earl of Northumberland, in Henry VIIIth's time. †

SIR GEORGE LANCASTRE PATENT OF XX MERKS BY YERE.

" HENRY Erle of Northumberland, &c. Knowe youe that I
" the said Erle, in consideration of the diligent and thankfull
" service, that my wellbeloved Cheplen Sir GEORGE LANCASTRE
" hath don unto me the said Erle, and also for the goode and
" vertus dispotion that I do perceive in him: And for that he
" shall have in his daily recommendation and praiers the good
" estate of all suche noble Blode and other Personages, as be now
" levynge ;

---

* Psal. xlii. 3.   † Clisted, F. I. No. 1. penes Duc. Northumb.

" levynge ; And the Soules of such noble Blode as be departed
" to the mercy of God owte of this prefent lyve, Whos Names
" are conteyned and wrettyn in a Table upon perchment figned
" with thande of me the faid Erle, and delivered to the cuftodie
" and keapynge of the faid fir George Lancafter : And further,
" that he fhall kepe and faye his devyn fervice in celebratyng
" and doynge Maffe of *Requiem* every weke accordinge as it is writ-
" ten and fet furth in the faide Table : HAVE geven and graunted,
" and by thefe prefentes do gyve and graunte unto the faid fir
" George, myn ARMYTAGE belded in a Rock of ftone within
" my Parke of WARKWORTH in the Countie of Northumbre-
" land in the honour of the bleffed Trynete, With a yerly
" Stipende of twenty Merks by yer*, from the feeft of feint Michell
" tharchaungell laft paft afore the date hereof yerly duryng the
" natural lyve of the faid fir George : and alfo I the faid Erle
" have geven and graunted, and by thefe Prefents do gyve and
" graunte unto the faid fir George Lancafter, the occupation of
" one litle Gresground of myn called Cony-garth nygh ad-
" joynynge the faid Harmytage, only to his own ufe and proufit
" wynter and fumer durynge the faid terme ; THE Garden and
" Orteyarde belongyng the faid Armytage ; THE Gate † and
" Pafture of Twelf Kye and a Bull, with their Calves fuking ;
" AND two Horfes goyin and beyng within my faid Parke of
" Warkworth wynter and fomer ; ONE Draught of Fiffhe every
" Sondaie in the yere to be drawen fornenft ‡ the faid Armytage,
" called The Trynete Draught ; AND Twenty Lods of Fyrewode
" to be taken of my Wodds called Shilbotell Wode, duryng the
" faid term.   The faid Stipend of xx Merks by yer to be taken
" and perceived § yerly of the rent and ferme of my Fiffhyng of
" Warkworth, by thands of the Fermour or Fermours of the fame
" for the tyme beynge yerly at the times ther ufed and ac-
                    O   " cuftomed

* This would be equal to £.100 per annum now. See the Chronicon Pretiofum.
† i. e. Going : from the verb, To Gae. ‡ Or fore anenft i. e. oppofite. § So MS.

" cuſtomed by evyn Portions. In wytnes
" whereof to thes my Letters Patentes I
" the ſaid Erle have ſet the Seale of myn
" Armes : Yeven undre my Signet at my
" Caſtell of Warkworth, the third daye of Decembre, in the
" xxiii[th] Yer of the Reigne of our Sovereyn Lorde kyng Henry
" the eight."

Allowe in recompenſe
herof yerly x[li] *.
Richerd Ryche.

On the diſſolution of the Monaſteries, the above Patent was
produced before the Court of Augmentation in Michaelmas-Term,
20 Oct. A. 29. Hen. VIII. when the ſame was allowed by the
Chancellor and Councel of the ſaid Court, and all the profits confirmed to the incumbent Sir George Lancaſter ; Excepting that
in compenſation for the annual Stipend of Twenty Marks, he was
to receive a Stipend of Ten Marks, and to have a free Chapel called
The Rood Chapel, and the Hoſpital of St. Leonard, within the
Barony of Wigdon, in the County of Cumberland.

After the peruſal of the above Patent it will perhaps be need-
leſs to caution the Reader againſt a Miſtake, ſome have fallen into ;
of confounding this Hermitage near Warkworth, with a Chantry
founded within the town itſelf, by Nicholas de Farnham, biſhop
of Durham, in the reign of Henry III. who appropriated the Church
of Brankeſton for the maintenance there of two Benedictine
Monks from Durham ‖. That ſmall monaſtic foundation is
indeed called a Cell by biſhop Tanner † : but he muſt be very
ignorant, who ſuppoſes that by the word Cell is neceſſarily to be
underſtood a Hermitage ; whereas it was commonly applied to any
ſmall conventual eſtabliſhment, which was dependant on another.

As

---

* Sic MS.   † So the MS. The above Sir Richard Rych was Chancellor of
the Augmentations at the Suppreſſion of the Monaſteries.

‖ Ang. Sacr. p. 738.   † Not. Mon. p. 395.

As for the Chapel belonging to this endowment of bishop Farnham, it is mentioned as in ruins in several old Surveys of Queen
Elizabeth's time; and its scite, not far from Warkworth Church, is
still remembered.   But that there was never more than ONE Priest
maintained, at one and the same time, within the HERMITAGE,
is plainly proved (if any further proof be wanting) by the following Extract from a Survey of Warkworth, made in the Year
1567, * viz.

  " Ther is in the Parke (sc. of Warkworth) also one Howse
" hewyn within one Cragge, which is called the HARMITAGE
" CHAPEL. In the same ther haith bene ONE PREAST keaped,
" which did such godlye Services as that tyme was used and cele-
" brated.   The Mantion House [sc. the small building adjoining
" to the Cragg] ys nowe in decaye : the Closes that apperteined
" to the said Chantrie is occupied to his Lordship's use."

* By Geo. Clarkson, MS. penes Duc. North.

To compleat the Subject of the HERMITAGE OF WARK-
  WORTH, it may be proper to subjoin here, from Captain Groce's
  " Antiquities of England and Wales, 1775, 4 Vols. 4to,"

AN EXTRACT OF A LETTER FROM NEWCASTLE UPON TYNE,
    DATED THE SIXTH OF SEPTEMBER, 1771.

  * * * * * I shall now, in compliance with your request, attempt to give you
  a Description of the ruins of the ancient Hermitage at Warkworth, which the
  very interesting Ballad, lately published on that subject, excited in me so great a
  desire to see.

As

As I went from Newcastle, I quitted the great Northern Road at a small village called Felton, (which stands about mid-way between Morpeth and Alnwick) and had a most romantic ride for the most part down a most beautiful rocky Vale, worne by the current of the river Coquet, which afforded a succession of very picturesque scenes.

I was much pleased with the situation of Warkworth itself; particularly with the Castle, which, although in ruins, is a fine Monument of ancient Grandeur, being one of the proud Fortresses, which heretofore belonged to the noble House of Percy, and from them descended to the present Duke and Duchess of Northumberland; who, together with the princely possessions, have inherited the generosity and magnificence of that great family.

Warkworth Castle deserves itself a particular description: I shall, therefore, at present only observe, that it is very boldly situate on an eminence, and overlooks the river Coquet, where it discharges its waters into the sea, and almost washes an Island of the same name; which, from its circular form, easy distance from the shore, and a little antique Tower, the remains of a small Monastic Edifice erected upon it, is a most beautiful object seen from every part of the coast.

From the Castle we ascended not more than half a mile up the river, before we came to the Hermitage; which is probably the best preserved and most intire now remaining in these kingdoms. It still contains three Apartments, all of them hollowed in the solid Rock, and hanging over the river in the most picturesque manner imaginable, with a covering of ancient hoary Trees, Reliques of the venerable Woods, in which this fine solitude was anciently embowered.

As the Hermitage, with all its striking peculiarities, is very exactly described in the Ballad of the *Hermit of Warkworth*, I might be content to transcribe the descriptive part of that Poem: but as you have insisted upon my relating to you what I saw myself, I shall endeavour to obey you.

The Cave contains three Apartments; which, by way of distinction, I will venture to call the Chapel, Sacristy, and Antichapel. Of these, the Chapel is very intire and perfect but the two others have suffered by the falling down of the rock at the west end. By this accident a beautiful Pillar, which formerly stood between these two apartments, and gave an elegant finishing to this end of the Sacred Vaults, was, within the memory of old people, destroyed.

The Chapel is not more than eighteen feet long, nor more than seven and a half in width and height; but is modelled and executed in a very beautiful style of Gothic Architecture. The Sides are ornamented with neat Octogon Pillars,

all

all cut in the solid Rock, which branch off into the cieling, and forming little pointed Arches, terminate in Groins. At the East end is a handsome plain Altar, to which the Priest ascended by two Steps: These in the course of ages, have been much worn away through the soft yielding nature of the stone. Behind the Altar is a little Nich, which probably received the Crucifix, or the Pix. Over this Nich is still seen the faint outline of a Glory.

On the North-side of the Altar is a very beautiful Gothic Window, executed like all the rest, in the living Rock. This Window transmitted light from the Chapel to the Sacristy; or what else shall we call it? being a plain oblong room which runs parallel with the Chapel, somewhat longer than it, but not so wide. At the east end of this apartment are still seen the remains of an Altar, at which Mass was occasionally sung, as well as in the Chapel. Between it and the Chapel is a square Perforation, with some appearance of Bars, or a Lattice, through which the Hermit might attend Confession, or behold the elevation of the Host without entering the Chapel. Near this Perforation is a neat Door-case opening into the Chapel out of this Side-room or Sacristy, which contains a Benching cut in the rock, whence is seen a most beautiful View up the river, finely overhung with woods. Over the Door case, within the Chapel, is carved a small neat Scutcheon, with all the emblems of the Passion, sc. the Cross, the Crown of Thorns, the Nails, the Spear, and the Spunge.

On the south side of the Altar is another Window, and below it a neat Cenotaph or Tomb, ornamented with three human Figures elegantly cut in the rock. The principal Figure represents a Lady lying along, still very intire and perfect: over her breast hovers what probably was an Angel, but much defaced: and at her feet is a Warrior erect, and perhaps originally in a praying posture; but he is likewise mutilated by Time. At her feet is also a rude sculpture of a Bull's or Ox's Head; which the Editor of the Ballad not unreasonably conjectures to have been the Lady's Crest. This was, as he observes, the Crest of the Widdrington Family, whose castle is but five Miles from this Hermitage. It was also the ancient Crest of the Nevilles, and of one or two other families in the North.

On the same side is another Door-case, and near it an Excavation to contain the Holy Water. Over both the Door-cases are still seen the traces of Letters, vestiges of two ancient Inscriptions; but so much defaced as to be at present illegible. I must refer you to the Poem for a further account of them.

This Door opens into a little vestibule, containing two square niches, in which the Hermit sat to contemplate; and his view from hence was well calculated to inspire meditation. He looked down upon the River which washes the foot of

the

the Hermitage, and glides away in a conftant murmuring lapfe; and he might thence have taken occafion, like the Author of the Night Thoughts, to remind fome young thoughtlefs Vifitant',

> " Life glides away, Lorenzo! like a ftream,
> " For ever changing, unperceiv'd the change.
> " In the fame ftream none ever bath'd him twice;
> " To the fame life none ever twice awoke.
> " We call the ftream the fame, the fame we think
> " Our life, though ftill more rapid in its flow;
> " Nor mark the Much irrevocably laps'd,
> " And mingled with the fea.

Over the Inner Door, within the Veftibule, hangs another Scutcheon with fome Sculpture, which we took for the reprefentation of a Gauntlet; perhaps it was the Founder's Arms or Creft. On the outward face of the Rock, near the fmall Veftibule above-mentioned, is a winding ftair-cafe cut alfo in the living ftone, and leading through a neat arched Door-cafe in the fame, up to the top of the Cliff which joins the level of the ancient Park; and here was planted the Hermit's Orchard. This has long fince been deftroyed; but Cherry-trees propagated from his Plantations are ftill fcattered over the neighbouring thicket. His Garden was below at the foot of the hill, as we were informed; and indeed fome ftraggling flowers and one little folitary Goofeberry-bufh, which ftill grows out of a cleft in the rock, confirm the tradition.

As all the Apartments above-defcribed feem to have been appropriated to facred ufes, you will naturally enquire where was the Dwelling of the Hermit, or at leaft of his Succeffors? This was a fmall fquare Building, erected at the foot of the Cliff, that contains the Chapel. It confifted of one fingle dwelling-room, with a Bed-chamber over it, and a fmall Kitchen adjoining; which is now fallen in and covered with earth; but the ruins of the Oven ftill mark its fituation, and fhew that fome of the inhabitants of this Hermitage did not always diflike good chear.

This little Building, erected below the Chapel, being compofed of materials brought together by human hands, has long fince gone to ruin; whereas the Walls of the Chapel itfelf, being as old as the World, will, if not purpofely deftroyed, probably laft as long as it, and continue to amufe the lateft pofterity. It gave me particular pleafure to obferve, that the prefent noble Proprietors have thought this curiofity not unworthy their attention, and have therefore beftowed a proper care to have it kept clean and neat; have cleared the Hermit's Path, which was choaked up, by the River's fide, have reftored his Well, (a fmall bubbling Fountain of

clear

clear water, which iffues from the adjoining Rock), and have renewed the Wood by new Plantations at the top of the Cliff, where the Trees had been thinned or deftroyed by Time.

In this delightful folitude, fo beautiful in itfelf, and fo venerable for its antiquity, you will judge with what pleafure I perufed the very amufing and interefting Tale of the Hermit of Warkworth: having the whole Scene before me, and fancying I was prefent at the Hermit's tender relation.

And this leads me to your laft query; what foundation the author of the poem had for his Story, which he gives as founded on truth? By all the enquiries I could make in the neighbourhood, it is the received tradition, that the Founder of this Hermitage was one of the Bertram family, who were anciently Lords of Bothal Caftle, and had great poffeffions in this County. He is alfo thought to be the fame Bertram, who having built Brinkburn Abbey, and Brinkshaugh Chapel higher up the River, at laft retired to end his life in this fequeftered valley. But the Editor has given reafons, why he thinks the Hermitage was founded at a later period than thofe Buildings, by another of the fame Name and Family. It is alfo the univerfal tradition, That he impofed his penance upon himfelf to expiate the murder of his Brother. As for the Lady, I could not find that any thing particular is remembered concerning her; but the elegant Sculpture of her Figure upon the Tomb, and the Creft at her feet, feem fufficiently to warrant the Story of the Ballad.

The old Record of the Endowment of this Hermitage by the Percy Family, which the Editor has printed at the end of his Poem, is a curiofity very fingular in its kind. When I perufed it, I could not help fmiling at the Article of the Trinity Draught of Fifh, to be taken oppofite to the Chapel, which was to be the Hermit's Perquifite every Sunday. It was, I affure you, no contemptible Perquifite for there is a very rich Salmon-Fifhery in this River belonging to the Duke and Duchefs of Northumberland; and I was told, that at one fingle draught this fummer, more than Three Hundred fifh had been taken oppofite to the Hermitage.*

I fhall conclude my long, tedious Defcription, with a Stanza from Spencer; which, if you will pardon a few alterations, will give you a pretty exact Picture of the place.

* I have been affured that more than Four Hundred Fifh, chiefly Salmon, Salmon-Trouts, and Gilts, have been taken at one Draught between the Hermitage and the Sea, which is about two miles diftant.

" A little

"A little lonely Hermitage there ſtood
  "Down in a Dale, hard by a River's ſide,
"Beneath a moſſy Cliff, o'erhung with Wood,
  "And in the living Rock, there cloſe beſide,
"A holy Chapel, entering we deſcried;
  "Wherein the Hermit duly wont to ſay
"His lonely prayers, each morn and even tide:
  "Thereby the cryſtal ſtream did gently play,
"Which thro' the woody Vale came rolling down alway."

F I N I S.

BOOKS Printed for T. EVANS in the Strand.

I. OLD BALLADS, Hiſtorical and Narrative, with ſome of modern Date, none of which are included in Dr. Percy's Collection, and to which this Work may be conſidered as a proper Supplement. Two Vols. 8s. bound.

A Third Volume is in the Preſs, and will be ſold ſeparate to complete Sets.

II. BIOGRAPHIA DRAMATICA; or, A Companion to the Play Houſe: containing Hiſtorical and Critical Memoirs, and original Anecdotes of Britiſh and Iriſh Dramatic Writers, from the Commencement of our Theatrical Exhibitions; amongſt which are ſome of the moſt celebrated Actors, and alſo of anonymous Writers. By David Erſkine Baker, Eſq. A new Edition, greatly enlarged, and continued from 1764 to 1782. In Two large Volumes, 8vo. Price in Boards 12s.

III. The POETICAL WORKS of Mr. William Collins, with his Life, and Obſervations on his Writings, by Dr. Langhorne. Price Bound 3s.

IV. The HISTORY of the PELOPONNESIAN WAR. Tranſlated from the Greek of Thucydides. To which are added, three Preliminary Diſcourſes: 1. On the Life of Thucydides: 2. On his Qualifications as an Hiſtorian: 3. A Survey of the Hiſtory. By Dr. Smith, Dean of Cheſter. In 2 Vols. 8vo. with Maps. Price bound 12s.

V. The INSTITUTES of ELOQUENCE. Tranſlated from Quintilian, by Mr. Parſal. 2 Vols. 8vo. Price bound 12s.

VI. DESIDERATA CURIOSA. A Collection of curious Tracts on Britiſh Hiſtory and Antiquities, publiſhed from the Originals, by Francis Peck, Rector of Godeby. In 2 Vols. Royal Quarto, with Plates. Price in Boards 1l. 11s. 6d.

THE KING's HOUSE AT CLYPESTON, NOTTINGHAMSHIRE.

CLYPESTONE, Clipſton or Kyngeſclypeſton lies on the weſtern ſide of the country, a ſmall diſtance north-eaſt of Mansfield.

BEFORE the conqueſt Clypſton belonged to Oſborne and Ulſi, and being taken from them, became the property of Roger de Buſti; after the conqueſt it was the Royal demeſne, but when or by whom the manſion or palace was built is unknown; it is mentioned in a record quoted in Madox's Hiſtory of the Exchequer, as early as the 29th of Henry II, when 36s. and 6d. was laid out in utenſils for it, in obedience to the King's writ.

KING John frequently reſided here, both while Earl of Mortain and after his acceſſion to the crown, as appears by ſeveral deeds dated at this place, particularly the charter granted by him to the town of Nottingham in the firſt year of his reign; by him the park is ſaid to have been added.

THOROTON, in his hiſtory of Nottinghamſhire ſays, " Clipſton was burned it " ſeems and repaired again before the 5th of Henry III;" but whither he means the King's Houſe or the village, ſeems doubtful.

A PARLIAMENT was held at Clpston by Edward I, anno 1290, whither in the King's House or elsewhere is not certain; it is however at least probable that the King resided here at that time, and that the Parliament was therefore assembled at this place; an ancient oak on the edge of the park, now bears the name of the Parliament oak.

EDWARD II, used also, at times, to retire hither, several writs recited by Madox being dated from Clypston in the 9th year of his reign: Clypston manor and park, says Thoroton, 2d Edward III, were by the King, committed, during his pleasure, to be kept by Robert de C . . . . . so that he should answer to the Exchequer for the issues, and keep the manor in repair at the King's cost, and the park pale at his own, receiving for the reparation of the said pale, timber of the dry wood there, and taking every day for himself the parcars and making the said pale, 7d.

GALFRIDUS DE KNEVETON, 16 July 22d Henry VI, was made keeper of the castle at Nottingham, Rochingham, and manor of Clypston, and the lodge of Beskwode, in Shirewood for life.

THIS manor with Mansfield and Lyndeby were, by Henry VI, settled on Edmund, Earl of Richmond, and Jasper, Earl of Pembroke; but reverting to the crown, Henry VIII granted it to Thomas Howard, Earl of Surry, when created D. of Norfolk; and it shortly after becoming again vested in the crown, Edward VI gave it to John Earl of Warwich and Henry Sidney, as the possessions of Jasper, Duke of Bedford; they having forfeited it, it remained sometime in the crown till the reign of James I, when it was passed to the feoffees of Gilbert, Earl of Shrewsbury; it afterwards belonged to the heirs of William and John, Dukes of Newcastle, and the manor and park is at present the property of his grace the Duke of Portland.

IT appears from Thoroton's account, published anno 1677, an hundred years ago, that very little more was then standing of this mansion, than is still remaining, "There is (says he) scarcely any ruins left of the King's old House, except a piece of stone wall." These ruins stood in a field of about five acres, close to the village of Clypeston and a quarter of a mile from the park, which is near eight miles in circumference, and was once famous for its fine oaks, many of which were destroyed during the troubles under Charles I.

NEWARK CASTLE, NOTTINGHAMSHIRE.

THIS castle stands on the eastern part of the county. It was built in the reign of King Stephen by Alexander Bishop of Lincoln, who built also the castles of Banbury in Oxfordshire and Sleford in Lincolnshire. Henry of Huntingdon says, this castle, emphatically called The New-work, gave name to the town. As these kind of military erections were deemed rather improper for an ecclesiastic, the last-cited author and William Parvus say, that by way of expiation he founded also two monasteries: but this did not satisfy King Stephen, who having seized this Bishop and his uncle, did not release them till they had surrendered to him all their strong holds. The Governor of this castle refused to deliver it up till directed by the Bishop in person, who informed him that the King had made a vow that he, the Bishop, should have neither meat nor drink till that fortress was surrendered.

DURING the troubles in the latter end of the reign of King John, this castle was in the hands of the royal party, and stoutly defended for the King. The garrison likewise frequently sallying out, wasted the lands and possessions of such of the insurgent Barons as lay in their neighbourhood; the Dauphin therefore, to put a stop to their depredations, detached Gilbert de Gaunt, lately by him created Earl of Lincoln, with a considerable force, but he hearing of the King's approac at the head of a powerful army, retired towards London. In the mean time the King having in his march over the washes loft a great part of his army, with his carriages and military cheft, all furprized and overwhelmed by the tide, came to this caftle extremely fick, and in great anguifh of mind, and here ended his unfortunate reign, October the 19th, in the year 1216.

STOWE adds, " that immediately on the King's death, his fervants taking all " that was about him fled, not leaving fo much of any thing (worth the carriage) " as would cover his dead carkafe."

AT the acceffion of Henry III. this caftle was in the hands of the Barons, being probably yielded to them by Robert de Gangi, Governor thereof, in the former reign, in whofe keeping it was continued. Henry directed it to be reftored to the Bifhop of Lincoln, but with this order Gangi, under pretence of money due to him for victualling it, refufed to comply; whereupon the King, with William Marfhal, Earl of Pembroke, laid fiege to it, but on the eighth day, by the mediation of friends, Gangi agreed to furrender the caftle to the Bifhop on being paid an hundred pounds fterling for the provifions with which he had furnifhed it.

IN the year 1376, in the reign of Edward III. Sir Peter de la More was imprifoned here at the inftigation of Lord Latimere and Sir Richard Stirie.

IN the year 1530 Cardinal Wolfey lodged in this caftle with a great retinue, in his way to Southwell, where he fpent great part of that fummer.

IN Peck's Defiderata Curiofa, Newark caftle is mentioned among the other caftles of royal manfions belonging to Queen Elizabeth. The fee of the conftable is there ftated at 6l. 13s. 4d. per annum, and that of the porter at 5l.

THIS caftle and town of Newark is particularly famous in hiftory for the firm adherence of its garrifon and inhabitants to the royal intereft during the whole time of the civil wars in England between the King Charles I. and the Parliament, when it formed a ftrong and moft ufeful poft, from whence many fuccefsful excurfions were made; it proved alfo an occafional place of retreat for the King.

IT was twice unfuccefsfully befieged by Sir John Meldrum, but furrendered on the 6th of May 1646, in obedience to the King's fpecial commands, when the Lord Bellafis, Governor thereof, obtained for himfelf and garrifon very advantageous and honourable conditions.

THIS view, which reprefents the north afpect, was drawn anno 1776.

NEWSTED PRIORY, NOTTINGHAMSHIRE.

Published as the Act directs by Edward Wm. Wallis June 1st 1770.

NEWSTED ABBEY was formerly a small PRIORY founded by HENRY II. and given by HENRY VIII. to Sir JOHN BIRON, and is now the feat of Lord BIRON.

This house is situated in a vale, in the midst of an extensive park, finely planted. On one side of the house, a very large winding lake has been made by the present Lord Biron, and is a noble water. On the other side is a very fine lake, which flows almost up to the house. The banks on one side are fine wood, which spread over the edge of a hill down to the water; on the other shore, scattered groves, and park. On the banks are two castles washed by the water of the lake: they are uncommon, though picturesque; but it seems rather unfortunate, that the cannon should be levelled at the parlour windows. A twenty-gun ship, with several yachts and boats lying at anchor, throw an air of most pleasing chearfulness over the whole scene. The ridings up the hill, leads to a Gothic building, from whence the view of the lakes, the abbey and its fine arch, the plantations and the park, are seen at once, and form a very noble landscape.

Newstead, in Nottinghamshire, the Seat of Lord Byron.

NEWSTED PRIORY, in NOTTINGHAMSHIRE,

The Seat of Lord BYRON.

Drawn by PAUL SANDBY, Esq. R. A.

Engraved by Mr. WALKER.

IN the Twenty-first Number of the work, (see Plate 61) we gave a different view of this
seat. To the description which accompanied it, we take this opportunity of adding, that
this building was by the founder, Henry II. dedicated to the Virgin Mary. He endowed it
with the several possessions of the church of *Paplewick*, the washes of *Kigel, Bavenshead*, &c.
which was confirmed in the sixth year of the reign of king John, and conveyed in the reign of
Henry the Eighth to Sir John Byron, who was steward of Manchester and Rochdale, constable
of the castle of Nottingham, and lieutenant of the forest of Shirwood. Its revenue was then
valued at 219l. a year. This priory has belonged to that gentleman's posterity ever since, and
is the seat of the present Lord Byron. The greatest part of the priory is converted into a dwelling house, which is very large and convenient, though not regular. At the end is the beautiful frontispiece of the old priory, in the Gothic taste, and of very curious architecture. Large
plantations and a park have been taken out of the forest, and inclosed with pales.

THE PALACE OF THE ARCHBISHOPS OF YORK AT SOUTHWELL, NOTTINGHAMSHIRE.

It is not agreed by whom this palace was first built; some say by one of the Booths, Archbishop of York, for there were two of that name; William, who died anno 1464, and Lawrence his half-brother, and save one immediate successor, who died in the year 1480; others attribute its erection to the magnificent Wolsey, whilst Archbishop of this See. In support of the first opinion, reference is made to a chapel by the south wall near it, called at this hour Booth's Chapel, supposed to be built at the same time with the palace by one of the afore-named Archbishops. In favour of the contrary opinion, besides the tradition, it is urged that Wolsey was in general a great builder, and laid out much money in his see. Probably truth may lie between both. The palace might have been first founded by one of the Booths, but afterwards so much repaired and added to by Wolsey, as to make it almost a new edifice.

Leland in his Itinerary says of it, " The Bishop of York hath ther a preaty " palace," but mentions nothing concerning its founder. It was situated on the south side of the Minster Yard, within a park called Little or New Park, and was demolished during the civil war in the time of Charles I. The site of the manor still belongs to the see of York.

This view was drawn anno 1776.

ISLEY CHURCH, OXFORDSHIRE

IFLEY, EYFLEY, OR YFTELE CHURCH, OXFORDSHIRE.

This church stands in the hundred of Bullington, about two miles south of Oxford, on the banks of the Isis, near its junction with the Cherwell.

This edifice is undoubtedly of great antiquity; its massive construction, its circular arches, and the stile of many of its original parts, exhibit a very good specimen of the stile commonly called Saxon. The arch of its west door, which is richly ornamented, has among other decorations, two, somewhat resembling the heads of kings joined to the beaks of birds. This door has been engraved in one of Dr. Ducarrel's publications; I think his Anglo-Norman Antiquities; but the drawing is by no means accurate. The south door, which is blocked up by a porch, is extremely beautiful; among the ornaments is the head of a Saxon king. Within the church there are several very fine circular arches, particularly a cross one in the chancel, which building seems to have been enlarged by modern additions. There was a circular window over the weft door; this, to judge from what remains, muft have been very rich.

THE font is rather an uncommon one; the upper part confifts of a large block of black marble, polifhed only in fome places; its furface is a fquare, each fide meafuring three feet feven inches, containing a bafon of a yard in diameter, lined with lead. It is fupported by four fhort and thick pillars, three of them fluted in a waving line, the other plain. This circumftance, as well as thofe of the colour and meafure of the ftone, are all nearly to be found in the ancient font at the cathedral at Winchefter. The only remarkable monument in this church, is that of Arthur Pitts, who deceafed the 15th of May, 1579, from which the brafs plates have been long taken. This Arthur Pitts, and others of his name, dwelt in the impropriation houfe adjoining to the church, and were tenants to the archdeacon of Oxford.

THIS church, with its appurtenances, was, according to one of Anthony Wood's manufcripts, No. 8474, kept under the mufeum at Oxford, given by Jeffry de Clinton to the canons of Kenilworth in Warwickfhire, alfo a yard land in Couley; and in No. 8505, it is faid this Jeffry de Clinton came in with William the Conqueror. Dugdale, among the charters of this priory, has one of Henry de Clinton, confirming the gifts of his anceftors; wherein he fays, " I alfo grant and comfirm to them, the church of Yftele, and one virgate of land in Covele, with all its appurtenances and liberties;" the gift of Juliana de Sancto Remigio. This directly contradicts Wood, who fays it was given by Jeffry. The vicarage at prefent is annexed to the archdeaconry of Oxford, and valued in the king's books at 8 l. per annum.

THE yew tree, fhewn in this view, which exhibits the north eaft afpect, feems fcarcely younger than the church. The fhaft of the crofs near it, is of no very modern workmanfhip. The manor of Yfele belongs to an hofpital at Donnington, near Newbury, Berks.

THIS view was drawn anno 1774, and was the only one that could be conveniently taken, the weft and fouth fides being encumbered with buildings of different kinds, or furrounded by private property.

Tickencote Chapel, Rutlandshire.

TICKENCOTE CHURCH, RUTLANDSHIRE.

THIS church exhibits evident marks of great antiquity. Mr. Gough, in his British Topography, says that Dr. Stukeley supposed it to be the oldest church now remaining in England, and that it was built by Peada, son of Penda, king of Mercia, about the year 746. It is a rectory, valued in the king's books at six pounds five shillings and eight-pence. The advowson was anciently in the abbot and convent of Osveston in Leicestershire, who in the 28th of Edward I. presented to it; and sir Britius Daneys, then lord of the manor, pretending a right to it, presented William his son. He however afterwards revoked his presentation.

THE following account of this place, is given by Wright in his History and Antiquities of Rutlandshire:

TICKENCOTE lyes in the east hundred; at the conqueror's survey, Grimbaldus held of the countess Judith three hides, bating one bovate, in Tichecote; the arable land was six carucates; in demesne one, eight sockmen, twelve villains, and one cottager; all possessing five carucates. Here was also one mill of 24s. and twelve acres of meadow, formerly valued at 30s. and then at 50s.

IN the reign of Ed. II. Britius Daneys was lord of this manour; which Britius Daneys was one of those eminent persons in this county, who in the 29th Ed. I.

received the king's writ of fummons to attend him at Berwick upon Tweed, well fitted with horfe and armes, from thence to march againſt the Scots.

IN the 18th Ed. III. Roger Daneys did releaſe to Rowland Daneys his brother, and to his heirs, all his right in the mannour of Tikencote, and in all ſuch lands and tenements which did at any time belong to Britius Daneys in Empingham.

IN the 10th Hen. IV. it was found that John Daneys, ſon and heir of John Daneys, held of the king the mannour of Tikencote, in the county of Rotel, by the ſervice of one knight's fee; and two carucates of land, with the appurtenances in Horum (i. e. Horn) in the ſaid county, by the ſixth part of a knight's fee.

IN the 5th Ed. VI. John Campynet and his wife obtained licenſe to alienate the mannour of Tikencote, in the county of Rutland, to John Bevercots and John Foxton, and their heirs, to the uſe of the ſaid John Campynet, &c. which mannour was held of the king in capite by knight's ſervice. But of later time a younger branch of the Wingfield's, of Upton in Com. Northampton, became lords of this mannour.

THIS view was drawn A. D. 1785.

Haghmond Abbey Shropshire.

HAGHMOND, or HAUGHMOND ABBEY, SHROPSHIRE.

This Abbey lies about two miles north east of Shrewsbury, and probably derived its name from being, situated on a high mound or eminence.

It was an abbey for canons regular of the order of St. Augustine, founded in the year 1110, by William Fitz-Alan, Lord of Clun, dedicated to St. Mary and St. John the Evangelist. Leland places this foundation as early as the first of Henry I. which according to Tanner was before those canons were brought into England; at the instance of Alured, abbot of this monastery, King Henry II. granted to the founder the patronage thereof in all vacancies. The family of the Says, of Richard's castle, were great benefactors to this house. Osbert de Say granted to them his mill at Wichbald, and his brother and heir Hugh de Say, confirmed to the canons here one yard land, lying in a place called Wydebroke, within his lordship of Richard's castle; and moreover gave to them his mill at Rocheford, with the toll thereof.

Walter Lord Clifford, called the son of Richard de Ponce, gave also to these canons, his mills at Tamedbury, and certain lands in Sinetune; to which Walter his son and heir added his mills at Almitone and Sinetune, for the maintenance of their kitchen, with one yard land in Sinetune, and a messuage belonging to the mills there. Robert de Clifford also in the 14th of Edward III. gave them the moiety of the hamlet of Winderton, in Warwickshire, and Ralph le Strange, endowed them with the patronage of his chapel at Crockin. All these lands and revenues given by several benefactors were confirmed to them by King Edward, in the 13th year of his Reign. Several Welch Princes are said to have made considerable donations to this house.

In the third of Henry V. Ralph then abbot of this house, at the recommendation of Thomas Earl of Arundel and Surrey, granted unto Robert Lee, residing with him as his Esquire, a corody for life, of meat, drink, and apparel, for himself, a boy, and two horses, as had before been customary to Esquires of other abbots; so long as he should abide in the said monastery.

In the time of Henry VI. Thomas Holden, Efq; granted to the Prior of the Holy Trinity of London, and his fucceffors, in behalf of the whole order of canons regular, one meffuage and garden, in the parifh of St. Peter and St. Michael, near the North Gate in Oxford, for a college for thofe of that order to ftudy in. Richard, bifhop of Coventry, likewife granted to thefe canons, that the facriftan under the abbot, might baptize as well Jews, as children, in that monaftery, and might ufe parochial rights within the fame. Nicholas, abbot of this houfe, in the year 1332, allotted certain revenues for the main-tenance of the kitchen, and for the purchafe of twenty hogs, to be made into bacon for the ufe of the houfe.

Richard Burnell, abbot, in the year 1459, made certain ordinances refpecting the offices of the prior and fub prior, whereby their privileges and authority were fettled ; Pope Alexander the IIId, granted diverfe liberties and advantages to this abbey. Such as not to pay tithes for the land and caftle in their own occupation ; a free burial place, and authority to prefent clerks to the parochial churches, which they held, referving the profits for the benefit of the houfe, to celebrate divine offices privately, in the time of a general interdiction, and to pay no tithes of their mills or meadows, unlefs the ufage had been otherwife ; Pope Boniface the IXth granted indulgences to fuch penitents as fhould vifit this church on certain days in the year, being confeffed, and truly repenting of their fins.

At the diffolution, the yearly revenues of this houfe were valued at 259l. 1s. 7d. 9 Dugdale—294l. 12s. 9d. Speed. The fite was granted 32d Henry VIII. to Edmund Lyttleton.

Leland in his Itinerary fays, " Ther was an Hermitage, and a chapell before the erectyng of the abbey. W. Fitz Allyn and his wyffe, with Richard Fitz-Allen and other, ar ther buried, and Richard Fitz Alan, a child, which child fell as is fayde by the necligence of his norice out of hir armes frym the battle-ments of the caftle of Shrawardig. The abat of Haghmon told me, that he hath hard that the caftell of Acton Burnell, a goodly manor place, where the parlia-ment was kepte, was firfte made by one Burnell a Byfhope."

Names of fome of the Abbats out of the Monafticon, Bifhop Tanner's and Dr. Wilks's Collections.

Alured is the firft I meet with, he occurs temp. Henry II.

Engelarde was fucceeded, anno 1241, by Gilbert.

John le Strange, anno 1243, 28th Henry III, and

Alexander, 1259.

Henry de Aftley, anno 1283, 10th Edward I. his fucceffor was

Gilbert de Caumpidon, elected by virtue of the Royal affent, dated July 27th, 1285. He refigned anno 1307, to

Richard de Brook, whom I find inftated abbot, June 15, 1307, his fucceffor, as I prefume was one

Nicholas. He built the new kitchen, &c. about the year 1332, temp. Edw. III. The next I find is

Ralph. He occurs abbat, anno 1414, and might probably be fucceeded by

Richard Burnel, whom I find elected, anno 1420. He prefided in the year 1459, but how long after I know not.

Richard Pontefbury, 1495.

Thomas Corvefar was the laft abbat ; he with ten Monks furrendered this Convent, 9th Sept. 1539, and had a penfion of 40l. per ann. affigned him.

Anno 1535, here remained in charge 11l. in annuities and corodies, and thefe penfions, viz. To Chriftopher Hunt, 10l. William Rilaunde, Hugh Coke and Roger Mekins, 6l. each. William Rigge, Thomas Leighe, John Mathew and William Owen, 5l. 6s. 8d. each.

This view was drawn anno 1778.

St. Wenelm's Chapel, in the County of Salop.

Published by G. Kearsly No. 46 Fleet Street January 1st 1778

Stoke Castle, Shropshire.

STOKE CASTLE, SHROPSHIRE.

THIS was rather a caftellated manfion than a caftle of ftrength; it ftands on the road fide between Bifhops Caftle and Ludlow; very little is mentioned refpecting it by the topographical writers. Leland only fays that it was built like a caftle, that it fometime belonged to the Ludlow's, and at the time when he wrote, was the property of the Vernon's. The prefent owner is the Lord Craven, whofe tenant lives in an adjoining farm-houfe.

BUCK, who has engraved this caftle, gives the following account of it, from what authority I know not. "This caftle ftands on the river Team; it anciently "belonged to the family of Verdun; iffue male failing in Theobald de Verdun, it "went by his daughter Elizabeth and her daughter Ifabel, by marriage, to Henry "Lord Ferrers, of Groby, who died in 17th Ed. III. It continued in this noble "family for many fucceffions, in that branch of it called Ferrers of Tamworth, "but it is now in the noble family of Cravon, William Lord Cravon, of Hamfted "Marfhal, being the prefent lord thereof;" i. e. A. D. 1731, when that view was publifhed.

THE entrance into this caſtle lies through a wooden gateway, covered with lath and plaiſter, on ſeveral parts of which, more particularly on the inſide, are carved a number of very groteſque figures.

ALL the other parts of the building are of ſtone, except ſome other apartments on the north ſide, which appear more modern than the hall or tower.

THE hall is ſpacious, and is lighted by four large church-like windows, with pointed arches, and has a door on the eaſt ſide of the ſame conſtruction. The hall is covered with ſtones, cut like tiles, and is ſeemingly in good repair. The tower conſiſts of a ſingle chamber on each ſtory, and on the north face has a re-entering angle, dividing it ſo as to have the appearance of a double tower.

THIS view was drawn anno 1785.

Charlcombe Church Somersetshire

CHARLCOMBE CHURCH, SOMERSETSHIRE.

THIS fingular little church ftands in a moft retired and picturefque fpot under the eaft fide of Landfdown hill, about a mile north of the city of Bath.

THE date of its erection is not known, but it is fuppofed to be older than the firft church of Bath abby, to which at the diffolution, it belonged.

INDEED its general appearance, and particularly that of its porch, bears evident marks of antiquity; its font is old, but here are no ancient monuments or braffes.

IT is a vicarage, valued in the king's books, at 5 l. 15 s. 10 d. The patronage was conveyed to the corporation of Bath by

the Reverend Walter Robins, LL. D. to be annexed to
the mafterfhip of the public grammar fchool, founded by
king Edward the Sixth, of which he was mafter.

THIS view, which fhews the north and weft fides, was
drawn anno 1784.

Combe Sydenham, Somersetshire.

COMBE SYDENHAM, SOMERSETSHIRE.

THIS is part of the remains of the manorial house of Combe Sydenham, in the hundred and parish of North Petherton, in the county of Somersetshire.

IT was purchased A. D. 1388, 12 of Rich. II. by Richard de Sidenham, a judge of the Common Pleas, and from him obtained the adjunct of Sidenham to its former name. This Richard was son of Roger de Sidenham, and had issue, Henry Sidenham, his son and heir, 19 Rich. II.

JOHN Sidenham, great-grandson of Henry, married Joan, daughter and co-heir of John Sturton, of Preston in the county of Somerset, with whom he had the manor of Brimpton in that county, which the family seem afterwards to have made their principal seat: she died 12 Edward IV. He the 8th of the said reign, seized of the manors of Sydenham and Comb Sidenham, leaving Walter his son and heir, who died the year following. From this Walter was lineally descended sir John Sydenham, knt. who was living and possessed of Brimpton and Comb Sydenham in 1623; whose son, sir John, was created a baronet, and was ancestor to sir Philip Sidenham, the last baronet of the family, who represented the county of Somerset in several parliaments. The Baronetage, published 1727, gives Comb Sidenham as one of his seats. He died unmarried, 10th Sept. 1739, and the title became extinct. The estates probably devolved to the female line.

THIS view, which shews a gate of the old mansion, was drawn A. D. 1765.

www.ingramcontent.com/pod-product-compliance
Lightning Source LLC
Chambersburg PA
CBHW030902270326
41929CB00008B/534